GREEK LYRIC

IV

LCL 461

GREEK LYRIC
IV

BACCHYLIDES, CORINNA, AND OTHERS

EDITED AND TRANSLATED BY

DAVID A. CAMPBELL

HARVARD UNIVERSITY PRESS
CAMBRIDGE, MASSACHUSETTS
LONDON, ENGLAND
1992

Library of Congress Cataloging-in-Publication Data

Greek lyric / with an English translation by
David A. Campbell.

(The Loeb classical library)
Text in Greek with translation in English.
Includes index.
Bibliography.
Contents: v. 1. Sappho, Alcaeus — v. 2. Anacreon,
Anacreontea — v. 3. Stesichorus, Ibycus, Simonides,
and others — v. 4. Bacchylides, Corinna, and others.
1. Greek poetry.   Greek poetry — Translations into
English.   I. Campbell, David.   II. Series.
PA3622.C3   1982   884'.01'08   82–178982
ISBN 0–674–99157–5 (v. 1)
ISBN 0–674–99158–3 (v. 2)
ISBN 0–674–99525–2 (v. 3)
ISBN 0–674–99508–2 (v. 4)

Typeset by Chiron, Inc, Cambridge, Massachusetts.
Printed in Great Britain by St Edmundsbury Press Ltd,
Bury St Edmunds, Suffolk, on acid-free paper.
Bound by Hunter & Foulis Ltd, Edinburgh, Scotland.

CONTENTS

CONTENTS

INTRODUCTION

THE poets who are included in this volume, with the probable exception of Corinna, wrote their poetry in the fifth century B.C. The earliest of them were younger contemporaries of Simonides, who lived until 468, and exact contemporaries of Aeschylus (525/4–456) and Pindar (518–438). Two of the most distinguished tragedians, Sophocles and Euripides, are represented by their lyric poems; and Old Comedy developed in the lifetime of Diagoras and Ion, both of whom were mentioned by Aristophanes.

CORINNA

Corinna's dates are disputed, and it is almost certain that her poetry belongs to the 3rd century B.C. Alexandrian scholars did not know her (unless they simply ignored her). She is not named or referred to by any writer before 50 B.C., perhaps not by any before the Augustan period (since the text of fr. 670, which may ascribe a commentary on her works to Alexander Polyhistor, is insecure): Propertius knows her (test. 5), Ovid is likely to have named his Corinna after her, Antipater of Thessalonica lists

her in his epigram on nine Greek poetesses (fr. 667),
and the scholars Habron and Tryphon seem familiar
with her work (fr. 664). The *terminus ante quem* for
her poems is 200 B.C. ±25 years, since they are
spelled in the Boeotian orthography of that date.

The alternative view, that she was a contem-
porary of Pindar and that her poems were lost until
c. 200 B.C., rests on very poor evidence, the anecdotes
transmitted by Plutarch, Aelian and Pausanias
(testt. 2–4). According to these, she had the better
of him, either when she preached the importance
of good judgement (test. 2) or when she actually
defeated him in poetic competition (testt. 3–4).
What is certain is that she referred to Pindar,
calling him 'son of Scopelinus' (fr. 695A), and
found fault with Myrtis 'in that, a woman, she
entered into competition with Pindar' (664a; see
also 688). But this by no means proves her to be
contemporary with these two; later biographers
predictably took the words that way, deducing a
teacher-pupil relationship between Myrtis and
Corinna (test. 1: cf. Myrtis test. 3). The tales of
rivalry between Corinna and Pindar, whom she
clearly admired, may go back to the fatuous inter-
pretation of Pindar's 'Boeotian sow' (*Ol.* 6. 89f.) as
an insult to Corinna: if Pindar insulted her so, he
must have had a reason; and since both were
poets, she must have had the better of him in
competition; compare the tales that Simonides
competed against Lasus and against Aeschylus.

2

The most that can be said in favour of the early dating is that Propertius seems to believe it, since he calls her *antiqua Corinna,* having alluded to Sappho in his previous couplet, and that Plutarch, who believes it, was a learned Boeotian.

Her home seems to have been Tanagra (fr. 655, test. 4), and her poems with the possible exception of the *Orestes* (fr. 690) tell Boeotian myths. Her five books (test. 1) may have been called ϝεροῖα (frr. 655–657), a mysterious term, perhaps to be linked with εἴρω and ἐρέω and explained as 'Tales' or 'Narratives' (D. L. Clayman, *Classical Quarterly* 72, 1978, 396 f.). Whether the other titles, *Boeotus, Seven against Thebes,* and so on, are to be identified with the ϝεροῖα and the 'lyric nomes' mentioned by the *Suda* (test. 1) is unclear. Our knowledge of her work is derived mainly from papyrus texts written in the first three centuries A.D. (frr. 654–655, 690–694).

TELESILLA

The *floruit* of Telesilla of Argos is set by Eusebius in or near the year 450 B.C. (test. 2), but we cannot say on what grounds the entry was based. The tale of her military prowess against Cleomenes of Sparta, improbable in itself, implies that she was a mature woman by 494 (test. 3 n.1); but it is likely that it was an Argive fabrication, designed to explain in part the obscure Delphic oracle which spoke of female defeating and driving out male and making the Argive women tear their cheeks in grief (test. 4). Maximus of Tyre said that Telesilla's poems roused the men of Argos to action (test. 5), and this suggests that some at least of her poetry was sung on public occasions. One of her poems was addressed to girls (717). She sang of Apollo and Artemis and perhaps of the marriage of Zeus and Hera, and she may have concentrated on local themes as Corinna did.

TIMOCREON

Timocreon of Ialysus in Rhodes is chiefly known as the composer of invective against Themistocles. Poem 727 may have been written in 479 or 478 before Pausanias and Leotychides fell into disgrace. Frr. 728–730 must be later than c. 471 when Themistocles had been ostracized and condemned. Timocreon medized in the Persian war (fr. 729), and an anecdote told about him by the late fifth century sophist Thrasymachus tells of a visit to the Persian court. He was a boxer and pentathlete with an athlete's reputation for gluttony (test. 2).

The symposium is the likely setting for his songs, and fr. 731 is in fact quoted as a σκόλιον or drinking-song. In 727 he uses the language and metre of choral lyric, perhaps because his invective begins in the manner of an encomium.

BACCHYLIDES

Bacchylides like his uncle Simonides was born in the city of Iulis on the island of Ceos. His grandfather, Bacchylides, was an athlete (test. 1), and his father, Meidylus or Meidon (testt. 1, 3), married Simonides' sister.

The dates of his birth and death are uncertain, but Severyns was probably correct to put his birth *c.* 518/517, so making him an exact contemporary of Pindar. The drinking-song for Alexander of Macedonia (fr. 20B) may have been written before 490, since its content suggests that author and addressee were young. The earliest datable epinician (13) belongs to 485 or at the latest 483; the latest (6, 7), to 452. Eusebius sets his *acme* in 468/7 (test. 4a), perhaps because Hiero's great Olympic victory, celebrated in poem 3, was won in 468. He offers a second date, 451/450 (test. 4b), which might originally have been posited as the date of his death. His third entry, under 431/430 (test. 4c) is puzzling, since we have no evidence that Bacchylides was alive after 452 or that he lived to be an old man.

Bacchylides wrote choral poetry of all types except the dirge, and his patrons belonged not only to his native Ceos and the nearby Aegina and Athens but to Sparta, Phlius, Thessaly, Macedonia and in the Greek West Metapontion and Syracuse. By far the most important was Hiero, tyrant of Syracuse, for whom he composed epinicians 5, 4 and

3 in 476, 470 and 468 B.C. Hiero was also the patron of Pindar at this time, but it does not follow that the scholiasts were correct in seeing uncomplimentary reference to Bacchylides in Pindar's poems (testt. 8–10); perhaps a passage in the second *Olympian* (test. 8) has the strongest claim to be interpreted in this way, since the context is clearly the σοφία or skill of poets.

Little else is known of his life. He was exiled from Ceos for a time and lived in the Peloponnese (test. 6). Severyns assigned his poetic activity to three periods: the years *c.* 498 to *c.* 486, when he was given commissions in Thessaly, Macedonia and Aegina; the period of his maturity and greatest success *c.* 486 to *c.* 466, when he wrote for the Athenian democracy and later for Hiero in Sicily; and the final years, during which he composed the poems for Cean victors but also spent some ten years as an exile in the Peloponnese, where he wrote for Sparta and Phlius (and, we may now add with our improved knowledge of fr. 4, for Asine).

Only some hundred lines of his poetry were known from quotation when a papyrus find restored extensive portions of fourteen epinician odes and six dithyrambs; F. G. Kenyon's *editio princeps* appeared in 1897. Bacchylides' works were collected in nine books: epinicians, dithyrambs, paeans, hymns, prosodia, partheneia, hyporchemata, erotica and encomia. In the first century B.C. Didymus wrote a commentary on the epinicians (test. 11), and the

INTRODUCTION

Alexandrians Callimachus and Aristarchus are among scholars known to have expressed views about the classification of the poems (test. 11 n.1).

DIAGORAS OF MELOS

Diagoras must have been born in the first half of the fifth century, and it is possible that Eusebius' dates for his *floruit,* 482/481 and 468/467 (test. 2), were originally posited as the date of his birth. He seems to have left Melos for the Peloponnese, where he became the friend of the Mantinean Nicodorus, boxer and statesman; he wrote a poem for him and also an encomium of the Mantineans (see *P.M.G.* 738). By 423 (or at the latest 416) he was sufficiently well known in Athens for his sceptical view of Zeus to prompt a joke of Aristophanes in his *Clouds* (test. 4). Later he was accused in Athens of impiety for his mockery of the Eleusinian Mysteries, and he fled to Pellene in Achaea to escape the death penalty; in the *Birds* of 414 B.C. (test. 5) Aristophanes referred to the decree by which he was outlawed, and it is likely that the decree belongs to the months immediately before the production, when the mutilation of the Hermae and the profanation of the Mysteries resulted in many prosecutions. No more is known of him, except that Pellene refused to hand him back to Athens. The Arab scholar Mubaššir (see test. 3 n.1) says that he lived for fifty-four years after the outbreak of the Peloponnesian

War, but his chronology is jumbled and the figure fifty-four may in fact, as Jacoby argued, represent the gap between 468/7 (Eusebius' second date) and 415/4 (the year in which Diagoras was accused).

He is said to have composed dithyrambs (test. 4, Sextus Empiricus at *P.M.G.* 738) and a paean (*Suda*, test. 1, in an anecdote explaining the origin of his atheism). Only two authentic fragments of his poetry remain (738), both from poems (encomia or epinicians?) for Peloponnesians. Later writers noted the contrast between the traditional piety of these lines and his reputation for atheism, and scholars, notably Woodbury and Winiarczyk, have argued that his atheism is the construct of a subsequent period.

ION OF CHIOS

Since Ion says he met Cimon on his arrival in Athens when 'still only a youth' (παντάπασι μειρά-κιον: test. 3) and since the meeting can be dated *c.* 465 (Jacoby), the date of Ion's birth will be somewhere between 485 and 480. He produced his first tragedies in Athens in 451/448 (test. 1), took first prize on at least one occasion (testt. 1, 2) and came third in 428 (test. 1 n.3). Aristophanes' mention of him in the *Peace* (test. 2) suggests that he had died shortly before the performance of the comedy in the spring of 421.

His versatility, which impressed Callimachus (test. 2 last n.), is indeed astonishing: in addition to his tragedies and satyr-plays he wrote elegiacs and lyric poetry of several kinds: dithyrambs (successfully produced in Athens: test. 2), paeans, hymns, drinking-songs and encomia. The epigrams attributed to him in the *Anthology* are spurious. His prose works included philosophical writing and the remarkable *Visits,* an account of his meetings with famous Athenians: Athenaeus 13. 606c–604d gives a long excerpt in which he paints an engaging picture of the 55-year-old Sophocles as a witty and flirtatious party-goer.

The third-century B.C. writer Baton of Sinope composed a monograph 'On Ion the poet' (see eleg. 31).

SELECT BIBLIOGRAPHY

Barker, A. (ed.), *Greek Musical Writings.* Vol. i: *The Musician and His Art,* Cambridge 1984

Bergk, T. *Poetae Lyrici Graeci,* vol. iii⁴, Leipzig 1882

Blumenthal, A. von, *Ion von Chios. Die Reste seiner Werke,* Stuttgart 1939

Bowra, C. M., *Greek Lyric Poetry from Alcman to Simonides*², Oxford 1961 (= *G.L.P.*)

Burnett, A. P., *The Art of Bacchylides,* Cambridge, Mass., and London 1985

Cambridge History of Classical Literature, vol. i: *Greek Literature,* ed. P. E. Easterling and B. M. W. Knox, Cambridge 1985

Campbell, D. A. *Greek Lyric Poetry: A Selection of Early Greek Lyric, Elegiac and Iambic Poetry,* London 1967 (repr. Bristol 1982); *The Golden Lyre: The Themes of the Greek Lyric Poets,* London 1983

Diehl, E. *Anthologia Lyrica Graeca,* vol. ii², Leipzig 1942

Dover, K. J., 'Ion of Chios: His Place in the History of Greek Literature', in *Chios: a Conference at the Homereion in Chios,* edited by Joan Boardman and C. E. Vaphopoulou-Richardson, Oxford 1986

Edmonds, J. M. *Lyra Graeca,* vol. iii², London 1940

Fränkel, H. *Early Greek Poetry and Philosophy,* trans. by M. Hadas and J. Willis, Oxford 1975

Gerber, D. *Euterpe: An Anthology of Early Greek Lyric, Elegiac and Iambic Poetry,* Amsterdam 1970; *Lexicon in Bacchylidem,* Hildesheim 1984

10

BIBLIOGRAPHY

Jacoby, F., 'Some Remarks on Ion of Chios', *Classical Quarterly* (1947) 1–17

Jebb, R. C., *Bacchylides: The Poems and Fragments,* Cambridge 1905

Maehler, H., *Bakchylides: Lieder und Fragmente* (Griechisch und Deutsch), Berlin 1968; *Die Lieder des Bakchylides: Erster Teil, Die Siegeslieder,* Leiden 1982

Page, D. L. *Corinna,* London 1953 (repr. 1963); *Poetae Melici Graeci,* Oxford 1962 (= *P.M.G.*: rev. ed. by M. Davies, vol. i, 1991); *Lyrica Graeca Selecta,* Oxford 1968 (= *L.G.S.*); *Supplementum Lyricis Graecis,* Oxford 1974 (= *S.L.G.*); *Epigrammata Selecta,* Oxford 1975; *Further Greek Epigrams,* Cambridge 1981 (= *F.G.E.*)

Severyns, A., *Bacchylide: Essai Biographique,* Liège 1933

Snell, B., and H. Maehler, *Bacchylidis Carmina cum fragmentis* [10], Leipzig 1970

West, M. L., 'Corinna', *Classical Quarterly* 20 (1970) 277–87; *Iambi et Elegi Graeci ante Alexandrum Cantati,* 2 vols., Oxford 1971 (= *I.E.G.*); *Studies in Early Greek Elegy and Iambus,* Berlin and New York 1974; *Greek Metre,* Oxford 1982; 'Ion of Chios', *Bulletin of the Institute of Classical Studies* 32 (1985) 71–78

Winiarczyk, M., 'Diagoras von Melos—Wahrheit und Legende', *Eos* 67 (1979) 191–213, 68 (1980) 51–75; *Diagoras Melius, Theodorus Cyrenaeus,* Leipzig 1981

Woodbury, L., 'The Date and Atheism of Diagoras of Melos', *Phoenix* 19 (1965) 178–211

GREEK LYRIC

BACCHYLIDES, CORINNA,
AND OTHERS

MYRTIS

TESTIMONIA VITAE ATQUE ARTIS

1 Plut. *Qu. Gr.* 40 (ii 357 Nachstädt-Sieveking-Titchener)

. . . ὡς Μυρτὶς ἡ Ἀνθηδονία ποιήτρια μελῶν ἱστόρηκε.

2 *Sud.* Κ 2087 (iii 157 Adler)

Κορίννα . . . , μαθήτρια Μύρτιδος.

3 *Sud.* Π 1617 (iv 132 Adler)

Πίνδαρος . . . · μαθητὴς δὲ Μυρτίδος γυναικός, γεγονὼς κατὰ τὴν ξε' Ὀλυμπιάδα . . .

4 *Anth. Pal.* 9. 26. 7s. = Antipater of Thessalonica xix 7s. Gow-Page

. . . ἰδὲ γλυκυαχέα Μύρτιν,
πάσας ἀενάων ἐργατίδας σελίδων.

MYRTIS

LIFE AND WORK[1]

1 Plutarch, *Greek Questions*[2]

... as Myrtis, the lyric poetess from Anthedon,[3] has told.

[1] For the most important testimony see Corinna 664(a). Tatian, *Against the Greeks* 33 attributes to one Boiscus a bronze statue of Myrtis; on his veracity in these matters see A. Kalkmann, *Rh. Mus.* 42 (1887) 489 ff., D. L. Page, *Corinna* 73 n. 6.   [2] See fr. 716 below.   [3] Coastal town of north Boeotia.

2 *Suda* (on Corinna)

She was the pupil of Myrtis.

3 *Suda* (on Pindar)

He was the pupil of Myrtis, a woman, and was born in the 65th Olympiad (520/516 B.C.) ...

4 *Palatine Anthology*: Antipater of Thessalonica (on nine poetesses)

... and sweet-voiced Myrtis; all craftswomen of immortal pages.

GREEK LYRIC

716 *P.M.G.* Plut. *Qu. Gr.* 40 (ii 357 Nachstädt-Sieveking-Titchener)

τίς Εὔνοστος ἥρως ἐν Τανάγρᾳ καὶ διὰ τίνα αἰτίαν
τὸ ἄλσος αὐτοῦ γυναιξὶν ἀνέμβατόν ἐστιν; Ἐλιέως τοῦ
Κηφισοῦ καὶ Σκιάδος Εὔνοστος ἦν υἱός, ᾧ φασιν ὑπὸ
νύμφης Εὐνόστας ἐκτραφέντι τοῦτο γενέσθαι τοὔνομα.
καλὸς δ᾽ ὢν καὶ δίκαιος οὐχ ἧττον ἦν σώφρων καὶ
αὐστηρός. ἐρασθῆναι δ᾽ αὐτοῦ λέγουσιν Ὄχναν, μίαν
τῶν Κολωνοῦ θυγατέρων ἀνεψιὰν οὖσαν. ἐπεὶ δὲ
πειρῶσαν ὁ Εὔνοστος ἀπετρέψατο καὶ λοιδορήσας
ἀπῆλθεν εἰς τοὺς ἀδελφοὺς κατηγορήσων, ἔφθασεν ἡ
παρθένος τοῦτο πράξασα κατ᾽ ἐκείνου καὶ παρώξυνε
τοὺς ἀδελφοὺς Ἔχεμον καὶ Λέοντα καὶ Βουκόλον ἀπο-
κτεῖναι τὸν Εὔνοστον ὡς πρὸς βίαν αὐτῇ συγγεγενη-
μένον. ἐκεῖνοι μὲν οὖν ἐνεδρεύσαντες ἀπέκτειναν τὸν
νεανίσκον, ὁ δ᾽ Ἐλιεὺς ἐκείνους ἔδησεν. ἡ δ᾽ Ὄχνη
μεταμελομένη καὶ γέμουσα ταραχῆς, ἅμα μὲν αὑτὴν
ἀπαλλάξαι θέλουσα τῆς διὰ τὸν ἔρωτα λύπης, ἅμα δ᾽
οἰκτείρουσα τοὺς ἀδελφούς, ἐξήγγειλε πρὸς τὸν Ἐλιέα
πᾶσαν τὴν ἀλήθειαν, ἐκεῖνος δὲ Κολωνῷ. Κολωνοῦ δὲ
δικάσαντος οἱ μὲν ἀδελφοὶ τῆς Ὄχνης ἔφυγον, αὐτὴ δὲ
κατεκρήμνισεν ἑαυτήν, ὡς Μυρτὶς ἡ Ἀνθηδονία ποιή-
τρια μελῶν ἱστόρηκε. τοῦ δ᾽ Εὐνόστου τὸ ἡρῷον καὶ τὸ
ἄλσος οὕτως ἀνέμβατον ἐτηρεῖτο καὶ ἀπροσπέλαστον
γυναιξίν, ὥστε πολλάκις σεισμῶν ἢ αὐχμῶν ἢ διοση-
μιῶν ἄλλων γενομένων ἀναζητεῖν καὶ πολυπραγμονεῖν
ἐπιμελῶς τοὺς Ταναγραίους μὴ λέληθε γυνὴ τῷ τόπῳ
πλησιάσασα.

16

716 *P.M.G.*   Plutarch, *Greek Questions*

Who was the hero Eunostus at Tanagra, and why are women forbidden to enter his grove?

Eunostus was the son of Elieus, son of Cephisus, and of Scias, and they say he got his name from the nymph Eunosta, who brought him up. Handsome and honourable, he was also chaste and strict. They say that his cousin, Ochna, one of Colonus' daughters, fell in love with him, but Eunostus rejected her advances and heaping abuse on her went off to denounce her to her brothers. The girl got there first, however, denounced him and urged her brothers, Echemus, Leon and Bucolus, to kill Eunostus, telling them that he had raped her. So they ambushed the boy and killed him, and Elieus put them in prison. Ochna now repented and was greatly upset: she wanted to be rid of the grief caused by her love, and she also felt pity for her brothers. So she told the whole truth to Elieus, who told Colonus. At his decree Ochna's brothers went into exile and she threw herself from a cliff, as Myrtis, the lyric poetess from Anthedon, has told. Women were so strictly prohibited from entering or approaching Eunostus' sanctuary and grove that often when there were earthquakes or droughts or other portents the people of Tanagra enquired with great diligence to discover whether a woman had approached the place without being seen.[1]

[1] For Eunostus see A. Schachter, *Cults of Boeotia* i 222.

CORINNA

TESTIMONIA VITAE ATQUE ARTIS

1 *Sud.* K 2087 (iii 157s. Adler)

Κόριννα, Ἀχελῳοδώρου καὶ Προκατίας, Θηβαία ἢ
Ταναγραία, μαθήτρια Μύρτιδος· ἐπωνόμαστο δὲ
Μυῖα· λυρική. ἐνίκησε δὲ πεντάκις ὡς λόγος Πίνδα-
ρον. ἔγραψε βιβλία ε' καὶ ἐπιγράμματα καὶ νόμους
λυρικούς.

cf. K 2088, 2089

2 Plut. *glor. Athen.* 4. 347f–348a (ii 128 Nachstädt-
Sieveking-Titchener)

ἡ δὲ Κόριννα τὸν Πίνδαρον, ὄντα νέον ἔτι καὶ τῇ
λογιότητι σοβαρῶς χρώμενον, ἐνουθέτησεν ὡς ἄμουσον
ὄντα μὴ ποιοῦντα μύθους, ὃ τῆς ποιητικῆς ἔργον εἶναι
συμβέβηκε, γλώσσας δὲ καὶ καταχρήσεις καὶ μεταφο-
ρὰς καὶ μέλη καὶ ῥυθμοὺς ἡδύσματα τοῖς πράγμασιν

18

CORINNA

BIOGRAPHY

1 *Suda*[1]

Corinna, daughter of Acheloodorus and Procatia, from Thebes or Tanagra,[2] pupil of Myrtis; nicknamed Myia, 'Fly'[3]; lyric poetess; said to have defeated Pindar five times[4]; wrote five books[5] and epigrams and lyric nomes.[6]

[1] There is confusion in the *Suda,* which lists also Corinna, a lyric poetess from Thespiae (cf. 674) or Corinth, and 'a younger Corinna', a lyric poetess from Thebes.   [2] See 655 fr. 1.   [3] A Spartan poetess called Myia is attested, e.g. by the *Suda*; Clement of Alexandria 4. 19. 122. 4 lists four poetesses, Corinna, Telesilla, Myia and Sappho; Eustathius *Il.* 326. 43 gives five: Praxilla, Sappho, Corinna, Erinna, Charixena.   [4] See test. 3.   [5] See 657.   [6] No epigrams survive, although 657 and 674 are hexameters; the nomes were probably her narrative poems.

CORINNA AND PINDAR[1]

2 Plutarch, *On the Glory of Athens*[2]

When Pindar was still young and flaunting his eloquence, Corinna warned him that he was no poet: instead of introducing myths, the true business of poetry, he based his works on rare words, extensions of meaning, paraphrases, melodies and rhythms,

GREEK LYRIC

ὑποτιθέντα. σφόδρ' οὖν ὁ Πίνδαρος ἐπιστήσας τοῖς
λεγομένοις ἐποίησεν ἐκεῖνο τὸ μέλος (fr. 29 Snell)·

Ἰσμηνὸν ἢ χρυσαλάκατον Μελίαν
ἢ Κάδμον ἢ Σπαρτῶν ἱερὸν γένος ἀνδρῶν
<ἢ τὰν κυανάμπυκα Θήβαν>
ἢ τὸ πάντολμον σθένος Ἡρακλέος
ἢ τὰν <Διωνύσου πολυγαθέα τιμὰν> ...

δειξαμένου δὲ τῇ Κορίννῃ γελάσασα ἐκείνη τῇ χειρὶ
δεῖν ἔφη σπείρειν ἀλλὰ μὴ ὅλῳ τῷ θυλάκῳ. τῷ γὰρ
ὄντι συγκεράσας καὶ συμφορήσας πανσπερμίαν τινὰ
μύθων ὁ Πίνδαρος εἰς τὸ μέλος ἐξέχεεν.

3 Ael. *V.H.* 13. 25 (p. 163 Dilts)

Πίνδαρος ὁ ποιητὴς ἀγωνιζόμενος ἐν Θήβαις ἀμα-
θέσι περιπεσὼν ἀκροαταῖς ἡττήθη Κορίννης πεντάκις.
ἐλέγχων δὲ τὴν ἀμουσίαν αὐτῶν ὁ Πίνδαρος σῦν ἐκάλει
τὴν Κόρινναν.

4 Paus. 9. 22. 3 (iii 41 Rocha-Pereira)

Κορίννης δέ, ἢ μόνη δὴ <ἐν> Τανάγρᾳ ᾄσματα
ἐποίησε, ταύτης ἔστι μὲν μνῆμα ἐν περιφανεῖ τῆς πό-
λεως, ἔστι δὲ ἐν τῷ γυμνασίῳ γραφή, ταινίᾳ τὴν κε-
φαλὴν <ἡ> Κόριννα ἀναδουμένη τῆς νίκης ἔνεκα ἣν
Πίνδαρον ᾄσματι ἐνίκησεν ἐν Θήβαις. φαίνεται δέ μοι

all mere embellishment. Pindar took her advice to heart with a vengeance and composed the famous song, 'Shall we sing of Ismenus or gold-distaffed Melia or Cadmus or the holy race of Sown Men or dark-snooded Thebe or the all-daring might of Heracles or the glorious honour of Dionysus . . . ?' When he showed it to Corinna, she laughed and said that one should sow with the hand, not the whole sack. For Pindar had in fact mixed together a jumbled hotchpotch of myths and emptied it into his song.

[1] See also test. 1, frr. 664(a), 688, 695A; for the dubious worth of the testimony see Introduction. [2] Cf. Eustathius *Il.* 327. 10, metrical Life of Pindar (i 8 Drachmann) 9 ff.

3 Aelian, *Historical Miscellanies*[1]

When the poet Pindar was competing in Thebes, he encountered ignorant audiences and was defeated five times by Corinna. By way of exposing their lack of poetic judgement he called Corinna a sow.[2]

[1] Cf. Themistius 27. 334. [2] The anecdote is based on misinterpretation of Pindar *Ol.* 6. 89 f., 'to know whether we have truly escaped the old insult, Boeotian sow'.

4 Pausanias, *Description of Greece*

The tomb of Corinna, the only lyric poet of Tanagra, is in a conspicuous part of the city, and in the gymnasium there is a painting of her tying her hair back with a ribbon to mark the victory she won over Pindar in Thebes with a lyric poem. In my

νικῆσαι τῆς διαλέκτου τε ἕνεκα, ὅτι ᾖδεν οὐ τῇ φωνῇ
τῇ Δωρίδι ὥσπερ ὁ Πίνδαρος, ἀλλὰ ὁποίᾳ συνήσειν
ἔμελλον Αἰολεῖς, καὶ ὅτι ἦν γυναικῶν <τῶν> τότε ᾖδε
καλλίστη τὸ εἶδος, εἴ τι τῇ εἰκόνι δεῖ τεκμαίρεσθαι.

5 Prop. 2. 3. 19ss.

> et quantum Aeolio cum temptat carmina plectro,
> par Aganippaeae ludere docta lyrae,
> et sua cum antiquae committit scripta Corinnae,
> carmina quae quivis non putat aequa suis.

6 Stat. *Silv.* 5. 3. 156ss. (p. 121 Marastoni)

> tu pandere doctus
> carmina Battiadae latebrasque Lycophronis atri
> Sophronaque implicitum tenuisque arcana Corin-
> nae.

view she defeated him partly because of her dialect, since she composed not in Doric like Pindar but in a dialect that Aeolians were likely to understand,[1] partly because she was the most beautiful woman of her day, if one may judge by the portrait.[2]

[1] Cf. schol. Dion. Thr. p. 469. 29 Hilgard, 'the Boeotian tongue which Corinna uses'.   [2] Tatian, *Against the Greeks* 33 speaks of a statue of C. by Silanion (4th c. B.C.); see Myrtis test. 1 n. 1. For the extant portrait see G. M. A. Richter, *The Portraits of the Greeks* i 144 with figs. 780–781.

VERDICT OF ANTIQUITY[1]

5 Propertius, *Elegies*

(not so much . . .)[2] as when she sets about singing with Aeolian plectrum,[3] so skilled as to rival the Aganippean[4] lyre, or when she matches her writings against the songs of ancient Corinna (which any judge reckons inferior to hers?).[5]

[1] See also fr. 667 and for scholarly activity on her poetry frr. 664, 670. Ovid must have named the Corinna of his *Amores* after her.   [2] P. is captivated less by his girl's good looks than by her skill as dancer, singer and poet.   [3] I.e. sings Sappho's poems to her lyre accompaniment.   [4] Aganippe was a spring of the Muses on Mt. Helicon.   [5] Text and translation insecure.

6 Statius, *Silvae*

You[1] were skilled at expounding the songs of the Battiad,[2] the puzzles of dark Lycophron, complex Sophron and the mysteries[3] of slim Corinna.

[1] Statius' father; see Ibyc. test. 14 with notes.   [2] Callimachus.
[3] Result of the Boeotian orthography.

7 Comment. Melamp. seu Diomed. in Dion. Thrac. (p. 21 Hilgard)

γεγόνασι δὲ λυρικοὶ οἱ καὶ πραττόμενοι ἐννέα, ὧν τὰ ὀνόματά ἐστι ταῦτα· Ἀνακρέων, Ἀλκμάν, Ἀλκαῖος, Βακχυλίδης, Ἴβυκος, Πίνδαρος, Στησίχορος, Σιμωνίδης, Σαπφώ, καὶ δεκάτη Κόριννα.

7 Melampus or Diomedes on Dionysius of Thrace

The lyric poets on whom commentaries are written are nine in number: Anacreon, Alcman, Alcaeus, Bacchylides, Ibycus, Pindar, Stesichorus, Simonides, Sappho, and a tenth, Corinna.[1]

---

[1] Cf. anon. in *Schol. Pind.* (i 11 Drachmann), 'some say Corinna also'; Tzetzes, *prol. Lycophr.* (p. 2 Scheer), *diff. poet.* (*C.G.F.* p. 34 Kaibel) includes her among the *lyrici*, Didymus (p. 395 Schmidt) does not.

CORINNA

FRAGMENTA

654 P. Berol. 284, prim. ed. Wilamowitz, *B.K.T.* v 2
(1907) 19ss.

(a) col. i

1 ε]ὐστέφανον   3]ἐπ' ἄκρυ   4]χορδάς
5] ρῶντ' ὀρίων   6] ν φοῦλον ὀνι-   9]ἠΐ
10 γ]ενέθλα·

12   ]ευ [. . . .] Κώρει-
τες ἔκρου]ψαν δάθιο[ν θι]ᾶς
βρέφο]ς ἄντροι, λαθρά[δα]ν ἀγ-
15 κο]υλομείταο Κρόνω, τα-
νίκά νιν κλέψε μάκηρα Ῥία

μεγ]άλαν τ' [ἀ]θανάτων ἔσ-
ς] ἔλε τιμάν. τάδ' ἔμελψεμ·
μάκαρας δ' αὐτίκα Μώση
20 φ]ερέμεν ψᾶφον ἔ[τ]αττον
κρ]ουφίαν κάλπιδας ἐν χρου-
σοφαῖς· τὺ δ' ἄμα πάντε[ς] ὦρθεν·

πλίονας δ' εἷλε Κιθηρών·
τάχα δ' Ἑρμᾶς ἀνέφαν[έν
25 νι]ν ἀούσας ἐρατὰν ὡς
ἔ]λε νίκαν, στεφ[ά]νυσιν

26

CORINNA

FRAGMENTS

Frr. 654–5 are papyrus finds; 656–63 are from titled poems, 664–89 from unidentified poems.

654 Berlin papyrus from Hermopolis, 2nd c. A.D.

(a) col. i

(THE CONTEST OF HELICON AND CITHAERON)

'... well-garlanded[1] ... on the top ... lyre-strings ... (of) the mountains[2] ... tribe of (asses?) ... always ... family[3] ... the Curetes hid the holy babe of the goddess in a cave without the knowledge of crooked-witted Cronus, when blessed Rhea stole him and won great honour from the immortals.' That was his song; and at once the Muses instructed the blessed ones to put their secret voting-pebbles into the gold-shining urns; and they all rose together, and Cithaeron won the greater number; and Hermes promptly proclaimed with a shout that he had won his desired victory, and the blessed ones

---

[1] Of a goddess or city. The mountain Cithaeron is singing in a contest against Helicon; his song, almost at an end, tells how the infant Zeus, child of Cronus and Rhea, was hidden on Crete to save him from his father.   [2] The marginal scholion has 'hunting'.
[3] Scholion 'snow' opposite next line.

i 24s. suppl. Lobel

δ . .] ατώ . αν ἐκόσμιον
μάκα]ρες· τῶ δὲ νόος γεγάθι·

ὁ δὲ λο]ύπησι κά[θ]εκτος
30 χαλεπ]ῆσιν ϝελι[κ]ὼν ἐ-
σερύει] λιττάδα [π]έτραν,
. . . . .]κεν δ' ὄ[ρο]ς· ὐκτρῶς
δ . . . .]ων οὐψ[ό]θεν εἴρι-
σέ [νιν ἐ]μ μου[ρι]άδεσσι λάυς·

36 ἀμ]βροσίας   38]ος μελ[ί]ων   40]ς ὄρουσεν
44s.]ιω φέγ-γος   45 μα]κάρων τῦ-   46]νἴον-
τασάσα[47]δρεοσινεῖς   48s.]ᾳ Διὸς Μνα-
[μοσούνας τ']   49]κώρη.

col. ii 11–12 marg. sin. coronis

schol. marg. dext. i 5 θηραν   11 χιονα   ii 2 επικλη-
θησεσθαι

27 δ' ἐλατάων νιν Bolling   31, 34 suppl. Page, 48s. Croenert

col. ii

12 γ[13 Μω[σάων   ]ων   14 δῶ[ρ-   ἐ]νέπω
15]μέλι   18 ὦτ[   ]ἀέλιος   19 θ]ουσίας
20s.]ο φιλα | ες δ'[23 ἰών[26   Ἀσωπ[ ]ἐν
νομόν   30 τείν[ἐς μελ]άθρων   32 ἐμ πε[ιμονὰν
33   ὢν Ἤγ[ιναν   γε]νέθλαν
    Δεὺς[ἀ]γαθῶν
35   πατρο[ἐ]ς,

28

CORINNA

adorned him with garlands (of firs?), and his heart
rejoiced; but the other, Helicon, gripped by cruel
anguish, tore out a smooth rock, and the mountain
(shuddered?); and (groaning?) pitiably he dashed it
from on high into ten thousand stones; ... immortal
(?) ... limbs (?)[4] ... (he) rushed ... the light ... of
the blessed ones ... daughters (of Zeus and
Mnemosyne?) ...[5]

[4] Or 'songs'.   [5] End of poem is indicated after 14 more frag-
mentary lines. Ten lines from the end the scholiast gives 'will be
invoked'.

coll. ii–iv

(THE DAUGHTERS OF ASOPUS)

(Having the gifts of the Muses?) I tell[1] ... in my
song ... like ... the sun ... sacrifices ... dear[2] ... I
... Asopus (went) to his haunts ... from your[3] halls
... into woe ...

Of these (daughters) Zeus, (giver?) of good things,
(took) his child Aegina ... from her father's ...[4],

[1] The opening of a poem at least 145 lines long. A title is given in
v. 12, perhaps 'Book X of the Tales'.   [2] Perhaps 'loving to
blow' or 'loving the Dawn' (West).   [3] The second person is
puzzling, unless Asopus is apostrophised.   [4] The text of the
catalogue of Asopus' nine lost daughters is insecure and difficult to
supplement e.g. at 34 f.; Zeus' other two victims were probably
Thebe and perhaps Plataea.

ii 12 ϝ deletum, sscr. γ   ϝ[εροίων tent. West   26 interpr.
West   34 δωτείρ ά] Wilamowitz

Κορκού[ραν δὲ κὴ Σαλαμῖ-]
ν᾽ εἶδ[᾽ Εὔβοιαν ἐράνναν]

Ποτι[δάων κλέψε πα]τείρ,
Σιν[ώπαν δὲ Λατοῖδα]ς
40 Θέσ[πιαν τ᾽   ἔ]στιν ἔχων·
τε[   ]ες
λο[   ]

τ[οῖ δ᾽ οὔ τις   ]ον

45]σαφές·   46 θ[ᾶς   iii 5]αρα θιῶν

7 [   ]ας
  [   ]ε τίως
  οὔ]ποκ᾽ αὐτὸ[. . . . .]θων
10   ]α γὰρ θιὰς[. . . . . .]
  ε]ὐδήμων [. . . . εἰ]δει.

τᾶν δὲ πήδω[ν τρῖς μ]ὲν ἔχι
Δεὺς πατεὶ[ρ πάντω]ν βασιλεύς,
τρῖς δὲ πόντ[ω γᾶμε] μέδων
15 Π[οτιδάων, τ]ᾶν δὲ δουῖν
Φῦβος λέκτ[ρα] κρατούνι,

τᾶν δ᾽ ἴαν Μή[ας] ἀγαθὸς
πῆς Ἑρμᾶς· οὔ[τ]ω γὰρ Ἔρως
κὴ Κούπρις πιθέταν, τὼς
20 ἐν δόμως βάντας κρουφάδαν
κώρας ἐννί᾽ ἐλέσθη·

while Corcyra (and Salamis) and (lovely Euboea) (were stolen by) father Poseidon, and (Leto's son) is in possession of Sinope and Thespia . . .[5]

But to Asopus no one (was able to make the matter) clear, until[6] . . .

'. . . (of) the gods . . . you[7] . . . your . . . never . . . for . . . goddesses . . . happy soon.[8] And of your daughters father Zeus, king of all, has three; and Poseidon, ruler of the sea, married three; and Phoebus is master of the beds of two of them, and of one Hermes, good son of Maia. For so did the pair Eros and the Cyprian persuade them, that they should go in secret to your house and take your nine daughters.

[5] The catalogue will have ended in v. 41 f. with Tanagra, seized by Hermes; Paus. 9. 20. 2 says that Corinna made her a daughter of Asopus, and Tanagra was a cult centre of Hermes.   [6] In the words which follow the seer Acraephen is prophesying to Asopus.   [7] Supplied from the scholiast.   [8] Perhaps a prediction that Asopus' wife Metope will be happy.

36, 38–40 tent. Wilamowitz, 37 Page   44, 46 e schol. suppl. West

τᾴ ποκ' εἰρώων γενέθλαν
ἐσγεννάσονθ' εἰμ[ιθί]ων,
κἄσσονθη π[ο]λου[σπ]ερίες
25 τ' ἀγείρω τ' · ἐς [μ]α[ντοσ]ούνω
τρίποδος ὤιτ[. . . . . . .].

τόδε γέρας κ[εκράτειχ' ἰὼ]ν
ἐς πεντείκο[ντα] κρατερῶν
ὁμήμων πέρ[οχο]ς προφά-
30 τας σεμνῶν [ἀδο]ύτων λαχὼν
ἀψεύδιαν Ἀκ[ρη]φείν ·

πράτοι [μὲν] γὰ[ρ Λατ]οΐδας
δῶκ' Εὐωνούμοι τριπόδων
ἐσς ἱῶν [χρε]ισμὼς ἐνέπειν,
35 τὸν δ' ἐς γᾶς βαλὼν Οὐριεὺς
τιμὰ[ν] δεύτερος ἴσχεν,

πῆς [Ποτ]ιδάωνος · ἔπι-
τ' Ὠα[ρί]ων ἁμὸς γενέτωρ
γῆα[ν ϝ]ὰν ἀππασάμενος ·
40 χὠ μὲν ὠραν[ὸ]ν ἀμφέπι,
τιμὰν δ'[ἔλλαχο]ν οὕταν.

τώνεκ' [εὖ τ' ἔγνω]ν ἐνέπω
τ' ἀτ[ρ]έκ[ιαν χρει]σμολόγον ·
τοὺ δέ [νου ϝίκέ τ' ἀ]θανάτυς
45 κὴ λού[πας ἄππαυε] φρένας
δημόν[εσσ' ἑκου]ρεύων.'

32

One day they shall give birth to a race of heroes
half-divine, and they shall be fruitful and ageless; so
(I was instructed) from the oracular tripod.

This privilege I alone out of fifty strong brothers
have obtained, preeminent spokesman of the holy
sanctuary, gifted with truthfulness, I Acraephen[9]:
for Euonymus was the first to whom Leto's son
granted the utterance of oracles from his tripods;
and Hyrieus, throwing him out of the land, was the
second to obtain the honour, son of Poseidon; and
then Orion, our father, having regained his own
land; and he now dwells in the sky, and (I obtained)
this honour. Therefore (I came to know well) and I
utter oracular truth; do you then yield to the immor-
tals and make your heart cease from grief, since you
are father-in-law to gods.'

[9] Eponymous hero of Acraephia, town near Apollo's sanctuary on
Mt. Ptoios; for the uncertainty of the reading see A. Schachter,
Cults of Boeotia i 61 ff.

---

iii 26 ἐδιδάχθειν suppl. Croenert   27 suppl. West, 29
Lobel   31 ἀκρηφ<ν>εἱν (adiect.) Lobel   42 suppl.
Jurenka   45 e.g. West

ὡς ἔφα [μάντις] π[ε]ράγείς·
τὸν δ' Ἀ[σωπὸς ἀσ]πασίως
δεξιᾶς ἐ[φαψάμ]ενος
50 δάκρού τ' [ὀκτάλ]λων προβαλ[ὼν
ὧδ' ἀμίψ[ατο φ]ωνῇ·

iv 2 φωρ[4 βεβεί λ[5 ἀπιθα[6 τεοῦς δ[
7 ϝάδο[μη   8 παυόμ[η   10 τέκν[12 πανθ[
13 εν θια[14 διὰ νι[15 ταω[16 ἔδν[17 δώσω[
20 τειν λαῦς . [21 τόσον ἔφα σ . [22 Πάρνεις
ἀντ—   23 ϝάδονή τε θ[24 κ]αδείαν τρ[
25 κεῖνο τεοῦς   26 τουχ . . ε[29 στέργω τ' ἀ[
31 Κιθηρὼ[ν] . [32 ἠτίως . [.] . [33 Πλειά[δ
34 μειδὲ[37 θουμο[38 ἐν πολ[39 κὴ γὰρ[
40 δ' εἶς κ[41 κὴ Κιθ[42 Πλάτη[α   43 δ' ἄγετ' ω[
44 κλᾶρος· ι[45 τῦς πλ[46 Πάρνε[48 θανοντ[
49 Πάρνε[50 φιλούρ[51 ὅς ποκε[52 μαντ[

schol. marg. dext. ii 26 ες   32 πημοναν   35 εκ   43 τωιδ'
ουτ<ι>ς   46 μεχρι   iii 7 σεαι   8 εντιεσδε   9 ουποτ'
11 ηδη   19 τεους   20 ες   22 ται   23 εκγεννα-
σονται   25 ηρωεκ   34 εκ   39 ανακτησαμ'ς   44 εικε
45 γ[αμηθεισς | [ ]ηρη του γη | [μαν]τος
iv 23 ϝάδομή Wilamowitz

(b) eiusdem pap. fragmenta incerti loci

1. 2 δημον[3 δευτ[4 βείλον[τη
2. 3 ὧδε δ[

3 schol. marg. dext.   1 ἀγρι]ελαια, πα[ρ' Ὁ]μηρω[ι   2 αιψα

4. 4]πόρεν φ[6]ἄειτι

34

So spoke the reverend prophet, and Asopus hap-
pily grasped him by his right hand and shedding
tears from his eyes answered him thus: '... (theft?)
... (it is my wish?) ... (not unpersuasive?) ...; and
of you ... I am glad ... I cease (grieving) ... my chil-
dren ... all ... (goddesses?) ... through ... (of
them?) ...; wedding-gifts I shall give ... (for your
peoples?) ...'

So much he said; ... Parnes[10] (spoke in turn) ...:
'Pleasures[11] ... connection by marriage ... that ...
of you ... fortune ... I am content ... Cithaeron[12]
... (them) responsible ... Pleiad(s) ... nor ... heart
... into much(?) ... for ... was ... and Cithaeron ...
Plataea[13] ... is brought(?) ... the lot[14] ... to the ...
Parnes ... having died ... Parnes ... (he) who once
... seer ...[15]

---

[10] Mountain between Boeotia and Attica.   [11] Or 'I take
pleasure'.   [12] The Boeotian mountain; see Paus. 9. 3. 1.
[13] Daughter of Asopus (Paus. loc. cit.).   [14] See fr. 677.   [15] Three
verses are needed to complete the stanza, and probably several
more stanzas to complete the tale introduced by 'who once'.

(b) (scraps of the same papyrus)

... god(s) ... second (?) ... (they) wish ... and
thus ... wild olive[1] ... suddenly ... gave ... (storm)
blows ...

---

[1] Scholiast's explanation of $\phi ov\lambda ia = \phi v\lambda ia$ (cf. *Od.* 5. 478) (Wila-
mowitz)

655 P.Oxy. 2370, prim. ed. Lobel

fr. 1   (a)]Ἀ[πο]λλώνιος
       (b) εἰ᾽Ἄρεις

ἐπί με Τερψιχόρα [καλὶ
καλὰ Ϝεροῖ᾽ ἀίσομ[έναν
Ταναγρίδεσσι λ[ευκοπέπλυς,
μέγα δ᾽ ἐμῆς γέγ[αθε πόλις
5 λιγουροκω[τί]λυ[ς ἐνοπῆς.
ὅττι γὰρ μεγαλ.[
ψευδ[.]σ.[.]αδομε[
.[.]. ω γῆαν εὐρού[χορον·
λόγια δ᾽ †ἐπ᾽† πατέρω[ν
10 κοσμείσασα †Ϝιδιο[
παρθ[έ]νυσι κατά[ρχομη·
πο]λλὰ μὲν Καφ[ισὸν ἰών-
γ᾽ ἀρχ]αγὸν κόσμ[εισα λόγυ]ς,
πολλὰ δ᾽ Ὠρί[ωνα] μέγαν
15 κὴ πεντεί[κοντ᾽] οὐψιβίας
πῆδα[ς οὓς νού]μφησι μιγ[ί]ς
τέκετο, κὴ]Λιβούαν κ[αλάν
.].[..]θησ[
Ϝιρίω κόραν.[
20 καλὰ Ϝιδεῖν αρ[
γ]ῆαν ἂν τίκτ[
.].τέκετο τυ[

cf. Heph. *Ench.* 16. 3 (p. 56s. Consbruch) (ἐν τοῖς Κορίννης), schol. A
(p. 164)

CORINNA

655 Oxyrhynchus papyrus (*c.* 200 A.D.)

(TALES)[1]

fr. 1 ... Apollonius[2]; or Ares[3]

Terpsichore summons me to sing fine tales for the white-robed women of Tanagra; and greatly does the city rejoice in my clear-coaxing utterances: for whatever ... great ... false ... the spacious earth; and having adorned (with my art?) stories from our fathers' time I begin them for the girls: often I adorned our ancestor Cephisus[4] with my words, often great Orion and the fifty sons of high strength[5] whom (he fathered) by intercourse with the nymphs, (and fair) Libya[6] ... (I shall tell of?) the girl ... (things) fine to see ... earth, whom ... bore ... fathered ...

---

[1] Perhaps the beginning of Book 1: see West, *C.Q.* 20 (1970) 283. Vv. 2–5 and 15 are ascribed to Corinna by Hephaestion.   [2] Part of introductory material with mention of the scholar Apollonius? [3] An alternative title?   [4] Boeotian river-god.   [5] Mentioned also in fr. 654.   [6] The nymph from whom Cadmus, founder of Thebes, was descended?

---

fr. 1. 1 suppl. West   2 κ. γέροια Heph. cod. A   καλαγέρεια cod. I εἰσομένα codd.   4 ἐμὴ codd.   5 -λαις codd.   8 π[ο]ντω ed. pr. τ[ε]ρπτω Page   9 εν sscr. π pap.   ἐς Lobel   ἀπ Lloyd-Jones   10 -ασ' ἰδίο[ι λόγοι tent. Lloyd-Jones   12s. suppl. ed. pr., Page   17 tent. West   19 ex ϝιρίων corr. pap.

37

fr. 2   1 π]αρθένυ τ[2]η ἐρουσιμ[βροτ- 3]ας δαφν[

fr. 4   3 τ' ἐϝῖδον ˌ[4 βάρβαρον κ[

6 βὰς δὲ Οὔριε[ύς   6s. ἐσ | σείλκουσε, ν[

fr. 2. 2 tent. West

ϝΕΡΟΙΩΝ α'

656 Anton. Lib. 25 (*Myth. Gr.* ii 1. 103 Martini)

Μητιόχη καὶ Μενίππη. ἱστορεῖ Νίκανδρος Ἑτεροιουμένων δ' καὶ Κόριννα ϝεροίων α' (γεροίων α' cod.).

(ϝΕΡΟΙΩΝ ?) ε'

657 Heph. *Ench.* 2. 3 (p. 9 Consbruch) (περὶ συνεκφωνή-σεως)

. . . ἢ δύο βραχεῖαι εἰς μίαν βραχεῖαν (sc. παραλαμβάνονται) . . . · ἔστι μέντοι καὶ ἐν ἔπει, ὡς παρὰ Κορίννῃ ἐν τῷ πέμπτῳ·

ἢ διανεκῶς εὕδεις; οὐ μὰν πάρος ἦσθα, Κόριννα, <οὔπναλέα>

cf. Choerob. ad loc. (p. 211 C.) τινὲς δέ φασιν ἐν δευτέρᾳ, κρεῖττον δέ ἐστιν ἐν πέμπτῃ.

d̄ιανεκέως (ἢ del.) Bergk   2 suppl. Hermann

CORINNA

fr. 2 ... girls ... (mortal-saving?) ... laurel ...

fr. 4 ... I[1] saw ... foreign ... and Hyrieus, having come ..., dragged (him) out ...

[1] Or 'they'.

TALES: BOOK 1

656 Antoninus Liberalis, *Collection of Metamorphoses*

'Metioche and Menippe'[1]: told by Nicander in Book 4 of his *Transformations* and by Corinna in Book 1 of her *Tales*.

[1] Daughters of Orion who in time of plague saved their city Orchomenus by sacrificing themselves; Persephone and Hades turned them into comets, and they were worshipped at Orchomenus under the title Coronides. Cf. Ov. *Met.* 13. 685 ff.

BOOK 5 (of *Tales*?)

657 Hephaestion, *Handbook on Metres* (on synizesis)

... or two short syllables are run together to give one short ...: this occurs even in a hexameter, as in Corinna in Book 5[1]:

Are you asleep for ever? In time past, Corinna, you were not (a lie-abed).

[1] 'In book 2 according to some' (Choeroboscus ad loc.).

ΒΟΙΩΤΟΣ

658 Hdn. π. μον. λέξ. a 11 (ii 917 Lentz)

παρὰ δὲ τῷ ποιητῇ (Ποσειδάων)· παρὰ μέντοι Βοιωτοῖς Ποτειδάων τραπέντος τοῦ σ εἰς τ. Κόριννα Βοιωτοῖ·

τοὺ δὲ μάκαρ Κρονίδα, τοὺ Ποτειδάωνι ϝάναξ Βοιωτέ

Wilamowitz: τοῦδε μάκαρ Κρονίδη· τοῦ Ποτειδάωνος ἄναξ Βοίωτε codd.

ΕΠΤΑ ΕΠΙ ΘΕΙΒΗΣ

659 Ap. Dysc. *Pron.* 119b (i 93 Schneider)

Δωριεῖς ὑμές ... Αἰολεῖς ὕμμες ... Βοιωτοὶ μετὰ διφθόγγου τοῦ ου·

οὐμὲς δὲ κομισθέντες,

Κόριννα Ἔπτ᾽ ἐπὶ Θήβαις.

ΕΥΩΝΟΥΜΙΗ

660 Ap. Dysc. *Pron.* 136b (i 107 Schneider)

Αἰολεῖς (τὴν 'ὅς') μετὰ τοῦ ϝ κατὰ πᾶσαν πτῶσιν καὶ γένος ...· ὁμοίως καὶ Βοιωτοί· Κόριννα Εὐωνυμίης·

πῆδα ϝὸν θέλωσα φίλης
ἀγκάλησ᾽ ἑλέσθη.

1 Boeckh: πηδεϝον cod.   2 ἀγκάλησιν? Page (ut evadat pherecr.)
Boeckh: ελησθε cod.

---

[1] Interpretation of *Euonymiae* uncertain; for Euonymus the prophet (son of Cephisus and father of Aulis) see fr. 654 col. iii.   [2] Cf. Sa. 164, Alcm. 103.

CORINNA

BOEOTUS

658 Herodian, *On Anomalous Words*

In Homer (the form is Poseidaon), but in the Boeotians it is Poteidaon with the s changed to t: cf. Corinna in her *Boeotus*:

you, blessed son of Cronus, you, lord Boeotus (fathered by?) Poseidon[1] . . .

[1] Text, metre and interpretation uncertain: Boeotus was son of Poseidon, Poseidon and Zeus were sons of Cronus. See also frr. 670, 671.

THE SEVEN AGAINST THEBES[1]

659 Apollonius Dyscolus, *Pronouns*

The Dorian form of ὑμεῖς, 'you' (pl.), is ὑμές, the Aeolic ὔμμες; the Boeotian has the diphthong ου:

and you, having been brought[2] . . .

So Corinna in her *Seven against Thebes*.

[1] Cf. 692 frr. 5–7. [2] From Argos to Thebes?

DAUGHTERS OF EUONYMUS[1]

660 Apollonius Dyscolus, *Pronouns* (on ὅς, 'his', 'her' etc.)

The Aeolians have the form with digamma (ϝός) in all cases and genders[2]; . . . so do the Boeotians: cf. Corinna in her *Daughters of Euonymus*:

wishing to take her son in her loving arms.

41

ΓΙΟΛΑΟΣ

661 Ap. Dysc. *Pron.* 113b (i 88 Schneider)

διὰ τοῦ ε ἡ νῶε παρὰ Ἀντιμάχῳ (fr. 50 Wyss) . . . καὶ

τού τε νῶε

ἐν Ἰολάῳ Κόριννα.

ΚΑΤΑΠΛΟΥΣ

662 Ap. Dysc. *Pron.* 98bc (i 77 Schneider)

ἑοῦς· αὕτη ἀκόλουθος Δωρικῇ τῇ τεοῦς. ᾗ συνεχῶς καὶ Κόριννα ἐχρήσατο· ἐν Καταπλῳ·

νίκασ' ὃν μεγαλοσθενεὶς
Ὠαρίων χώραν τ' ἀπ' ἑοῦς
πᾶσαν ὠνούμηνεν.

1 Hermann: νίκασ' ὁ μ. cod.

663 Ap. Dysc. *Pron.* 105b (i 82 Schneider)

λέγεται δὲ καὶ τίν (sc. ἡ σοί) . . .· τίθεται παρὰ Κορίννῃ καὶ ἐπ' αἰτιατικῆς ἐν Καταπλῳ·

οὐ γὰρ τὶν ὁ φθονερὸς
†δαμωτ†

ἀντὶ τοῦ σέ, καὶ σαφὲς ὡς κατ' ἐναλλαγὴν πτώσεως.

2 δαμίωτ' (= ζημιοῦται) ci. Edmonds, δήμων Ahrens

CORINNA

IOLAUS

661 Apollonius Dyscolus, *Pronouns*

The pronoun νώ (1st pers. dual) has the form νῶε in
Antimachus; so Corinna in her *Iolaus*:

> and you ... us two[1]

[1] Or 'both you and we two'.

VOYAGE HOME[1]

662 Apollonius Dyscolus, *Pronouns*

The form ἐοῦς, 'of him(self)', corresponds to the Doric
τεοῦς, 'of you'. Corinna used it often, e.g. in her *Voyage
Home*:

> whom[2] mighty Orion conquered, and named[3] all
> the land after himself.

[1] Orion's voyage?   [2] Text uncertain.   [3] Perhaps 'was for
naming'.

663 Apollonius Dyscolus, *Pronouns* (on σοί, dative, 'to
you')

The form τίν is also found ... Corinna has it in the
accusative case too in her *Voyage Home*:

> for this envious man does not (harm?) you,

where τίν stands for σέ and there is clearly an interchange
of cases.

664 Ap. Dysc. *Pron.* 64b–65a (i 51 Schneider)

Βοιωτοὶ <ἰών>, ὡς μὲν Τρύφων ... ὡς δὲ ἔνιοι, ὧν ἐστιν ὁ
Ἄβρων, θέμα ἐστίν, ὃ συζύγως οἱ αὐτοί φασι, τῇ μὲν ἐγών τὴν ἰών,
<τῇ δὲ ἐγώνη τὴν ἰώνει>, εἴγε τὸ παρὰ Δωριεῦσιν η εἰς ει μετα-
βάλλεται, τῇ δ' ἐγώνγα τὴν ἰώνγα. Κόριννα·

(a) μέμφομη δὲ κὴ λιγουρὰν
    Μουρτίδ' ἰώνγ' ὅτι βανὰ φοῦ-
    σ' ἔβα Πινδάροι πὸτ ἔριν,

καὶ ἔτι

(b) ἰώνει δ' εἰρώων ἀρετὰς
    χειρωάδων

cf. Hdn. π. μον. λέξ. α 18 (ii 924 Lentz) τὸ γὰρ παρὰ Κορύννη βανά ...
ἴδιον θέμα Βοιωτῶν τασσόμενον ἀντὶ τοῦ γυνή; Hsch. Β 184, 187

(a) 3 Wilamowitz: Πινδαριοιο cod.   Π. post ὅτι transp. West

665 Anton. Lib. 10 (*Myth. Gr.* ii 1. 80 Martini)

Μινυάδες· ἱστορεῖ Νίκανδρος Ἑτεροιουμένων δ' καὶ Κόριννα.

666 Ap. Dysc. *Pron.* 95bc (i 74 Schneider)

ἀλλὰ μὴν καὶ τῇ ἐμοῦς Δωρίῳ (sc. σύζυγος) ἡ τεοῦς ... · καὶ
ἔτι Κόριννα·

    περὶ τεοῦς Ἑρμᾶς πὸτ Ἄρεα
    πουκτεύει

1 Wilamowitz: ποτ αρ'ευα cod.

CORINNA

664 Apollonius Dyscolus, *Pronouns* (on ἐγώ, 'I')

The Boeotians use ἰών, according to Tryphon[1] ...; but according to some, Habron[2] among them, ἰών is a primary form, used by the same writers conjointly, ἰών with ἐγών, ἰώνει with ἐγώνη, if the Dorian η is altered to ει, and ἰώνγα with ἐγώνγα. So Corinna:

(a) and I find fault also with clear-voiced Myrtis[3] in that, a woman, she entered into competition with Pindar;

and again,

(b) but I for my part (sing of) the excellences of heroes and heroines.

[1] Grammarian of Augustan period.   [2] Grammarian, 1st c. A.D.   [3] The Boeotian poetess; see above, p. 14.

665 Antoninus Liberalis, *Collection of Metamorphoses*

'The Daughters of Minyas'[1]: told by Nicander in book 4 of his *Transformations* and by Corinna.

[1] Reluctant worshippers of Dionysus, whose fate resembled that of Agave and her sisters in Eur. *Bacchae*. Minyas was founder of Orchomenus.

666 Apollonius Dyscolus, *Pronouns* (on ἐμοῦ, 'of me')

Indeed side by side with the Dorian ἐμοῦς (= ἐμοῦ)[1] stands τεοῦς (= σοῦ), 'of you' ...: cf. also Corinna:

for your sake[2] Hermes boxes against Ares.

[1] See fr. 682.   [2] Tanagra's? See fr. 654 col. ii p. 31 n. 5.

667 *Anth. Pal.* 9. 26. 5s. = Antipater of Thessalonica xix 5s. Gow-Page

καὶ σέ, Κόριννα,
θοῦριν Ἀθηναίης ἀσπίδα μελψαμέναν.

668 [Plut.] *Mus.* 14. 1136b (p. 117 Lasserre, vi 3. 12 Ziegler)

ἡ δὲ Κόριννα καὶ διδαχθῆναί φησι τὸν Ἀπόλλω ὑπ' Ἀθηνᾶς αὐλεῖν.

669 Prisc. *Inst. Gramm.* i 36 (ii 27s. Keil)

(Aeoli) enim θουγάτηρ dicunt pro θυγάτηρ, ου corripientes, vel magis υ sono u soliti sunt pronuntiare; ideoque ascribunt o, non ut diphthongum faciant, sed ut sonum υ Aeolicum ostendant, ut

καλλιχόρω χθονὸς Οὑρίας θουγάτειρ

670 Schol. Ap. Rhod. 1. 551a (p. 47 Wendel)

Ἀρμενίδας δὲ ἐν τοῖς Θηβαϊκοῖς (*F.Gr.H.* 378 F1) Ἀμφικτύονος υἱὸν Ἴτωνον ἐν Θεσσαλίᾳ γεννηθῆναι, ἀφ' οὗ Ἴτων πόλις καὶ Ἰτωνὶς Ἀθηνᾶ. μέμνηται καὶ Ἀλέξανδρος ἐν τῷ α' τῶν Κορίννης ὑπομνημάτων (*F.Gr.H.* 273 F 97).

τῶν Κορίννης cod. L, Καρικῶν cod. P   ἐν τῷ α' τῶν Καρικῶν ὑπομνημάτων, Κορίννης ὑπομνησθείς ci. Crönert

CORINNA

667 *Palatine Anthology*: Antipater of Thessalonica (on nine poetesses)

... and you, Corinna, who sang of Athena's warlike shield.

668 'Plutarch', *On Music*

Corinna actually says that Apollo was taught by Athena to play the pipes.

669 Priscian, *Grammar*

The Aeolians say θουγάτηρ instead of θυγάτηρ, 'daughter', keeping the ου short; or rather they pronounce Greek υ with the sound of Latin u, and that is why they add the o: not to make a diphthong, but to indicate the Aeolic sound of υ; e.g.

daughter of Hyria,[1] land of fair dances.

[1] Place in Boeotia; the daughter is Antiope (Hes. fr. 181 M.-W., Steph. Byz. s.v. Ὑρία).

670 Scholiast on Apollonius of Rhodes

Armenidas[1] in his *Theban History* says Itonus, Amphictyon's son, was born in Thessaly, and that the city of Iton and Itonian Athena were named after him. This is mentioned also by Alexander[2] in Book 1 of his commentaries on Corinna.[3]

[1] 5th c. B.C.   [2] Polyhistor, historian, 1st c. B.C.   [3] Text insecure: with Crönert's reading, 'Alexander in Book 1 of his *Carian History*, quoting Corinna'.

GREEK LYRIC

671 Schol. Ap. Rhod. 3 1177–87a (p. 250s. Wendel)

Ὠγυγίας δὲ τὰς Θήβας ἀπὸ Ὠγύγου τοῦ βασιλεύσαντος αὐ-
τῶν. Κόριννα δὲ τὸν Ὤγυγον Βοιωτοῦ υἱόν. ἀπὸ τούτου δὲ καὶ τῶν
Θηβῶν πύλαι.

672 Schol. Eur. *Phoen.* 26 (i 251 Schwartz)

τινὲς δὲ καὶ τὴν μητέρα αὐτῷ (sc. τῷ Οἰδίποδι) φασιν ἀνῃρῆ-
σθαι. ἀνελεῖν δὲ αὐτὸν οὐ μόνον τὴν Σφίγγα ἀλλὰ καὶ τὴν Τευμη-
σίαν ἀλώπεκα, ὡς Κόριννα.

673 Schol. Nicand. *Ther.* 15 (p. 5 Keil, p. 41 Crugnola)

οἱ δὲ πλείους Ταναγραῖον εἶναί φασι τὸν Ὠρίωνα. Κόριννα δὲ
εὐσεβέστατον λέγει αὐτὸν καὶ ἐπελθόντα πολλοὺς τόπους ἡμερῶσαι
καὶ καθαρίσαι ἀπὸ θηρίων.

cf. Parthen. 20 (*Myth. Gr.* ii 35s. Sakalowski)

674 Gramm. anon. ed. Egenolff, *Philol.* 59 (1900) 249

τὸ δὲ Θέσπεια ὁ Ὦρος διὰ τῆς ει διφθόγγου γράφει τῷ τῶν προ-
παροξυτόνων κανόνι. ὁ δὲ Ἡρωδιανὸς ἐν τῇ Ὁμηρικῇ προσῳδίᾳ
(cf. i 280, ii 520 Lentz) διὰ τοῦ ι γράφει, ἐπειδὴ γὰρ εὔρηται ἡ πι
συλλαβὴ συνεσταλμένη, ὡς παρὰ Κορίννῃ·

Θέσπια καλλιγένεθλε φιλόξενε μωσοφίλειτε.

cf. Steph. Byz. s.v. Θέσπεια (i 310 Meineke), schol. A Hom. *Il.* 2. 498
(i 292 Erbse), Eust. *Il.* 266. 6 (i 406 Van der Valk), *Epim. Hom.* i
212 Dyck, *Anecd. Par.* iii 137 Cramer

μουσοφίλητε cod.

48

671 Scholiast on Apollonius of Rhodes

Thebes is called Ogygian after Ogygus who ruled over it. Corinna makes Ogygus the son of Boeotus. From him came also the gates of Thebes.

672 Scholiast on Euripides, *Phoenician Women*

Some say also that Oedipus' mother was killed by him; and that he killed not only the Sphinx but also the Teumessian fox[1]; so Corinna.

[1] Teumessus was a Boeotian village. In the usual version Cephalus killed the fox to oblige Amphitryon.

673 Scholiast on Nicander, *Poisonous Bites and their Antidotes*

Most authorities say that Orion was from Tanagra. Corinna calls him most pious and says he visited many places,[1] reclaiming the land and clearing it of wild beasts.

[1] E.g. Chios, according to Parthenius.

674 Anonymous grammarian

Thespeia is written with the diphthong $\epsilon\iota$ by Orus[1] in accordance with the rule for proparoxytones[2]; but Herodian in his *Homeric Prosody* writes it with the ι, since the syllable $\pi\iota$ is found shortened, as in Corinna:

Thespia of the beautiful offspring, lover of strangers, loved by the Muses.[3]

[1] Orthographer, c. 450 A.D.   [2] Words with acute accent on 3rd last syllable.   [3] It is close to Mt. Helicon; for the sanctuary of the Muses see A. Schachter, *Cults of Boeotia* ii 150 ff.

GREEK LYRIC

675 Heph. *Ench.* 16. 3 (p. 57 Consbruch)

ὁμοίως δὲ καὶ ἐπὶ τῶν γλυκωνείων τοιαῦτα σχήματα παραλαμβάνεται, οἷον ἐν τοῖς Κορίννης (fr. 655 i 2–5). ὧδε καὶ τόδε (fr. 655 i 15). ἔτι δὲ καὶ πλείοσιν αὕτη κέχρηται σχήμασιν·

(a) δώρατος ὧστ᾽ ἐπ᾽ ἵππω

(b) κατὰ μὲν βριμούμενοι

(c) πόλιν δ᾽ ἔπραθ᾽ ὁ μὲν προφανείς

(d) γλουκοὺ δέ †τις ἄδων†

(e) πελέκεσσι δονῖτη

cf. schol. A. (p. 164 Consbruch)

(a) δούρ-, ἐφ᾽ codd. (b) κάρτα ci. Hermann (d) δὲ τῦς ἄδων ci. Ahrens, Croenert (e) δονεῖται codd.

676 *Epim. Hom.* (*Anecd. Oxon.* i 172 Cramer; cf. i 160)

συνεμπίπτει δὲ ἡ ἐς καὶ ἄλλῃ Βοιωτικῇ προθέσει τῇ ἐξ·

(a)   ἐς Μωσάων

ἀντὶ τοῦ ἐκ Μουσῶν· ἂν δὲ φωνῆεν ἐπιφέρηται, διὰ δύο σσ·

(b)   ἐσσάρχι πτολέμω

(a) Μουσῶν cod. (b) Ahrens: ἐσσ᾽ Ἀρχιπτολέμου cod.

677 Ap. Dysc. *Pron.* 96a (i 75 Schneider)

τεῦς·... ἐστὶ δὲ καὶ Βοιωτιακὸν δῆλον ὡς·

τεῦς γὰρ ὁ κλᾶρος.

675 Hephaestion, *Handbook of Metres*

Similarly such forms occur in glyconics,[1] e.g. in Corinna's (fr. 655 i 2–5, 15); and she uses still more forms:

(a) on a plank as if on a horse[2]
(b) snorting at . . .
(c) and he appearing[3] sacked the city
(d) and (singing to them?) sweetly
(e) is shaken by axes

[1] The term embraces choriambic dimeters and pherecrateans; analysis of (b)–(e) is difficult.   [2] Cf. *Od.* 5. 371.   [3] Or 'conspicuous'.

676 *Homeric Parsings*

The preposition ἐς ('into') is identical with another, the Boeotian form of ἐξ ('out of'):

(a) out of the Muses,

where ἐς is for ἐκ; but if a vowel follows, it has the form ἐσσ:

(b) begins war[1]

[1] Ascribed to Corinna like other examples of Boeotian usage, 677, 679.

677 Apollonius Dyscolus, *Pronouns*

τεῦς (= σοῦ, 'of you') . . . is clearly Boeotian also:

for yours is the lot.[1]

[1] Maas suggested that the words belong to 654 iv 43 f.: see p. 35.

GREEK LYRIC

678 Ap. Dysc. *Pron.* 122b (i 96 Schneider)

Αἰολεῖς ὑμμέων . . . · οὐμίων Βοιωτοί ·

τὸ δέ τις οὐμίων ἀκουσάτω,

Κόριννα.

ουμμιων cod., corr. Bergk, Bechtel

679 Ap. Dysc. *Pron.* 121c (i 95 Schneider)

ἁμῶν · . . . ὁμοίως Βοιωτοί

ἁμίων,

ἐπὶ δὲ τῆς κτητικῆς ἁμῶν ·

ἁμῶν δόμων

680 Schol. T Hom. *Il.* 17. 197b (iv 366s. Erbse)

γηράς · ἀποκοπὴ τοῦ γηράσας, ὡς ὑποφθάς, ἐπιπλώς. καὶ Κόριννα ·

βροντάς

ἀντὶ τοῦ βροντήσας.

681 Ap. Dysc. *Pron.* 106b (i 82 Schneider)

ἐστὶ καὶ ἡ

ἑίν

ἀπὸ τῆς τεΐν παρὰ Ἀντιμάχῳ (fr. 92 Wyss) καὶ Κορύννη, ἐπ᾽ αἰτιατικῆς (Bekker: ἐπὶ δοτικῆς cod.) ἔσθ᾽ ὅτε παραλαμβανομένη.

CORINNA

678 Apollonius Dyscolus, *Pronouns* (on ὑμῶν, 'of you')

The Aeolians have ὑμμέων (Alc. 391). The Boeotians have οὐμίων; cf. Corinna,

> and let men hear this from you.

679 Apollonius Dyscolus, *Pronouns* (on ἡμῶν, 'of us')

Similarly the Boeotians have ἁμίων,

> of us,

and for the possessive pronoun ἁμῶν:

> of our houses

680 Scholiast on *Iliad* 17. 197 (γηράς, 'having grown old')

A shortened form of γηράσας; so ὑποφθάς (*Il.* 7. 144), and ἐπιπλώς (*Il.* 6. 291) and Corinna's βροντάς,

> having thundered,

for βροντήσας.

681 Apollonius Dyscolus, *Pronouns*

There is also a form ἐΐν,

> to him,

modelled on τεΐν, 'to you', in Antimachus and Corinna; it is sometimes used as an accusative.[1]

---

[1] As well as a dative.

682 Ap. Dysc. *Pron.* 95a (i 74 Schneider)

ἡ

ἐμοῦς

κοινὴ οὖσα Συρακουσίων καὶ Βοιωτῶν, καθὸ καὶ Κόριννα καὶ Ἐπί-
χαρμος (fr. 144 Kaibel) ἐχρήσαντο, πρὸς ἐνίων ἐδόκει <μᾶλλον>
κατωρθῶσθαι τῆς δίχα τοῦ ϛ προφερομένης.

683 Choerob. in Theodos. *Can.* (i 80 Gaisford) = *Anecd.
Gr.* iii 1381 Bekker (Hdn. i 44, ii 742 Lentz)

θρᾶνυξ,

θράνυκος, ἐπὶ τοῦ θρόνου παρὰ Κορίννῃ.

684 Theodos. π. κλίσ. τῶν εἰς -ων βαρυτόνων: *Excerpta Hdn.*
p. 18 Hilgard

τὸ Λάδων ὑπὸ Ἀντιμάχου (fr. 34 Wyss) διὰ τοῦ ω κλίνεται
. . . ˙ ἡ μέντοι Κόριννα διὰ τοῦ ντ τὴν κλίσιν ἐποιήσατο τῷ λόγῳ
τῶν μετοχικῶν, οἷον

Λάδοντος δονακοτρόφω

cf. Choerob. i 75 = *Anecd. Gr.* iii 1393 Bekker (Hdn. ii 729 Lentz),
ubi Νεδ- pro Λάδ-

Gaisford: -οστρόφου cod.

685 Hsch. T 1123 (iv 164 Schmidt)

τόνθων ˙

παρὰ Κορίννῃ. ἐπὶ νωτιαίου (νοτιβίου cod.) κρέως τὸ ὄνομα.

682 Apollonius Dyscolus, *Pronouns*

The form ἐμοῦς (= ἐμοῦ),

of me,

being common to the Syracusans and the Boeotians inasmuch as it was used by both Corinna and Epicharmus, seemed to some to be more correct than the form without the ς.

683 Choeroboscus, *On the Canons of Theodosius*

θρᾶνυξ, gen. θράνυκος, is used in the sense of θρόνος,

chair,

by Corinna.

684 Theodosius, *On the Declension of Barytone Words in -ων*

The word Λάδων, 'Ladon', is declined by Antimachus with the ω (i.e. gen. Λάδωνος) . . . ; but Corinna declined it with ντ like participles (i.e. gen. Λάδοντος), e.g.

of Ladon,[1] nurse of reeds

1 Earlier name of the Theban river Ismenus (Paus. 9. 10. 6).

685 Hesychius, *Lexicon*

τόνθων, in Corinna,

chine-meat;

the word refers to the flesh from the back of an animal.

686 Athen. 4. 174f (i 392 Kaibel)

τούτοις δὲ καὶ οἱ Κᾶρες χρῶνται ἐν τοῖς θρήνοις, εἰ μὴ ἄρα καὶ ἡ Καρία Φοινίκη ἐκαλεῖτο, ὡς παρὰ Κορίννῃ καὶ Βακχυλίδῃ (fr. 40 Snell) ἔστιν εὑρεῖν.

687 Heraclid. Miles. fr. 26 (p. 59 Cohn) (Eust. *Od.* 1654. 24; cf. *Il.* 824. 28, *Anecd. Oxon.* i 62 Cramer)

οὕτω δὲ καὶ φράζω φράσσω, τὸ λέγω. ἐκεῖθεν Κόριννα ἡ μελο-ποιὸς

φράττω

ἔφη ἐν δυσὶ τ Βοιωτικῶς.

688 Schol. Ar. *Ach.* 720 (p. 95 Wilson)

ἀγοράζειν· ἐν ἀγορᾷ διατρίβειν, Ἀττικῶς. ὅθεν καὶ ἡ Κόριννα ἐπιτιμᾷ (Geel: ἐπὶ Γ, ἐστὶ Ε) τῷ Πινδάρῳ ἀττικίζοντι (Geel: τοῦ Πινδάρου Ἀττικιστί ΕΓ), ἐπεὶ ἐν τῷ πρώτῳ τῶν Παρθενίων ἐχρή-σατο τῇ λέξει (fr. 94d Snell).

689 Phrynich. *Ecl.* 280 (p. 90 Fischer)

ψίεθος μιερός ὕελος· ἁμαρτάνουσιν οἱ διὰ τοῦ ε λέγοντες, ἀδόκι-μον γάρ. καὶ Κόριννα·

†τὸν ὑάλινον παῖδα θήσεις†

cf. Hsch. Θ 556 (ii 322 Latte) θήσω· αἰτήσω. Βοιωτοί.

τὸν : τοῦ δ' ci. Bergk   παῖδα b πόδα d   τὸν δ' ὑάλιον πεδαθή-σεις post Scaliger Hartung

CORINNA

686 Athenaeus, *Scholars at Dinner* (on the γίγγρας, a small Phoenician pipe)

The Carians also use these in their laments, unless of course the name Phoenice was being applied to Caria,[1] as one may find it in Corinna and Bacchylides.

[1] I.e. unless the pipe was truly Carian.

687 Heraclides of Miletus, *Grammar*

In the same way φράσσω is found for φράζω, 'I say'; and from it φράττω with the Boeotian ττ in the lyric poet Corinna,

I declare.

688 Scholiast on Aristophanes, *Acharnians*

ἀγοράζειν: to spend one's time in the agora, an Attic use of the word. That is why Corinna censures Pindar for atticising: he used the expression in Book 1 of his *Partheneia*.[1]

[1] See L. Lehnus, *R.I.L.* 107 (1973) 393 ff.

689 Phrynichus, Extracts from *The Atticist*

Those who use the letter ε (rather than α) in ψίεθος, μιερός, ὕελος ('glass') are in error: it is disreputable. Cf. Corinna:

(but you will change the?) glass.[1]

[1] Text and translation quite uncertain; with Bergk's text, 'but you will ask for a glass-like (i.e. beautiful) boy.'

690 *P.S.I.* 1174, prim. ed. Coppola

2]αυτοφονε [3] καρδίη σφαδδ . [4] . τονιν ·
κρούψε δ . [5] . δ' ἔδωκε δωρ' ε[6]ν πυρὶ ἔκηον
ηδα[.]τ[7] . σαντες ἐπ' ὠκουπόρω . [

ΟΡΕΣΤΑΣ

Ἄ]ας μὲν ὠκιανῶ λιπῶ-
σα π[αγὰς] ἱαρὸν φάος
σελάνας <σ>πάσα[τ' ὤραν]ῶ ·
Ὤρη δ' ἐς Διὸς ἀμβρότυ
5 [νίονθ]η ϝέαρος ἐν ἄνθεσι<ν>,
γέγα[θεν δὲ πόνυς πο]δῦν
χορὸς ἀν ἐπτάπουλον [πόλιν.

Orest. 1–7 (= 690. 8–12 *P.M.G.*) suppl. West

691 P.Oxy. 2371 (prim. ed. Lobel)

8] . ε μοῦθον · ἴ[9] . οτερυ τάχι[στα
10]μα, Εὐω[νουμ- 11]ν Ἄρειος ἀντι[

9 vel τάχι Lobel 10 tent. West

692 P.Oxy. 2372 (prim. ed. Lobel)

fr. 1 2]ν κῆν γαλά[νη 3 κο]ύνες · ἠὶν ὅτε[
4]δε θαλάττας [5]ταν κουπ . . . [6]νο . γ'
ἄνευ ἠ[7]ένηεν ἁδ' ἐπ[8] . ξ ἐπ' ἄνθι[α
9]λιπὼν επτ[10] . . η τόδε ϝ[

scholia inter lineas: 1–2] . ενος νωθρ . [2–3 κυ]νες θα-
λασσιοι ουκ[6–7 εναιεν 7–8] . . ανθη

Frr. 690–694 were regarded by Lobel and by Page in P.M.G. as 'Boeotian, of uncertain authorship'. West argues convincingly that they are almost certainly by Corinna (C.Q. 20, 1970, 278 f.).

690 Italian papyrus (1st c. A.D.)

... (killer?) with his own hands ... his heart (bade him?) slay ...; and he concealed ... and he gave gifts ... with fire (they) were burning ..., having (come?) on swift-travelling (ship? ships?).[1]

ORESTES[2]

(Dawn), leaving (the waters) of Ocean, (drew from the sky) the moon's holy light, while the Seasons (come) from immortal Zeus among spring's flowers; and the choir rejoices (in the toils of its feet?) in the seven-gated city ...

[1] End of poem.　　　[2] Perhaps composed for a girls' choir to perform at the Daphnephoria, Apollo's Theban festival (for which see A. Schachter, *Cults of Boeotia* i 83 ff.).

691 Oxyrhynchus Papyrus (*c.* 200 A.D.)

... story ... speed ... (Euonymus?) ... (of Ares?) ...

692 Oxyrhynchus Papyrus (*c.* 150 A.D.)

fr. 1 ... and in calm weather ... dogs[1]; always when ... (of) the sea ... without ... she dwelt ... to flowers ... (he) having left ... this ...

[1] The scholiast has 'sluggish' and 'sea-dogs, not (land-)dogs', presumably with reference to basking sharks.

fr. 2 (a)] ₁ ια (titulus)   1]υ παρθένυ κόρη[
2 Καφι]σὸν εὔδενδρον [3 ω]ν οὔπ' ὀμφᾶς κοῦφος [
4 λι]γοὺ δὲ μέλψον[θ ₂] [5]ν φιλόμολπον

scholia inter lineas: 1–2]ν ποταμον Βοιωτιας   2–3
]οργανων ειδη μουσικω[ν

3 λωτῶ]ν ci. Lobel

fr. 3, 4   1 Καφι]σὸν εὐρού [ῥέοντα   3]εὐρού
γάνουτ' ά ₂ [4 φ]ρένας· ἄγ' ἀντὶ τόυ ₂ [
5]ῥοθίων κατα[₂]ερύκι[6]παρθένον ἐι ₂ ἐν[
7 ἁι' ἔχωσα ₂ [8]ὠναϊστῶ[9]ἐνθι ενιδ[

scholia inter lineas: 4–5]ψεα ζητων εληλυθα   5–6]τιζη
η αδελφη   8–9 εισι ερωτ ₂ [

fr. 5 (a), (b)   2]ν γ' ἑκατα   3] ₂ ἐσκούλιξε
4 Μελά]νιππος λίον[5s.]φιλειπόλε | [μο-
6 καλὸν ἔγχος[7]άων διά τ' ὀγ-[

scholia inter lineas: 1 Αμ]φιαραου[2–3 εσκυλευσε
4–5 Μ]ελανιππος μ[ ] ₂ αναιρει Τυδ[7–8 βληθε[
cf. 5 (c)(d) scholia: Τυ[, Μη]κιστεα, Ετεοκλε[

60

fr. 2 (a) ... virgin daughters[1] ... well-wooded
Cephisus[2] ... the light (step) accompanying the
voice[3] ... and (they) will sing clearly ... song-loving
...

[1] Muses? The beginning of a poem, the title of which is given in the
previous line.   [2] Scholiast refers to 'the river of Boeotia'.
[3] Scholiast indicates that musical instruments were named: pipes?

frr. 3, 4 ... widely (flowing Cephisus?) ... (wide?)
... (was glad at?) heart. Come, (instead of?) ...
(breakers?) ... (wards off?)[1] ... girl[2] ... (she) hav-
ing ... (they) are[3] ...

[1] Scholiast gives 'I have come seeking ...' (the speaker is male).
[2] Scholiast gives 'his sister'.   [3] Scholiast mentions 'love'.

fr. 5 (a)(b)[1] ... (Hecate?)[2] ... stripped him of his
arms ... Melanippus ... lion ...[3] battle-lover ...
fine spear ... and through (the Oncaean gates?) ...[4]

[1] Frr. 5–7 deal with the attack of the Seven against Thebes (cf.
659): Amphiaraus, Tydeus, Mecisteus and Eteoclus were attackers,
Melanippus a Theban defender who killed Tydeus and Mecisteus
and was himself killed by Amphiaraus (or by Tydeus in one
version).   [2] The moon, emblem on Tydeus' shield? The scho-
liast mentions Amphiaraus one line earlier.   [3] Scholiast has
'... kills Tydeus' or 'Tydeus kills ...'.   [4] Scholiast has 'having
been struck'. In other frr. the scholiast speaks of Tydeus and Mec-
isteus and of Eteoclus (or Eteocles).

fr. 6 1 ἄ]μιβεγ · χῆρ᾽ ὦ Πολ[ούνικες   2]υμα
κατ᾽ ἐσχατια . [3 νέμ]ονθη φίλτατέ[4]περίφρων
μ.̣[5]ἀμείβετο λ[

scholia inter lineas: 1 ογερω[ν   2–3 νεμονται   4–5
οπο[λυνικης?

fr. 7 3 ὁ]μύων π[4]αν ἔσσοχον ἑ . [5] . α[ ]α̣ς
αὐτῖ λιπὼν πρα[7]ν ἀνδρ[άσι]ν · τε[ύ]χια δ᾽ ἐσσ[
8]δένινη[ ] . μ . [ ] . αγαθ[9 μ]έγαν ἐν[   ] .
νόον[

scholia inter lineas: 2–3 ο]μοιω μο[5–6]Μηκιστ[ε]υς

fr. 8 1 ᾽Α]πόλλωνο̣[2]α νυμφᾶν · ὦ . [4]α
σόφων [

fr. 9   2 μίγ]νουτη · δ[3 ε]ὐδήμων

fr. 20   3 Πολυν[ικ-   4 Καλ]λιόπας

fr. 22   3 Π]ολυνίκ[

fr. 33 (schol.) 4] . υς ελευσεται[ ]αι αυτος εγω[7]αις
κοσμησω το . [11]ευπορησον . [12]ν αϊσμα[ ]α̣τα
τον ελικω[ν-

fr. 36 2 λιγουφ[ων-   3 Θιομαχία (titulus)
4 Μῶσά μ[υ   5 Δευξίπ[πα (titulus)

4 e.g. West

62

CORINNA

fr. 6 ... he[1] answered: 'Greetings, Polynices ...
(of those who) dwell at the border ..., dearest one,
... wise ...'. Polynices answered ...

[1] 'The old man' (scholiast).

fr. 7 ... resembling ... excellent ... leaving there
...[1] (to) men; arms ... good ... mighty mind ...

[1] Scholiast has 'Mecisteus'.

fr. 8 ... Apollo ... Nymphs; oh ... wise (men) ...

fr. 9 ... has intercourse ... blessed ...

fr. 20 ... (Polyneices?) ... (Calliope?) ...

fr. 22 ... Polyneices ...

fr. 33 (scholiast) ... (he) will come ... I myself[1] ... I
shall adorn ... song ... down Helicon ...

[1] The speaker is male.

fr. 36[1] ... (title missing) ... clear-voiced (Muses?)
...; *Battle of the Gods*: Muse ... (to me?) ...;
Zeuxippe[2]: ...

[1] Titles of poems with their first lines.   [2] Daughter of Atha-
mas and mother of Ptous by Apollo.

63

693 P.Oxy. 2373 (prim. ed. Lobel)

fr. 1 2]εν εὐανεμ[3 μελιγ]άρουι φων[ῆ
4]προφωστε   7 πως ποκ' αὐδ[13 ε]ὺροὺ
πορφο[υρ-   14]δ' ἐπ' Εὐρίπυο [17]πων
Ὀλουμπ[19]ετε δεῦρ' ὀμει[ρίωση

19 tent. West

fr. 2 2 κατί]γνειτος · ὃς μετα [4 (ἐ)γεγ]άθι
χορῦς   5]ιτη πρὶν γα [6]πικιν ὄδον παρα [

fr. 3 2]α . [.] μαστός · [3]πολοι σαμ . [
4]θαλαμα . [

3 θαλαμα]πόλοι vel ἀμφι] vel προ] Lobel

fr. 5 (a) 2 δολερ[3καλως . [8 ἀϝύδιμος κ[
9 κὴ μέγα θο[10] . ον · εὐδημ[12]πάντη πα[
(c) 6] . ἀϊσμ[8]ελι[

CORINNA

693 Oxyrhynchus Papyrus (2nd or 3rd c. A.D.?)

fr. 1 ... enjoying kindly winds ... with melodious
voice ... how once song ... wide surging ... on the
Euripus ... Olympus[1] ... (come) here (to meet?) ...

[1] From the beginning of a song with a summons to the Muses?

fr. 2 ... (brother), who ... rejoiced in the choirs
... before ... road ...

fr. 3 ... breast ... (attendant?) ... chamber ...

fr. 5 (a) ... guileful ... fine ... famous in song ...
and great ... blessed ... everywhere ...

(c) ... song ... (Helicon?) ...

694 P.Oxy. 2374 (prim. ed. Lobel)

fr. 1 κὴ . [Πτ]οῖον ὄρος κ[
      κὴ . [   ] . Ἀθανήας[
   5 κὴ . [   ]πρωτερικα[
      κὴ . [Γάρ]γαρα σκιό[εντα
      ἴζον[θη   Ἡ]γίδαο θο[

6 vel σκιό[εσσα

fr. 2 3 ο]ὔπ᾽ ἀντελιᾶ[ν   4] . δήιον ϝυκτ[
6]αν ἀπέκοψ[αν   7]μίστουλλαν τ[

fr. 6(a) 2]ορεγον π[3 τ]ύγ᾽ οὔδρευο[ν
4]κη, στ[ο]ναχα[5]ε κάρμος ιδ

fr. 7 2]καρμ[ος ?   4]ας πολίτας [5]μαδ᾽
ὐμωγᾶς[6] . ι κώρας [7]ν Ὀλυμπ[

fr. 9 2 Εὐ]ειρίδα χο . [3]λα ϝέργα[

schol. sup. v. 1]τι νυκτος αυτω[1–2] . απο Ευηρους
Ηρα[κλεους υιου

fr. 11 4] ὤς ποκ᾽ . [5 τ]ῆν θιῆ[ν
6]δευρ᾽ ἴθ[ι

fr. 13 2 Ἐρού[θρος ? (titulus)

CORINNA

694 Oxyrhynchus Papyrus (late 2nd c. A.D.)

fr. 1 ... and the mountain Ptoios ... and Athena's ... and ... and shadowy Gargara[1] ... (they) will come ... of the son of Aegeus[2] ...

[1] Mountain in Troad with a sanctuary of Zeus.   [2] Theseus? Or a Boeotian Aegeid?

fr. 2 ... under the east ... hostile ... (pitiable?) ... they cut off ... they sliced (the meat) ...

fr. 6 (a) ... (they stretched out?) ... they drew water ... wailing ... (haircutting?) ...

fr. 7 ... (haircutting?) ... citizens ... lamentation ... maidens ... Olympus ...

fr. 9 ... (scholiast: night) ... son of Eueres[1] ... works

[1] Son of Heracles (scholiast).

fr. 11 ... as once ... (of the two goddesses?) ... come here! ...

fr. 13 ... (*Red* ...?)[1]

[1] A title.

MISCELLANEA

695 (a) Ap. Dysc. *Pron.*

64b Βοιωτοὶ <ἰών>; 69c Βοιωτοὶ τού καὶ τούν καὶ τούγα; 106a (οἶ) Βοιωτοὶ ... εἰς τὸ ϝῦ μεταλαμβάνουσι; 111c (νῶι) τεκμηριοῦνταί τε ἐκ τοῦ Βοιωτιακοῦ, ἐπεὶ οὐδέποτε παρὰ αὐτοῖς νοί διὰ τοῦ οι; 135a (τεός) ἐπὶ ταύτης τῆς λέξεως μεταβάλλουσι τὸ ε εἰς ι.

(b) Pap. Bibl. Univ. Giss. 40: vid. Simon. test. 18 n. 2

(c) Hsch. Γ 65, 70–72

γακέα (γακα cod.)· ἡδέως; γακού· ἡδύ, γλυκύ; γακούδια· ἡδύσματα; γακουπώνης (-τανης cod.)· ἡδυπότης.

695A P.Oxy. 2438 col. ii

υἱὸς δὲ (sc. ὁ Πίνδαρος) κατὰ μὲν Κόρ[ιννἀν] καὶ ἑτέρας ποιητρίας Σκοπελίνο[υ.

CORINNA

MISCELLANEOUS

695 (a) Examples of Boeotian usage given by Apollonius Dyscolus, *Pronouns*: ἰών, 'I'; τού, τούν, τούγα, 'you'; Ϝῦ, 'to him'; νῶε (= νῶι), not νοί, 'we two, us two', τιός, 'your'.

(b) See Simon. test. 18 n. 2 on Hyccara. Page took ὐκ[τ]ρ(ας) to be Boeotian, 'pitiable'.

(c) Hesychius, *Lexicon* lists γακέα, 'sweetly', γακού, 'sweet', γακούδια, 'seasonings', γακουπώνης, 'fond of drinking': Latte ascribes the forms to Corinna (i 502).

695A Oxyrhynchus papyrus (*c.* 200 A.D.): Life of Pindar

According to Corinna and other poetesses Pindar was the son of Scopelinus.

TELESILLA

TESTIMONIA VITAE ATQUE ARTIS

1 *Anth. Pal.* 9. 26. 5 = Antipater of Thessalonica xix 5
Gow-Page

Τελέσιλλαν ἀγακλέα

2 Euseb. *Chron.* Ol. 82.2 (p. 112 Helm)

Crates comicus et Telesilla ac Bacchylides lyricus
clari habentur. Praxilla quoque et Cleobulina sunt
celebres.

cf. Sync. p. 297 Mosshammer

3 Plut. *Mul. Virt.* 4. 245c-f (ii 232s. Nachstädt-Sieveking)

οὐδενὸς δ' ἧττον ἔνδοξόν ἐστι τῶν κοινῇ διαπε-
πραγμένων γυναιξὶν ἔργων ὁ πρὸς Κλεομένη περὶ Ἄρ-
γους ἀγών, ὃν ἠγωνίσαντο Τελεσίλλης τῆς ποιητρίας
προτρεψαμένης. ταύτην δέ φασιν οἰκίας οὖσαν ἐνδό-
ξου τῷ δὲ σώματι νοσηματικὴν εἰς θεοῦ πέμψαι περὶ
ὑγιείας· καὶ χρησθὲν αὐτῇ Μούσας θεραπεύειν, πειθο-
μένην τῷ θεῷ καὶ ἐπιθεμένην ᾠδῇ καὶ ἁρμονίᾳ τοῦ τε

---

[1] King of Sparta; for his attack on Argos *c.* 494 B.C. see Hdt. 6. 76 ff.
Hdt. does not mention Telesilla or the Argive women, but see test. 4.

TELESILLA

1 *Palatine Anthology*: Antipater of Thessalonica (on nine poetesses)[1]

> glorious Telesilla

[1] Cf. Corinna test. 1 n. 3.

2 Eusebius, *Chronicle*

Olympiad 82.2 (451/450 B.C.)[1]: the comic poet Crates and Telesilla and the lyric poet Bacchylides are regarded as famous. Praxilla also and Cleobulina are renowned.

[1] The Armenian version gives 449/8.

3 Plutarch, *Fine Deeds of Women*

As distinguished as any of the exploits performed by groups of women is the struggle against Cleomenes[1] for possession of Argos. It was Telesilla the poetess who urged the women to fight. They say that she was of distinguished family but had poor health and sent to Apollo's temple to ask how she might become well. On being told that she must do service to the Muses she took the god's advice and devoted herself to singing and playing the lyre, with

71

GREEK LYRIC

πάθους ἀπαλλαγῆναι ταχὺ καὶ θαυμάζεσθαι διὰ ποιη-
τικὴν ὑπὸ τῶν γυναικῶν. ἐπεὶ δὲ Κλεομένης ὁ βασι-
λεὺς τῶν Σπαρτιατῶν πολλοὺς ἀποκτείνας (οὐ μήν,
ὡς ἔνιοι μυθολογοῦσιν, ἑπτὰ καὶ ἑβδομήκοντα καὶ
ἑπτακοσίους πρὸς ἑπτακισχιλίοις) ἐβάδιζε πρὸς τὴν
πόλιν, ὁρμὴ καὶ τόλμα δαιμόνιος παρέστη ταῖς ἀκμα-
ζούσαις τῶν γυναικῶν ἀμύνεσθαι τοὺς πολεμίους ὑπὲρ
τῆς πατρίδος. ἡγουμένης δὲ τῆς Τελεσίλλης ὅπλα
λαμβάνουσαι καὶ παρ᾽ ἔπαλξιν ἱστάμεναι κύκλῳ τὰ
τείχη περιέστεψαν, ὥστε θαυμάζειν τοὺς πολεμίους.
τὸν μὲν οὖν Κλεομένη πολλῶν πεσόντων ἀπεκρού-
σαντο· τὸν δ᾽ ἕτερον βασιλέα Δημάρατον, ὡς Σωκρά-
της φησίν (F.Gr.H. 310 F6), ἐντὸς γενόμενον καὶ
κατασχόντα τὸ Παμφυλιακὸν ἐξέωσαν. οὕτω δὲ τῆς
πόλεως περιγενομένης . . .

4 Paus. 2. 20. 8–10 (i 153s. Rocha-Pereira)

ὑπὲρ δὲ τὸ θέατρον Ἀφροδίτης ἐστὶν ἱερόν, ἔμπροσ-
θεν δὲ τοῦ ἕδους Τελέσιλλα ἡ ποιήσασα τὰ ᾄσματα
ἐπείργασται στήλῃ· καὶ βιβλία μὲν ἐκεῖνα ἔρριπταί οἱ
πρὸς τοῖς ποσίν, αὐτὴ δὲ ἐς κράνος ὁρᾷ κατέχουσα τῇ
χειρὶ καὶ ἐπιτίθεσθαι τῇ κεφαλῇ μέλλουσα. ἦν δὲ ἡ
Τελέσιλλα καὶ ἄλλως ἐν ταῖς γυναιξὶν εὐδόκιμος καὶ
μᾶλλον ἐτιμᾶτο ἔτι ἐπὶ τῇ ποιήσει. συμβάντος δὲ Ἀρ-

---

[1] Tatian, *Against the Greeks* 33 attributes to Niceratus (*c.* 100 B.C.)
a statue of Telesilla; see Myrtis test. 1 n. 1.

72

the result that she was soon enjoying good health and was admired by the women for her poetry. When Cleomenes, the Spartan king, had killed many Argives (not however 7,777, the fabulous figure given by some authorities)[2] and was marching against Argos, those women who were in the prime of their lives were moved by a superhuman impulse of daring to ward off the enemy and save their native city. Under the leadership of Telesilla they took up arms and manned the battlements all round the circuit of the walls, with the result that the enemy were astonished. They beat back Cleomenes with heavy loss to his troops and drove out the other king Demaratus, who according to Socrates[3] had entered the city and seized the Pamphyliacum. That was how the city survived.[4]

[2] See Polyaenus 8. 33. Hdt. 7. 148 says 6,000.   [3] Historian of Argos, between 250 and 100 B.C.(?).   [4] See also Polyaenus loc. cit., Lucian, *Amores* 30, Clement of Alexandria, *Str.* 4. 19. 120. 3.

4 Pausanias, *Description of Greece* (on Argos)

Above the theatre there is a temple of Aphrodite, and in front of her seated statue is a slab with a representation of Telesilla, the composer of the songs: those books of hers have been thrown down at her feet, and she herself is gazing at a helmet which she holds in her hand and is about to place on her head.[1] Although Telesilla had a fine reputation among women on other grounds also, she won even greater honour for her poetry. The Argives had

γείοις ἀτυχῆσαι λόγου μειζόνως πρὸς Κλεομένην τὸν
Ἀναξανδρίδου καὶ Λακεδαιμονίους, καὶ τῶν μὲν ἐν
αὐτῇ πεπτωκότων τῇ μάχῃ, ὅσοι δὲ ἐς τὸ ἄλσος τοῦ
Ἄργου κατέφυγον διαφθαρέντων καὶ τούτων, τὰ μὲν
πρῶτα ἐξιόντων κατὰ ὁμολογίαν, ὡς δὲ ἔγνωσαν ἀπα-
τώμενοι συγκατακαυθέντων τῷ ἄλσει τῶν λοιπῶν,
οὕτω τοὺς Λακεδαιμονίους Κλεομένης ἦγεν ἐπὶ ἔρημον
ἀνδρῶν τὸ Ἄργος. Τελέσιλλα δὲ οἰκέτας μὲν καὶ ὅσοι
διὰ νεότητα ἢ γῆρας ὅπλα ἀδύνατοι φέρειν ἦσαν, τού-
τους μὲν πάντας ἀνεβίβασεν ἐπὶ τὸ τεῖχος, αὐτὴ δὲ
ὁπόσα ἐν ταῖς οἰκίαις ὑπελείπετο καὶ τὰ ἐκ τῶν ἱερῶν
ὅπλα ἀθροίσασα τὰς ἀκμαζούσας ἡλικίᾳ τῶν γυναικῶν
ὥπλιζεν, ὁπλίσασα δὲ ἔτασσε κατὰ τοῦτο ᾗ τοὺς πολε-
μίους προσιόντας ἠπίστατο. ὡς δὲ <ἐγγὺς> ἐγίνοντο
οἱ Λακεδαιμόνιοι καὶ αἱ γυναῖκες οὔτε τῷ ἀλαλαγμῷ
κατεπλάγησαν δεξάμεναί τε ἐμάχοντο ἐρρωμένως, ἐν-
ταῦθα οἱ Λακεδαιμόνιοι, φρονήσαντες ὡς καὶ διαφθεί-
ρασί σφισι τὰς γυναῖκας ἐπιφθόνως τὸ κατόρθωμα ἕξει
καὶ σφαλεῖσι μετὰ ὀνειδῶν γενήσοιτο ἡ συμφορά, ὑπεί-
κουσι ταῖς γυναιξί. πρότερον δὲ ἔτι τὸν ἀγῶνα τοῦτον
προεσήμηνεν ἡ Πυθία, καὶ τὸ λόγιον εἴτε ἄλλως εἴτε
καὶ συνεὶς ἐδήλωσεν Ἡρόδοτος·

ἀλλ' ὅταν ἡ θήλεια τὸν ἄρρενα νικήσασα
ἐξελάσῃ καὶ κῦδος ἐν Ἀργείοισιν ἄρηται,
πολλὰς Ἀργείων ἀμφιδρυφέας τότε θήσει.

---

[2] Hdt. 6. 77. 2: he does not explain the oracle, and it is likely that it
was the Argives who in later years saw reference to
Telesilla.   [3] See also *Suda* s.v. Telesilla (T 260).

74

suffered an indescribable disaster at the hands of Cleomenes, son of Anaxandridas, and the Spartans: some had fallen in the battle itself, and all who took refuge in the grove of Argus also perished: at first they came out under a truce, and then when they realised that they were being tricked the remainder were burned to death in the grove; and that is how Cleomenes was leading his Spartans against an Argos that had lost its menfolk. But Telesilla sent up to the wall slaves and all who had been too young or too old to bear arms, and gathering all the weapons that had been left in the houses or were in the temples armed those women who were in the prime of life and stationed them where she knew the enemy would attack. When the Spartans were close at hand, the women were not at all dismayed by the battle-cry but stood their ground and offered strong resistance. In those circumstances the Spartans reflected that if they defeated the women their success would be invidious, while if they failed their disaster would be ridiculed, and so they gave way before the women. The priestess at Delphi had foretold this conflict, and Herodotus quoted the oracle, whether or not he understood it[2]: 'But when the female defeats the male and drives him out and wins glory among the Argives, she shall leave many of the Argive women with torn cheeks.' That was the part of the oracle that referred to the women's exploit.[3]

5 Max. Tyr. 37. 5 (p. 432 Hobein)

καὶ Σπαρτιάτας ἤγειρεν τὰ Τυρταίου ἔπη καὶ Ἀργείους τὰ Τελεσίλλης μέλη καὶ Λεσβίους ἡ Ἀλκαίου ᾠδή.

5 Maximus of Tyre, *Orations*

The Spartans were roused by the lines of Tyrtaeus, the Argives by the lyrics of Telesilla, the Lesbians by the song of Alcaeus.

TELESILLA

717 Heph. *Ench.* 11. 2 (p. 35 Consbruch)

ἐστὶ τοίνυν ἐπίσημα ἐν τῷ ἰωνικῷ ἐφθημιμερῆ (πενθημιμερῆ ci.
Edmonds) μὲν τὰ τοιαῦτα, οἷς ἡ Τελέσιλλα ἐχρήσατο·

> ἁ δ' Ἄρτεμις, ὦ κόραι,
> φεύγοισα τὸν Ἀλφεόν

cf. *Ench.* 4. 4 (p. 14 Consbruch), epitom. (p. 361)

1 ἁ δ' bis cod. I: ἃδ' vel ἅδε rell., nisi οὐδ' epitom.   κόρα 4. 4 cod. D

718 Athen. 14. 619b (iii 365 Kaibel)

ἡ δὲ εἰς Ἀπόλλωνα ᾠδὴ

> φιληλιάς,

ὡς Τελέσιλλα παρίστησιν.

Musurus: φηλικίας cod.

719 Paus. 2. 35. 2 (i 190 Rocha-Pereira)

Ἀπόλλωνος δέ εἰσι ναοὶ τρεῖς καὶ ἀγάλματα τρία· καὶ τῷ μὲν
οὐκ ἔστιν ἐπίκλησις, τὸν δὲ Πυθαέα [[οὕτως]] ὀνομάζουσι, καὶ Ὅριον
τὸν τρίτον. τὸ μὲν δὴ τοῦ Πυθαέως ὄνομα μεμαθήκασι παρὰ Ἀρ-
γείων· τούτοις γὰρ Ἑλλήνων πρώτοις ἀφικέσθαι Τελέσιλλά φησι
τὸν Πυθαέα ἐς τὴν χώραν Ἀπόλλωνος παῖδα ὄντα.

TELESILLA

717 Hephaestion, *Handbook on Metres* (on the ionic *a maiore*)

Remarkable among the ionic metres are the three-and-a-half foot lines of the following type,[1] used by Telesilla:

> And Artemis, girls, fleeing from Alpheus . . .[2]

[1] The metre ($--\smile\smile-\smile-$) is called telesillean; perhaps read 'two-and-a-half foot lines' with Edmonds.   [2] Probably the beginning of a poem in spite of 'and'. Pausanias 6. 22. 9 tells how the river-god Alpheus pursued Artemis, who foiled his advances at Letrini, north of the river mouth.

718 Athenaeus, *Scholars at Dinner* (on the names of songs)

The song to Apollo is the *philhelias*,

> the sun-loving song,

as Telesilla has it.

719 Pausanias, *Description of Greece* (on Hermione)

There are three temples and three images of Apollo. One has no extra title, but they call the second Apollo Pythaeus and the third Apollo of the Boundaries. They have learned the name Pythaeus from the Argives, for according to Telesilla theirs was the first district of Greece to which Pythaeus, a son of Apollo, came.[1]

[1] Paus. had noted in Argos 'a temple of Apollo, first built by Pythaeus on his arrival from Delphi' (2. 24. 1).

720 Paus. 2. 28. 2 (i 172 Rocha-Pereira)

ἐπὶ δὲ τῇ ἄκρᾳ τοῦ ὄρους Κορυφαίας ἐστὶν ἱερὸν Ἀρτέμιδος, οὗ καὶ Τελέσιλλα ἐποιήσατο ἐν ᾄσματι μνήμην.

721 [Apollod.] *Bibl.* 3. 46s. (p. 120 Wagner)

ἐσώθη δὲ τῶν μὲν ἀρρένων Ἀμφίων, τῶν δὲ θηλειῶν Χλωρὶς ἡ πρεσβυτέρα (-τάτη Bergk), ᾗ Νηλεὺς συνῴκησε. κατὰ δὲ Τελέσιλλαν ἐσώθησαν Ἀμύκλας καὶ Μελίβοια, ἐτοξεύθη δὲ ὑπ' αὐτῶν καὶ Ἀμφίων.

722 Hsch. B 500 (i 323 Latte)

βελτιωτέρας·

τὰς βελτίους. Τελέσιλλα.

Lobeck, L. Dindorf: βελτιώτας codd. (cf. schol. BT Hom. *Il.* 2. 248 χερειότερον ὡς μειζονώτερον, βελτιώτερον)

723 Athen. 11. 467f (ii 28 Kaibel)

Τελέσιλλα δὲ ἡ Ἀργεία καὶ τὴν ἅλω καλεῖ

δῖνον.

cf. Eust. *Il.* 1207. 9

δεῖνον cod. A, δῖνον (ει sup. ῖ scr.) E

TELESILLA

720 Pausanias, *Description of Greece* (on Epidaurus)

On top of the mountain[1] there is a temple of Artemis Coryphaea,[2] mentioned by Telesilla in one of her songs.

[1] Coryphum, the Peak.   [2] Artemis of the Peak.

721 'Apollodorus', *Library* (on Niobe's children)

Of the males the only one to be saved was Amphion, of the females Chloris, the elder,[1] whom Neleus married.[2] According to Telesilla it was Amyclas and Meliboea who were saved, while Amphion also was shot by Apollo and Artemis.[3]

[1] Or with Bergk's emendation 'the eldest'.   [2] See *Od.* 11. 281 ff.; Nestor was their son.   [3] Telesilla presumably followed the usual version in which Amphion was Niobe's husband. Pausanias in his account of the temple of Leto at Argos (2. 21. 9) says that Meliboea was the original name of the daughter, Chloris (Green, Pale) the name given to her when she turned green with fright at the time of the killing.

722 Hesychius, *Lexicon*

βελτιωτέρας :

the better ones,[1]

used for βελτίους by Telesilla.

[1] Fem.: perhaps 'the better women'.

723 Athenaeus, *Scholars at Dinner*

Telesilla of Argos calls the threshing-floor δῖνος,

the round.

GREEK LYRIC

724 Pollux 2. 23 (i 88 Bethe)

οὐλοκίκιννε

δὲ Τελέσιλλα εἴρηκεν.

-κίκινε cod. F, -κίκινα cod. A

725 Schol. A Hom. *Od.* 13. 289 (ii 572 Dindorf)

καλῆ τε μεγάλη τε· ἐκ τῆς κατὰ τὴν ὄψιν κοσμιότητος καὶ αἰ-
δοῦς καὶ τοῦτο ὑπονοεῖν δίδωσι, καθὰ καὶ Ξενοφῶν καὶ Τελέσιλλα ἡ
Ἀργεία διαγράφουσιν Ἀρετῆς καὶ Καλοκαγαθίας εἰκόνα.

726   MISCELLANEA

(i) Phot. *Bibl.* 167 (ii 157 Henry)

(ποιηταὶ δὲ . . .) Τελέσιλλα . . .

(ii) [Censorin.] *de Musica* (*Gramm. Lat.* vi 608 Keil)

Telesilla etiam Argiva minutiores edidit numeros.

(iii) Schol. Theocr. 15. 64 (Hunt and Johnson, *Two Theo-
critus Papyri,* pp. 46, 76)

ad v. 60 (marg. sin.) ποιητριαν Τελεσιλλαν scriptum
deletumque; ad v. 64 (marg. sin.) θαυμαζει την ποιητριαν,
(marg. dext.) μια αυτων θαυμαζ[ει

TELESILLA

724 Pollux, *Vocabulary*

Telesilla used the form οὐλοκίκυννε,
curly-locks!

725 Scholiast on *Odyssey* ('Athena was like a beautiful, tall woman')

Homer conveys this also by means of the comeliness and modesty of her appearance,[1] just like Xenophon and Telesilla of Argos in their representation of Virtue and Nobility.

[1] Text and translation insecure: one would expect 'conveys by this means the comeliness . . .'.

726   MISCELLANEOUS

(i) Photius, *Library* in his account of the *Anthology* of Stobaeus names Telesilla as one of the poets from whom he made extracts. None survives in our Stobaeus.

(ii) 'Censorinus', *On Music*

Telesilla of Argos also composed shorter lines.

(iii) Antinoe papyrus (*c.* 500 A.D.): scholiast on Theocritus ('Women know everything, even how Zeus married Hera.')

(The speaker) is marvelling at the poetess.[1]

[1] Three lines above, the words 'the poetess Telesilla' have been written and then erased: Telesilla may have described the marriage, alluded to in *Il.* 14. 295 f. Hera had a famous temple at Argos.

TIMOCREON

TESTIMONIA VITAE ATQUE ARTIS

1 *Sud.* T 625 (iv 558 Adler)

Τιμοκρέων, Ῥόδιος, κωμικὸς καὶ αὐτὸς τῆς ἀρχαίας κωμῳδίας. διεφέρετο δὲ πρὸς Σιμωνίδην τὸν τῶν μελῶν ποιητὴν καὶ Θεμιστοκλέα τὸν Ἀθηναῖον, εἰς ὃν ἐξύφανε ψόγον δι' ἐμμελοῦς τινος ποιήματος. ἔγραψε δὲ κωμῳδίαν εἴς τε τὸν αὐτὸν Θεμιστοκλέα καὶ εἰς Σιμωνίδην τὸν μελοποιὸν καὶ ἄλλα.

2 Athen. 10. 415f–416a (ii 404s. Kaibel)

καὶ Τιμοκρέων δ' ὁ Ῥόδιος ποιητὴς καὶ ἀθλητὴς πένταθλος ἅδην ἔφαγε καὶ ἔπιεν, ὡς τὸ ἐπὶ τοῦ τάφου αὐτοῦ ἐπίγραμμα δηλοῖ ('Simon.' XXXVII)·

πολλὰ πιὼν καὶ πολλὰ φαγὼν καὶ πολλὰ κάκ' εἰπὼν
ἀνθρώπους κεῖμαι Τιμοκρέων Ῥόδιος.

Θρασύμαχος δ' ὁ Καλχηδόνιος ἔν τινι τῶν προοιμίων

TIMOCREON

1 *Suda*

Timocreon, a Rhodian,[1] likewise[2] a playwright of the Old Comedy. He was at loggerheads with Simonides, the lyric poet,[3] and with Themistocles the Athenian, against whom he composed a poem of censure in lyric metre.[4] He wrote a comedy on the same Themistocles and the lyric poet Simonides in addition to other works.[5]

[1] From Ialysus (727. 7).   [2] Like Timocles, subject of the previous entry.   [3] Cf. Diog. Laert. 2. 46, and see fr. 10 West.
[4] Fr. 727.   [5] Nothing is known of his comedies; it is probable that he was not a playwright but simply a composer of mockery in lyric metres. Philodemus, *On Vices* 10. 4 recounts an anecdote in which he appears as a conceited singer performing a Castor-song in a festival competition; see Wilamowitz, *S.u.S.* 146 n. 2.

2 Athenaeus, *Scholars at Dinner* (on gluttony)

Timocreon of Rhodes, poet and pentathlete, ate and drank his fill,[1] as is shown by the epigram on his tomb ('Simon.' XXXVII): 'After much drinking, much eating and much slandering of men I lie here, Timocreon of Rhodes.' Thrasymachus of Chalcedon[2]

[1] Cf. Aelian, *V.H.* 1. 27.   [2] The sophist and rhetorician (flor. c. 430–400 B.C.) known from Plato's *Republic*.

(fr. 4 Diels) τὸν Τιμοκρέοντά φησιν ὡς μέγαν βασιλέα ἀφικόμενον καὶ ξενιζόμενον παρ' αὐτῷ πολλὰ ἐμφορεῖσθαι. πυθομένου δὲ τοῦ βασιλέως ὅ τι ἀπὸ τούτων ἐργάζοιτο, εἶπε Περσῶν ἀναριθμήτους συγκόψειν. καὶ τῇ ὑστεραίᾳ πολλοὺς καθ' ἕνα νικήσας μετὰ τοῦτο ἐχειρονόμησε. πυνθανομένου δὲ τὴν πρόφασιν ὑπολείπεσθαι ἔφη τοσαύτας, εἰ προσίοι τις, πληγάς.

3 Ael. Arist. or. 3. 612 (i 496 Behr) = or. 46. 294 (ii 380 Dindorf)

μὴ τοίνυν ἡμεῖς ἐκεῖνον ὑπερβαλώμεθα, μηδὲ Τιμοκρέοντος τοῦ σχετλίου πρᾶγμα ποιῶμεν, ἀλλ' εἰδῶμεν εὐφημεῖν τὰ γιγνόμενα . . .

Schol. Oxon. ad loc. (iii 720 Dindorf)

οἱ μὲν λυρικὸν ποιητὴν τοῦτόν φασι, γεγραφότα ἰάμβους διαβολὰς ἔχοντας· οἱ δὲ ὅτι κακὸς ἦν καὶ καταγνωσθεὶς ὑπ' Ἀθηναίων περιῄει λέγων ὡς οὐκ ἐμὲ μόνον πεποιήκασι κακῶς ἀλλὰ καὶ Περικλέα.

tells in one of his *Introductions* how Timocreon went
to the king of Persia and stuffed himself full at his
table; and when the king asked what this was lead-
ing to, he said he was going to beat up countless
numbers of Persians. On the next day he defeated
many of them, one after the other, and then stood
punching the air; and on being asked why, he said
he had all those blows left if anyone wanted to take
him on.

3 Aelius Aristides, *In defence of the Four*

Let us not outdo him,[1] then, nor copy the wretch
Timocreon; let us know, rather, how to speak well of
events . . .

[1] Archilochus, who according to Aristides attacked not the best and
most famous of the Greeks, although he was so libellous, but
Lycambes, Charilaus, Batusiades and his contemporary Pericles.

Scholiast on the passage

Some say this Timocreon was a lyric poet who
wrote slanderous iambics, others that he was a
wicked man who when convicted by the Athenians
went about saying, 'I'm not the only one they
wronged: they wronged Pericles too.'[1]

[1] This cannot be our Timocreon; Pericles was tried and fined by the
Athenians in 430.

TIMOCREON

FRAGMENTA

727 Plut. *Them.* 21 (i 1. 182s. Ziegler)

ἦν δὲ καὶ τοῖς συμμάχοις ἐπαχθὴς περιπλέων τε τὰς νήσους καὶ
χρηματιζόμενος ἀπ' αὐτῶν· . . . Τιμοκρέων δ' ὁ Ῥόδιος μελοποιὸς
ἐν ᾄσματι καθάπτεται πικρότερον τοῦ Θεμιστοκλέους, ὡς ἄλλους
μὲν ἐπὶ χρήμασι φυγάδας διαπραξαμένου κατελθεῖν, αὐτὸν δὲ ξένον
ὄντα καὶ φίλον προεμένου δι' ἀργύριον. λέγει δ' οὕτως·

ἀλλ' εἰ τύ γε Παυσανίαν ἢ καὶ τύ γε Ξάνθιππον αἰνεῖς
ἢ τύ γε Λευτυχίδαν, ἐγὼ δ' Ἀριστείδαν ἐπαινέω
ἄνδρ' ἱερᾶν ἀπ' Ἀθανᾶν
ἐλθεῖν ἕνα λῷστον, ἐπεὶ Θεμιστοκλῆν ἤχθαρε Λατώ,

5 ψεύσταν ἄδικον προδόταν, ὃς Τιμοκρέοντα ξεῖνον
      ἐόντα
ἀργυρίοισι κοβαλικοῖσι πεισθεὶς οὐ κατᾶγεν
πατρίδ' Ἰαλυσὸν εἴσ<ω>,
λαβὼν δὲ τρί' ἀργυρίου τάλαντ' ἔβα πλέων εἰς ὄλεθρον,

τοὺς μὲν κατάγων ἀδίκως, τοὺς δ' ἐκδιώκων, τοὺς δὲ
      καίνων·
10 ἀργυρίων δ' ὑπόπλεως Ἰσθμοῖ γελοίως πανδόκευε

---

[1] After the battle of Salamis (480 B.C.); see Hdt. 8. 111 f.
[2] Pausanias and Aristides distinguished themselves at Plataea (479
B.C.), Xanthippus and Leotychidas at Mycale (479 B.C.); Themisto-

TIMOCREON

727 Plutarch, *Life of Themistocles*

Themistocles made himself offensive to the allies also by sailing round the islands and trying to exact money from them[1]; ... Timocreon, the lyric poet from Rhodes, makes a bitter attack on Themistocles in one of his songs, saying that he took bribes to arrange for the restoration of other exiles but abandoned Timocreon himself, his host and friend, and all for silver. This is what he says:

Well now, if you praise Pausanias and you, sir, Xanthippus and you Leotychidas, I commend Aristides[2] as the very best man to have come from holy Athens; for Themistocles incurred the hatred of Leto,[3] Themistocles the liar, the criminal, the traitor, who was bribed with mischievous silver and would not take Timocreon home to his native Ialysus, although he was his guest-friend. Instead he accepted three talents of silver and sailed off to the devil, restoring some to their homes unjustly, chasing others out, killing others. Gorged with silver, he made a ridiculous innkeeper at the

cles had been responsible for the victory at Salamis.   [3] Allusion uncertain: Leto was closely associated with Delos, and the Delian league was created in 478–477; see also 'Simon.' XIII.

ψυχρὰ <τὰ> κρεῖα παρίσχων·
οἱ δ᾽ ἤσθιον κηὔχοντο μὴ ὥραν Θεμιστοκλέος γενέσθαι.

4 ἐλθεῖν ἕνα λῶστον codd. UMA   ὃς ἦλθε λεκτὸς S   Wila-
mowitz: Θεμιστοκλῆα UMA   -κλέα δὲ S   6 Bergk: σκυβαλ-
UMAS (marg.)   κυμβαλ- S   7 Page: εἰς πατρῷ᾽ Ἰαλυσὸν codd.
10 Enger: ἀργυρίων ὑπόπλεως Ἰσθμοῖ (-οῖς M) δὲ πανδόκευε γελοίως
UMA   ἀργυρίου δὲ ὑπόπλεως κτλ. S   11 Page: ψ. κρέα παρέχων codd.
12 κηὔχοντο: εὐχόμενοι ci. Bowra   Ahrens: -κλέους codd.

728 Plut. *Them.* 21 (i 1. 183 Ziegler)

πολὺ δ᾽ ἀσελγεστέρᾳ καὶ ἀναπεπταμένῃ μᾶλλον εἰς τὸν Θεμι-
στοκλέα βλασφημίᾳ χρῆται μετὰ τὴν φυγὴν αὐτοῦ καὶ τὴν καταδί-
κην ὁ Τιμοκρέων, ᾆσμα ποιήσας οὗ ἐστιν ἀρχή·

> Μοῦσα τοῦδε τοῦ μέλεος
> κλέος ἀν᾽ Ἕλλανας τίθει,
> ὡς ἐοικὸς καὶ δίκαιον.

729 Plut. *Them.* 21 (i 1. 183 Ziegler)

λέγεται δ᾽ ὁ Τιμοκρέων ἐπὶ μηδισμῷ φυγεῖν συγκαταψηφισα-
μένου τοῦ Θεμιστοκλέους. ὡς οὖν ὁ Θεμιστοκλῆς αἰτίαν ἔσχε μηδί-
ζειν, ταῦτ᾽ ἐποίησεν ἐς αὐτόν·

> οὐκ ἄρα Τιμοκρέων μόνος
> Μήδοισιν ὁρκιατομεῖ,
> ἀλλ᾽ ἐντὶ κἄλλοι δὴ πονη-
> ροὶ κοὐκ ἐγὼ μόνα κόλου-
> 5 ρις· ἐντὶ κἄλλαι ᾽λώπεκες.

cf. Arsen. = Apostol. *Cent.* 7. 28 (ii 402 Leutsch-Schneidewin)

1 ἄρα, μοῦνος codd.   2 Hermann: ὅρκια τέμοι codd. UM   ὅρκια
τομῇ S   ὅρκια τέμνει A   4 Hermann: οὐκ codd.

90

Isthmus,[4] serving cold meat[5]: the guests would eat up and pray that no attention be paid to Themistocles.

[4] He failed to win first prize when the Greek commanders met at the Isthmus in autumn 480 to reward distinguished service against the Persians; see Hdt. 8. 123 f.   [5] He may have given a vote-catching dinner-party which turned out to be 'a frost'.

728 Plutarch, *Life of Themistocles* (continued)

Far more brutal and brazen slander is directed by Timocreon against Themistocles after his exile and condemnation,[1] when he composed a song which begins,

Muse, spread the fame of this song among the Greeks, as is fitting and just.

[1] *C.* 471 B.C.

729 Plutarch, *Life of Themistocles* (continued)

It is said that Timocreon was exiled on a charge of medism, Themistocles joining in the vote against him. So when Themistocles was accused of medizing, Timocreon composed the following lines against him:

Timocreon then is not the only one who swears a solemn oath with the Medes: there are other scoundrels too, and I am not the only animal with a brush[1]: there are other foxes too.

[1] Usually taken as 'I am not the only dock-tailed one' with reference to a mishap.

GREEK LYRIC

730 *P.S.I.* xi (1935) 1221, p. 152ss.: anon. περὶ αἴνου (ed. Bartoletti)

ὁ δὲ Κύπρι[ο]ς λεγό[μενος] αἶνος ὄνομα τοιο[ῦτον] ἤνεγκεν ὡς ἐφη. [διὰ τὸ] παρὰ Κυπρίοις ἐπ[ιχώριο]ς λέγεσθαι. κέχρη[ται δὲ τούτωι] Τιμοκρέων ἐν [ἄισματι κατὰ Θε]μιστοκλ[έο]υς ἐκ[πεσόντος] ἐκ τῆς ['Ελ]λάδος ἐ[φηδό]μενος αὐτοῦ τῆι φ[υγῆι· οὕτω δὲ λέ]γει·

λό[γ]ον δέ σοι λε[| . . .] ον ταυτα σοι π . . [
| . . τ]ῶν τριῶν ταλ[άντων | . . . .]ων ξένος[

[Diogenian.] praef. (i 180 Leutsch-Schneidewin)

κέχρηται δὲ καὶ τούτῳ (sc. τῷ Κυπρίῳ αἴνῳ) Τιμοκρέων, ἐμφαίνων ὡς οἱ ἄδικα πράσσοντες καὶ ἐς ὕστερον τῶν προσηκόντων τυγχάνουσι. καὶ γὰρ τῷ 'Αδώνιδι ἐν Κύπρῳ τιμηθέντι ὑπὸ τῆς 'Αφροδίτης μετὰ τὴν τελευτὴν οἱ Κύπριοι ζώσας ἐνίεσαν περιστεράς, αἱ δ' ἀποπτᾶσαι καὶ διαφυγοῦσαι αὖθις ἀδοκήτως εἰς ἄλλην ἐμπεσοῦσαι πυρὰν διεφθάρησαν.

cf. schol. anon. in Aphthon., *Rhet. Gr.* ii 12 Walz

731 Schol. Ar. *Ach.* 532 (p. 74 Wilson)

ἐτίθει νόμους· μιμούμενος τὸν τῶν σκολίων ποιητήν. Τιμοκρέων δὲ ὁ 'Ρόδιος μελοποιὸς τοιοῦτον ἔγραψε σκόλιον κατὰ τοῦ Πλούτου, οὗ ἡ ἀρχή·

ὤφελέν σ' ὦ τυφλὲ Πλοῦτε
μήτε γῇ μήτ' ἐν θαλάσσῃ
μήτ' ἐν ἠπείρῳ φανῆμεν,

730 Italian papyrus (2nd c. A.D.): anonymous writer, *On Fables*

The so-called Cyprian fable got its name, as (I said?), because it was told locally by the people of Cyprus. Timocreon uses it in a song against Themistocles after his banishment from Greece to express his delight in the man's exile. This is what he says:

(I shall tell) you a story . . . (these things?) to you . . . (of) the three talents . . . guest-friend . . .[1]

[1] Cf. 727. 5–8.

'Diogenian', preface to *Proverbs*

Timocreon uses the Cyprian fable also[1] to show that wrong-doers eventually meet their deserts. When Adonis had been honoured in Cyprus by Aphrodite after his death, the Cyprians threw live doves on his body; these flew away and escaped, but later they unexpectedly fell on another pyre and perished.

[1] Cf. 734.

731 Scholiast on Aristophanes, *Acharnians* ('Pericles . . . made laws worded like drinking-songs, that Megarians must remain neither on land nor in the agora nor on sea nor on the mainland.')

He imitates the composer of the drinking-songs. Timocreon, the lyric poet from Rhodes, wrote a drinking-song like this against Wealth; it begins,

Blind Wealth, if only you had appeared neither on land nor on sea nor on the mainland,[1] but had

[1] I.e. Asia.

GREEK LYRIC

ἀλλὰ Τάρταρόν τε ναίειν
5 κ'Ἀχέροντα· διὰ σὲ γὰρ πάντ'
αἰὲν ἀνθρώποις κακά.

cf. schol. Ald. *Ran.* 1302, *Sud.* Σ 645 (iv 383 Adler), Isid. Pelus. *Ep.* 2. 146

1 Ilgen: ὤφελες ὦ codd. (ὄφ-, ὄφειλ- *Sud.*)   2 Brunck: μήτ' ἐν γῇ codd. (τῇ γῇ *Sud.* V)   3 ἠπείρῳ: οὐρανῷ ci. Schneidewin Bergk: φανήμεναι codd.   6 αἰὲν Page: ἐν codd.

732 Heph. *Ench.* 12. 5s. (p. 39 Consbruch)

τῷ δὲ καθαρῷ (διμέτρῳ ἰωνικῷ) ἐφθημιμερεῖ ὅλον ᾆσμα Τιμο-κρέων συνέθηκε·

Σικελὸς κομψὸς ἀνὴρ
ποτὶ τὰν ματέρ' ἔφα

733 = 7 West   Ar. *Vesp.* 1060ss.

ὦ πάλαι ποτ' ὄντες ὑμεῖς ἄλκιμοι μὲν ἐν χοροῖς,
ἄλκιμοι δ' ἐν μάχαις,
καὶ κατ' αὐτὸ δὴ μόνον τοῦτ' ἄνδρες ἀλκιμώτατοι,
πρίν ποτ' ἦν πρὶν ταῦτα . . .

Schol. Ald. ad 1063s. (p. 170 Koster)

Δίδυμός φησιν (p. 259. 61 Schmidt) ὡς παρῴδησε ταῦτα ἐκ τῶν Τιμοκρέοντος τοῦ Ῥοδίου.

cf. Anacr. 426 πάλαι ποτ' ἦσαν ἄλκιμοι Μιλήσιοι.

lived in Tartarus and Acheron; for thanks to you men have all evils always.

732 Hephaestion, *Handbook on Metres* (on the ionic *a minore*)

Timocreon composed a whole song in the pure three-and-a-half foot dimeter[1]:

A clever Sicilian said to his mother . . .[2]

[1] Servius, *Cent. Metr.* (iv 464 Keil) calls the line a catalectic dimeter and labels it *timocratium* (for *timocreontium* ?).   [2] Plato, *Gorgias* 493a refers to 'a clever man, Sicilian perhaps or Italian'.

733 = 7 West   Scholiast on Aristophanes, *Wasps* ('Oh you who once long ago were valiant in the choral dance, valiant in battle, and in *this* respect particularly valiant men, that was in the past . . .')

Didymus says that this is parodied from the poems of Timocreon of Rhodes.[1]

[1] Perhaps so, but cf. Anacr. 426, 'Once long ago the Milesians were valiant.'

GREEK LYRIC

734 [Diogenian.] praef. (i 179 Leutsch-Schneidewin)

Καρικὸς δὲ αἶνος λέγεται, ὃν ἀναφέρουσιν εἰς γένει Κᾶρα ἄνδρα· τοῦτον γὰρ ἁλιέα τυγχάνοντα χειμῶνος θεασάμενον πολύποδα εἰπεῖν· εἰ μὲν ἀποδὺς κολυμβήσαιμι ἐπ' αὐτόν, ῥιγώσω, ἐὰν δὲ μὴ λάβω τὸν πολύποδα τῷ λιμῷ τὰ παιδί' ἀπολῶ. κέχρηται δὲ τῷ λόγῳ τούτῳ καὶ Τιμοκρέων ἐν μέλεσι, καὶ Σιμωνίδης [fr. 514]
. . .

cf. *Rhet. Gr.* ii 10 adnot. Walz

9 West Heph. *Ench.* 1. 3 (p. 2 Consbruch)

γίνεται δὲ τοῦτο κατὰ πέντε τρόπους· ἤτοι γὰρ λήξει εἰς δύο σύμφωνα, οἷον Τίρυνς κτλ (adesp. 1043 *P.M.G.*), μάκαρς κτλ (Alcm. 15) καὶ Τιμοκρέοντος ἐκ τῶν ἐπιγραμμάτων·

ᾧ ξυμβουλεύειν χὲρς ἄπο, νοῦς δὲ πάρα.

10 West *A.P.* 13. 31

Τιμοκρέοντος Ῥοδίου·

Κηΐα με προσῆλθε φλυαρία οὐκ ἐθέλοντα·
οὐ θέλοντά με προσῆλθε Κηΐα φλυαρία.

2 West: οὐκ ἐθέλοντα cod.

96

734 'Diogenian', preface to *Proverbs*

The Carian fable is the name of the one which is told of a Carian man, a fisher who encountered wintry weather after spotting an octopus and said, 'If I take off my clothes and dive for it, I shall freeze, and if I don't catch the octopus, I shall starve my children to death.' Timocreon uses this story in his songs, and Simonides mentions it (fr. 514).

9 West Hephaestion, *Handbook on Metres*

This (sc. the lengthening of syllables 'by position') occurs in five different ways: either the syllable will end in two consonants, as with 'Tiryns' (anon. fragment) or μάκαρς (Alcm. 15) or χέρς, 'hand', in the epigrams of Timocreon:

to plot with whom the hand keeps apart, although the mind stands ready.

10 West *Palatine Anthology*: Timocreon of Rhodes

Nonsense from Ceos came to me against my will. Against my will there came to me nonsense from Ceos.[1]

A hexameter followed by a trochaic tetrameter: presumably a reply to Simonides (of Ceos) eleg. 17; see also testt. 1, 2.

CHARIXENA

Phot. *Lex.* (ined.: v. Kassel-Austin *P.C.G.* iv 198) = *Et. Gen.*
B (*Et. Magn.* p. 367. 21)

ἐπὶ Χαριξένης· αὐλητρὶς ἡ Χαριξένη ἀρχαία καὶ
ποιήτρια κρουμάτων, οἱ δὲ καὶ μελοποιόν. Θεόπομπος
Σειρῆσιν (fr. 51 K.–A.)·

αὐλεῖ γὰρ σαπρὰ
αὕτη γε κρούμαθ' οἷα τἀπὶ Χαριξένης.

Κρατῖνος Ὀδυσσεῦσιν (fr. 153 K.–A.)·

οὐκ εἰδυῖα τάδ' οὐκέτ' ὄνθ'
οἷα τἀπὶ Χαριξένης.

Ἀριστοφάνης Ἐκκλησιαζούσαις (943)·

τἀπὶ Χαριξένης.

Prov. cod. Par. suppl. 676 = Hsch. E 5413 (ii 178 Latte)

ἐπὶ Χαριξένης· ἐπὶ μωρίᾳ ἡ Χαριξένη διεβεβόητο
ὅτι οὐκ ᾔδει (Kassel: οὐκ ᾄδει Prov. Par., om. Hsch.)
ἀρχαία οὖσα. ἔνιοι δὲ καὶ ποιήτριαν αὐτὴν ἐρωτικῶν
λέγουσιν. ἔστι δὲ καὶ παροιμία οἷα τὰ ἐπὶ Χαριξένης.

CHARIXENA

Photius, *Lexicon* = *Etymologicum Genuinum*

'In Charixena's day': Charixena was an old-fashioned pipe-player and a musical composer, some say a lyric poet too.[1] Theopompus in his *Sirens* says, 'She plays rotten music on her pipes, the kind of thing that belongs to Charixena's day.' Cratinus in his *Odysseuses*: '(she) not knowing that this no longer exists, the kind of thing that belongs to Charixena's day.' Aristophanes in his *Ecclesiazusae*: 'the things that belong to Charixena's day.'

Proverb (Paris ms.) = Hesychius, *Lexicon*

'In Charixena's day': Charixena was famous for her stupidity[2] in that she did not know that she was old-fashioned. Some say she was also a composer of erotic songs. There is also a proverb, 'the kind of thing that belongs to Charixena's day.'[3]

[1] Cf. Corinna test. 1 n. 3; but the evidence for Charixena's music and poetry is poor.   [2] Cf. *Suda* X 116 (iv 789 Adler), where she is also called a hetaira, schol. Ar. *Eccl.* 943.   [3] See Appendix to the Proverbs 2. 82 (i 411 Leutsch-Schneidewin).

BACCHYLIDES

TESTIMONIA VITAE ATQUE ARTIS

1 *Sud.* B 59 (i 449 Adler)

Βακχυλίδης, Κεῖος, ἀπὸ Κέω τῆς νήσου, πόλεως δὲ
Ἰουλίδος . . ., Μείδωνος (Neue: Μέδωνος codd.) υἱὸς
τοῦ Βακχυλίδου τοῦ ἀθλητοῦ παιδός· συγγενὴς Σιμω-
νίδου τοῦ λυρικοῦ, καὶ αὐτὸς λυρικός.

2 Str. 10. 5. 6 (ii 418 Kramer)

Κέως δὲ τετράπολις μὲν ὑπῆρξε, λείπονται δὲ δύο,
ἥ τε Ἰουλὶς καὶ ἡ Καρθαία, εἰς ἃς συνεπολίσθησαν αἱ
λοιπαί, ἡ μὲν Ποιήεσσα εἰς τὴν Καρθαίαν, ἡ δὲ Κορη-
σία εἰς τὴν Ἰουλίδα. ἐκ δὲ τῆς Ἰουλίδος ὅ τε Σιμωνί-
δης ἦν ὁ μελοποιὸς καὶ Βακχυλίδης ἀδελφιδοῦς ἐκεί-
νου, καὶ μετὰ ταῦτα Ἐρασίστρατος ὁ ἰατρὸς καὶ τῶν
ἐκ τοῦ περιπάτου φιλοσόφων Ἀρίστων . . .

BACCHYLIDES

BIOGRAPHY

1 *Suda,* Bacchylides

A Cean, from the island of Ceos and the city of
Iulis ...; son of Meidon,[1] whose father was Bacchy-
lides the athlete; kinsman[2] of the lyric poet
Simonides, and himself a lyric poet.

[1] See also test. 3. The mss. of *Suda* give 'Medon', the elegiacs in
schol. Pindar (i 11 Drachmann) 'Milon'. The form Meidon is known
from a 3rd c. B.C. inscription from Iulis (*I.G.* XII 5.610.26).
[2] B. was the son of Simonides' (younger?) sister: see test. 2.

BIRTHPLACE AND FAMILY

2 Strabo, *Geography*

Ceos was a tetrapolis, but only two of the cities
remain, Iulis and Carthaea; the other two, Poeëessa
and Coresia, were incorporated into Carthaea and
Iulis respectively. From Iulis came Simonides the
lyric poet and Bacchylides his nephew, and later
Erasistratus the physician and the peripatetic phi-
losopher Ariston ...[1]

[1] So Stephanus of Byzantium on 'Iulis': cf. fr. 43, Syrianus 1. 47
Rabe.

3 *Et. Gen.* (*Et. Mag.* 582.20)

Μειδύλος· οὕτω δὲ λέγεται ὁ πατὴρ Βακχυλίδου παρὰ τὸ μειδιῶ Μειδύλος, ὡς παρὰ τὸ φειδώ, ἐξ οὗ καὶ τὸ φείδομαι, Φείδυλος.

4 Euseb. *Chron.*

(a) Ol. 78.1 (p. 110 Helm, ii 103 Schöne)

Bacchylides et Diagoras atheus plurimo sermone celebrantur.

cf. *Chron. Pasch.* 162b, Sync. p. 297 Mosshammer

(b) Ol. 82.2 (p. 112 Helm, ii 105 Schöne)

Crates comicus et Telesilla ac Bacchylides lyricus clari habentur.

(c) Ol. 87.2 (p. 114 Helm, ii 109 Schöne)

Bacchylides carminum scriptor agnoscitur.

cf. Sync. p. 309 Mosshammer

5 Eust. *prooem. ad Pind.* (iii 297 Drachmann)

ὅς (sc. Πίνδαρος), φασί, καὶ Σιμωνίδου ἤκουσε, νεώτερος μὲν ἐκείνου ὤν, πρεσβύτερος δὲ Βακχυλίδου.

cf. Thom. Mag. *vit. Pind.* (i 5 Drachmann)

---

[1] P. was born in 518 B.C. The *Suda* entry on Diagoras dates the *floruit* of Diagoras to Ol. 78 (468/4 B.C.) and says he was 'younger

3 *Etymologicum Genuinum*

Meidylus: this is the name of Bacchylides' father, Μειδύλος being derived from μειδιῶ, 'smile', as Φειδύλος from φειδώ, φείδομαι, 'live thriftily'.

CHRONOLOGY[1]

4 Eusebius, *Chronicle*

(a) Olympiad 78.1 (468/7 B.C.)[2]

Bacchylides and Diagoras the atheist are much spoken of.

(b) Olympiad 82.2 (451/450 B.C.)

The comic poet Crates and Telesilla and the lyric poet Bacchylides are regarded as famous.

(c) Olympiad 87.2 (431/430 B.C.)[3]

Bacchylides, the writer of songs, is well-known.

[1] B.'s earliest datable poem is 13 (485 B.C.?), his latest 6 and 7 (452 B.C.). [2] B.'s *acme* seems to be made to coincide with the death of his uncle Simonides or with Hiero's greatest victory in the games (see poem 3). [3] Georgius Syncellus gives Olympiad 88 (428/424 B.C.). G. S. Fatouros, *Philol.* 105 (1961) 147 ff. argues that the entry refers to an aulete called Bacchylides.

5 Eustathius, *Proem to Pindar*

Pindar, they say, was a pupil of Simonides, younger than Simonides but older than Bacchylides.[1]

than Pindar and Bacchylides'. P. and B. may in fact have been roughly contemporary.

6 Plut. *de exilio* 14. 605CD (iii 526 Pohlenz-Sieveking)

καὶ γὰρ τοῖς παλαιοῖς ὡς ἔοικεν αἱ Μοῦσαι τὰ κάλλιστα τῶν συνταγμάτων καὶ δοκιμώτατα φυγὴν λαβοῦσαι συνεργὸν ἐπετέλεσαν· ... Βακχυλίδης ὁ ποιητής ('Ἰουλιήτης Cobet) ἐν Πελοποννήσῳ.

7 Pind. pae. 4 (= fr. 52d). 23s.

γινώσκ[ο]μα[ι] δὲ καὶ
μοῖσαν παρέχων ἅλις.

8 Schol. Pind. *Ol.* 2. 86ss. (154ss.) (i 99 Drachmann)
(σοφὸς ὁ πολλὰ εἰδὼς φυᾷ· | μαθόντες δὲ λάβροι | παγγλωσσίᾳ κόρακες ὡς ἄκραντα γαρύετον | Διὸς πρὸς ὄρνιχα θεῖον.)

154c ἀποτείνεται δὲ πρὸς τὸν Βακχυλίδην· γέγονε γὰρ αὐτῷ ἀνταγωνιστὴς τρόπον τινὰ καὶ εἰς τὰ αὐτὰ καθῆκεν.

BACCHYLIDES

EXILE

6 Plutarch, *On Exile*

Indeed the Muses, it seems, took Exile as their fellow-worker when they completed for the ancients the finest and most highly regarded of their compositions: ... the poet Bacchylides[1] in the Peloponnese.

[1] Plutarch lists Thucydides, Xenophon, Philistus, Timaeus, Androtion (all historians) and B., and goes on to say that the men who drove them out are now forgotten.

PINDAR AND BACCHYLIDES[1]

7 Pindar, Paean for Ceans

I[2] am known also for providing the Muses' art in abundance.[3]

[1] Hiero, tyrant of Syracuse, was patron of both, as also of Simonides. B. composed 3, 4, 5 for him. Cf. Ael. *V. H.* 4. 15. [2] I.e. the island of Ceos. [3] The reference must be to Simonides and B.

8 Scholiast on Pindar, *Olympian* 2. 86 ff. ('The skilled man is he who knows many things by the gift of nature: those who learned, boisterous in their garrulity, are like crows, the pair of them, uttering idle words against the holy bird of Zeus.')

154c This is directed against Bacchylides, who was in a sense his rival and competed in the same arena.

157a αἰνίττεται Βακχυλίδην καὶ Σιμωνίδην, ἑαυτὸν λέγων ἀετόν, κόρακας δὲ τοὺς ἀντιτέχνους.

158d εἰ δέ πως εἰς Βακχυλίδην καὶ Σιμωνίδην αἰνίττεται, καλῶς ἄρα ἐξείληπται τὸ γαρύετον δυικῶς.

9 Schol. Pind. *Pyth.* 2 (ii 48, 54, 58, 60 Drachmann)

(a) 52s. (97s.) (ἐμὲ δὲ χρεών | φεύγειν δάκος ἀδινὸν κακαγοριᾶν.)

αἰνίττεται δὲ εἰς Βακχυλίδην· ἀεὶ γὰρ αὐτὸν τῷ Ἱέρωνι διέσυρεν.

(b) 72s. (132s.) (καλός τοι πίθων παρὰ παισίν, αἰεί | καλός.)

131b ταῦτα δὲ ἔνιοι τείνειν αὐτὸν εἰς Βακχυλίδην· εὐδοκιμῆσαι γὰρ αὐτὸν παρὰ τῷ Ἱέρωνι.

132c ἢ οὕτως· ὥσπερ ὁ πίθηκος σπουδάζεται παρὰ τοῖς παισὶν φαῦλος ὤν, οὕτω καὶ Βακχυλίδης παρὰ παισὶ μὲν ἄφροσιν εὐδοκιμείτω, παρὰ σοὶ δὲ σοφῷ ὄντι πίθηκος ἔστω.

157a He is referring in riddling fashion to Bacchylides and Simonides, calling himself an eagle and his rival craftsmen crows.

158d If he is referring in riddling fashion to Bacchylides and Simonides, then the dual form γαρύετον, 'the pair of them utter', has been well chosen.

9 Scholiast on Pindar, *Pythian* 2

(a) v. 52 f. ('I must avoid the violent bite of slander.')

He is talking in riddling fashion of Bacchylides, who was always disparaging him to Hiero.

(b) v. 72 f. ('A monkey is beautiful in the eyes of children, always beautiful.')

131b Some say he is aiming these words at Bacchylides, who was highly regarded by Hiero.

132c Alternatively: as the monkey is taken seriously by children although it is worthless, so let Bacchylides enjoy high regard among foolish children but be a monkey in your wise judgement.

(c) 88s. (162ss.) (χρή | δὲ πρὸς θεὸν οὐκ ἐρίζειν, | ὃς ἀνέχει τοτὲ μὲν τὰ κείνων, τότ' αὖθ' ἑτέροις | ἔδωκεν μέγα κῦδος.)

163b ἄλλως· κἀγὼ οὐκ εἴξω τῷ Βακχυλίδῃ τὰ νῦν, παρὰ θεῶν εὖ πράττοντι, καὶ οὐκ ἀντιβήσομαι τῇ προαιρέσει †ἐπιπλεῖστον†.

(d) 90ss. (166ss.) (στάθμας δέ τινος ἑλκόμενοι | περισσᾶς ἐνέπαξαν ἕλ-|κος ὀδυναρὸν ἑᾷ πρόσθε καρδίᾳ ...)

166d ἡ ἀναφορὰ πάλιν πρὸς Βακχυλίδην. εἴληπται δὲ οὕτως ἡ διάνοια, διὰ τὸ παρὰ τῷ Ἱέρωνι τὰ Βακχυλίδου προκρίνεσθαι ποιήματα, καί φησιν ὅτι φέρειν δεῖ τὰ συμπτώματα τῆς τύχης.

cf. 171c, 171d

10 Schol. Pind. Nem. 3. 82 (143s.) (iii 62 Drachmann) (κραγέται δὲ κολοιοὶ ταπεινὰ νέμονται.)

δοκεῖ δὲ ταῦτα τείνειν εἰς Βακχυλίδην· ἦν γὰρ ὑφόρασις αὐτοῖς πρὸς ἀλλήλους. παραβάλλει δὲ αὑτὸν μὲν ἀετῷ, κολοιῷ δὲ Βακχυλίδην.

(c) v. 88 f. ('One must not strive against God, who at one moment supports the fortunes of those men, at the next gives great glory to others.')

163b Alternatively: and I therefore shall yield to Bacchylides now, since he is enjoying good fortune from the gods, and I shall not protest against the choice . . .[1]

(d) v. 90 ff. ('By pulling on an excessively long measuring-line they first inflict a painful wound on their own heart.')

166d The reference is again to Bacchylides. The passage is taken this way because Hiero preferred the poems of Bacchylides, and Pindar says he must put up with the chances of fortune.

[1] Hiero's preference for B.? The last part of the text is corrupt.

10 Scholiast on Pindar, *Nemean* 3. 82 ('Shrieking jackdaws inhabit low levels.')

He seems to be aiming these words at Bacchylides: each was jealous of the other. He compares himself to the eagle, Bacchylides to the jackdaw.

11 'Ammon.' *Diff.* 333 (p. 86 Nickau)

Δίδυμος (p. 300 Schmidt) ὁμοίως ἐν ὑπομνήματι Βακχυλίδου Ἐπινίκων.

cf. Eust. *Od.* 1954.4

12 'Longinus' *de subl.* 33. 5 (p. 42 Russell)

τί δέ; ἐν μέλεσι μᾶλλον ἂν εἶναι Βακχυλίδης ἕλοιο ἢ Πίνδαρος, καὶ ἐν τραγῳδίᾳ Ἴων ὁ Χῖος ἢ νὴ Δία Σοφοκλῆς; ἐπειδὴ οἱ μὲν ἀδιάπτωτοι καὶ ἐν τῷ γλαφυρῷ πάντη κεκαλλιγραφημένοι, ὁ δὲ Πίνδαρος καὶ ὁ Σοφοκλῆς ὁτὲ μὲν οἷον πάντα ἐπιφλέγουσι τῇ φορᾷ, σβέννυνται δ' ἀλόγως πολλάκις καὶ πίπτουσιν ἀτυχέστατα. ἢ οὐδεὶς ἂν εὖ φρονῶν ἑνὸς δράματος, τοῦ Οἰδίποδος, εἰς ταὐτὸ συνθεὶς τὰ Ἴωνος <πάντ'> ἀντιτιμήσαιτο ἑξῆς.

BACCHYLIDES

SCHOLARLY ACTIVITY[1]

11 'Ammonius', *On Similar but Different Words*[2]

Similarly Didymus in his commentary on the Epinicians of Bacchylides.

[1] The scholiast on B. mentions at fr. 20A. 19 a Ptolemaeus, for whom see Snell-Maehler p. 132, and the commentator on B.'s *Cassandra* (23), perhaps Didymus, mentions the views of Callimachus, Aristarchus and Dionysius of Phaselis on the classification of the poem. [2] Based on the work of Philo of Byblos (*c.* 100 A.D.). The point at issue is the supposed distinction between 'the Nereids' and 'the daughters of Nereus'; see 1. 8, 13. 123.

VERDICT OF ANTIQUITY[1]

12 'Longinus', *On sublimity*

Or take lyric poetry: would you choose to be Bacchylides rather than Pindar? Or in tragedy Ion of Chios rather than Sophocles? Certainly Bacchylides and Ion never put a foot wrong and in all their works show themselves masters of beautiful writing in the smooth style, whereas the other two sometimes set the world ablaze in their violent onrush, but often have their flame quenched for no reason and collapse miserably. Surely no one in his right mind would rate all the works of Ion put together as highly as one single play, the *Oedipus*.

[1] For the base, with feet, of a herm inscribed BAKXYΛIΔOY (Vatican inv. 16250; found in a villa near Tivoli) see G. M. A. Richter, *Portraits of the Greeks* i 142 with fig. 786.

13 *Anth. Pal.* 4. 1. 33s. = Meleager i Gow-Page

λείψανά τ' εὐκαρπεῦντα μελιστάκτων ἀπὸ Μουσέων
ξανθοὺς ἐκ καλάμης Βακχυλίδεω στάχυας.

14 *Anth. Pal.* 9. 184. 1s. = anon. xxxvi(a), 1194s. *F.G.E.*

Πίνδαρε, Μουσάων ἱερὸν στόμα, καὶ λάλε Σειρήν,
Βακχυλίδη, . . .

15 *Anth. Pal.* 9. 571. 4 = anon. xxxvi(b), 1207 *F.G.E.*

λαρὰ δ' ἀπὸ στομάτων φθέγξατο Βακχυλίδης.

16 Galen. in Hippocr. *Prorrhet.* 1 (p. 41 Diels)

ἤκουσα . . . γραμματικοῦ (sc. παραφρονοῦντος)
βιβλίον ἀναγιγνώσκειν οἰομένου Βακχυλίδειον ἢ
Σαπφικόν.

13 *Palatine Anthology*: Meleager, *The Garland*[1]

... and fruitful remnants[2] from his honey-dropping Muses, yellow ears from the corn-stalks of Bacchylides.

[1] Introductory poem to M.'s collection of epigrams in which he compares each poet's work to a flower or plant. Two epigrams are ascribed to B. in the *Anthology* (6. 53, 6. 313), a third to B. or Simonides (13. 28).　　[2] I.e. the epigrams formed only a small part of B.'s poetry.

14 *Palatine Anthology*: anon. on the nine Lyric Poets[1]

You, Pindar, holy mouth of the Muses, and you, talkative Siren, Bacchylides ...

[1] B. is listed as one of the nine in Schol. Pind. also (i 11 Drachmann).

15 *Palatine Anthology*: anon. on the nine Lyric Poets

... and Bacchylides uttered sweet sounds from his lips.

16 Galen, *On the Prorrhetics of Hippocrates*

I heard ... a mad schoolmaster who imagined that he was reading a book of Bacchylides or Sappho.[1]

[1] His favourite poets?

113

<ΒΑΚΧΥΛΙΔΟΥ ΕΠΙΝΙΚΟΙ>

1

<ΑΡΓΕΙΩΙ ΚΕΙΩΙ>
<ΠΑΙΔΙ ΠΥΚΤΗΙ (?) ΙΣΘΜΙΑ>

κλυτοφόρμιγγες Δ[ιὸς ὑ-
ψιμέδοντος παρθένοι,
–∪∪ Πι]ερίδες
– –]ενυφαι[∪∪– –
5 –∪∪]ους, ἵνα κ[–
– –∪] γαίας Ἰσθμί[ας
– –∪]ν, εὐβούλου ν[∪ –
–∪ γαμ]βρὸν Νηρέ[ος

∪∪–] νάσοιό τ᾿ ἐΰ-
10   ∪∪]αν, ἔνθ[–∪ –
–∪∪–∪∪ –
– –∪∪–∪∪ – –
ὦ Πέλοπος λιπαρᾶς
14   νάσου θεόδματοι πύλαι

suppl. ed. pr. (Kenyon) exceptis quae sequuntur   1s. comment.
ad Callim. Αἴτια (fr. 2a Pfeiffer) παρθένο]ς · θυγάτηρ ὡς [καὶ] Βακχυ-
λίδης [φησί·] κλυτ.... παρθένοι: hic locavit Maas   3 Blass
δεῦρ᾿ ἴτε Maas   4 ἐνυφαί[νετε δ᾿ ὕμνους Blass   5s. κ[υ]δαίνητε
Jebb   7 ἀρχαγό]ν Maas   8 Blass   9s. ἐΰ[|δρανί]αν ci. Maehler
10 ἔνθ[εν μολών Blass   13s. schol. Pind. Ol. 13. 4c πρόθυρον καὶ
θύρας εἰώθασι καλεῖν τὴν Κόρινθον διὰ τὸ ἀρχὴν ἢ τέλος εἶναι τῆς Πελοπον-
νήσου. Βακχ. ὦ ... πύλαι. hic locavit Blass

114

BACCHYLIDES

*All the major texts of Epinicians (1–14) and Dithyrambs
(15–20) are in the British Museum papyrus (A: 2nd c. A.D.);
14A and most of 14B are in P. Oxy. 2363.*

VICTORY-ODES

1[1]

FOR ARGEIUS OF CEOS
BOY BOXER,[2] ISTHMIAN GAMES

Famous lyre-players,[3] daughters of high-ruling
Zeus, (come hither), Pierians, and (inweave ...
songs of praise), so that (you may glorify the ruler?)
of the Isthmian land, the ... son-in-law[4] of wise
Nereus ..., and the well- ... of the island,[5] whence
(Argeius came?) ..., you god-built gates[6] of the
gleaming island of Pelops ...

[1] The first two lines are quoted by a commentator on Callimachus
to illustrate B.'s use of παρθένος, 'maiden', in the sense of 'daughter'.
Lines 13 f. are cited from B. by the scholiast on Pindar *Ol.* 13. 4 for
the description of Corinth as 'gateway'.   [2] Or pancratiast: he
is 'strong-handed' (v. 141): cf. 2. 4. An inscription from the Cean
city Iulis (*I.G.* XII 5.608) commemorates his Isthmian victory won
when a boy and a Nemean victory won when a youth; Maehler
dates the Isthmian victory to 452 or 454.   [3] The Muses, born
in Pieria.   [4] Poseidon, husband of Amphitrite. For Didymus'
note on the passage see test. 11 n. 2.   [5] Ceos.   [6] Corinth,
gateway of the Peloponnese.

19 −∪−ἔζευξεν ὑφ' ἄρ]μασιν ἵππου[ς·
20   οἰ δὲ π]έτοντο [∪−−
  −∪−−]εσσιν ἀν[δρῶν
−∪∪−∪]τον αὐτ[−
  −∪−] ἄλλαισιν [−−−∪−−

∪∪−−−]ν δ' ετε[−
25   ∪∪−]γονώτ[∪−
·26   ]πλ[

35   τοῖον [∪∪−∪∪−]ται
καλ[∪∪−∪∪−
  ..].[−∪−−]εμεν, ὅταν
−−∪−−]τει συνευ-
39   −∪−−−∪]ας

46   ]εοσ[

∪∪−−−]ν πυκ[ιν−
  ∪∪−−]. γοι κόρ[αι
−∪∪−]αγορα
50   −−]ο μελίφρονος ὕπ[νου
−∪∪ ἀμετ]έραν
  −−∪ ἀρ]χαίαν πόλιν
  −−∪−−]γοιμεν οἴ-
  κους δ' ἐπ'] ἀνθήροις ἁλός

4 lines missing

... yoked[1] his horses under his chariot, and they
flew ... (of men?) ... other ... and ... (another ...
more fruitful?) ...

8 lines missing

... such ... (fine?) ..., when ... (from need of bed-
mates?)[2] ...

7 lines mostly missing

... (shrewd?) ... maidens ... (Lysagora[3] said on
awakening from?) kindly sleep, ('If only we were
to flee from) our (lofty) ancient city[4] and (find) a
home [5] on the shore of the sea and open to the rays

---

[1] Zeus? The myth begins here, but the sequence of the small frag-
ments is uncertain. [2] The need of Dexithea and her
sisters? [3] One of Damon's daughters? See p. 119 n. 1. [4] Their
original Cean home. [5] Coresia? See p. 121 n. 2.

19–21 Blass 24 ἔτε[ρον, 25 εὐ]γονώτ[ερον Blass 38s. χή]τει
συνεύ[νων Blass 49ss. e.g. Blass: φθέγξατο Λυσ]αγόρα | λήξασα] μ.
ὕ. · | εἰθέ ποθ' ἁ. | αἰπεῖαν ἁ. π. | ... φεύ]γοιμεν, οἵ | κους δ' ἐπ'] ἁ. ἁ.

55 ὑπό τ' a]ὐγαῖς ἀελίου
56   ].ι.δ.[

72 –◡◡–]σαγόραι
     ––Μα]κελὼ δὲ τ[◡––
   –◡ φιλ]αλάκατος,
75   ––δ' ἐπ' εὐναῇ [πό]ρο[ν
     ––]α· προσφώνει τέ νιν·
   –◡–]σαίνουσ' ὀπί·

   ◡◡––μ]ὲν στέρομαι
     ◡◡ ἀμ]φάκει δύαι
80 –◡◡–π]ενίαι·
     ––◡◡–].'γετ[.] πάμπα[ν
   –◡◡–◡◡]ας.
83   ––◡–––]ομοι

111 –◡].αφθε[..].[◡◡–◡◡––
     –]ς· τριτάται μετ[◡––
   ἀμ]έραι Μίνως ἀρ[ῆι]ος
   ἦλ]υθεν αἰολοπρύμνοις
115 ναυσὶ πεντήκοντα σὺν Κρητῶν ὁμίλωι·
   Διὸς Εὐκλείου δὲ ἔκα-
     τι βαθύζωνον κόραν
   Δεξιθέαν δάμασεν·
     κα]ί οἱ λίπεν ἥμισυ λ[α]ῶν,
120 ἄ]νδρας ἀρηϊφίλους,

118

of the sun . . .'

16 lines mostly missing

. . . (to Lysagora?), and Macelo,[1] distaff-loving, . . . to
the fair-flowing stream,[2] and she addressed them,[3]
coaxing with (gentle) voice: 'I am without . . . (by?)
double-edged misery . . . (by?) poverty; . . . com-
pletely . . .'

30 lines mostly missing

On the third day thereafter[4] warlike Minos came
with a throng of Cretans on fifty glittering-sterned
ships, and by the favour of Zeus, god of glory, he
bedded the slim-waisted maiden Dexithea; and he
left her half of his force, warriors dear to Ares, and

---

[1] The myth is known from discrepant references in Pindar, *Paean*
4. 35 ff., Callimachus, *Aetia* 3 fr. 75, 64 ff., Ovid, *Ibis* 475 with scho-
lia and Nonnus, *Dion.* 18. 38; see also fr. 52 of B. The Telchines,
mythical craftsmen and wizards living on Ceos, angered the gods
by blighting the fruits of the earth. Zeus and Poseidon (or Apollo)
destroyed the island and its population, but spared Dexithea and
her sisters, daughters of Damon (or Demonax), the chief of the Tel-
chines, because Macelo had entertained the two gods: in Cal-
limachus Macelo is mother of Dexithea and is spared with her, in
Ovid and the scholia she is her sister and loses her life because her
husband had offended the gods.   [2] Strabo 10. 5. 6 mentions a
river Elixus near Coresia.   [3] Zeus and Poseidon (or Apollo).
Apollonius Dyscolus quoted the words from B. for his use of the pro-
noun νιν as a plural form (as at 9. 15).   [4] After the visit of the
gods?

---

72 Λυ]σαγόραι Blass   73, 75 Blass   76 Ap. Dysc. *Pron.* 108a (i
84 Schneider) ἔτι καὶ ἡ 'νιν' τάσσεται ἐπὶ πλήθους . . . · προσφωνεῖτέ νιν
ἐπινίκοις (ἐπὶ νίκαις codd.) Βακχυλίδης   77 μειλίχωι Wolff   112
μετ[έπειτα Kenyon   113 ἀρ[ῆι]ος Blass

το]ῖσιν πολύκρημνον χθόνα
νείμας ἀποπλέων ὤ[ιχε]τ' ἐς
Κ̣νωσὸν ἱμερτὰν [πό]λ̣ιν

β]ασιλεὺς Εὐρωπιά[δας]·
125   δεκάτωι δ' Εὐξ[άντι]ο̣ν
μηνὶ τέ]κ' εὐπλόκ[αμος
νύμφα φερ]εκυδέϊ [νάσωι
–∪∪–] πρύτανιν
129   ––∪–] ̣ δν ̣ [–∪–

138   –∪–––∪–] –̣ ξαν θύγατρες

πόλ[ιν –––]ν βαθυδεί-
140   ελον· [ἐκ το]ῦ̣ μὲν γένος
ἔπλε[το καρτε]ρόχειρ
Ἀργεῖο[ς ∪–∪] λέοντος
θυμὸ[ν ἔχων], ὁπότε
χρεί[α συνα]βολοῖ μάχας,
145   ποσσί[ν τ' ἐλα]φρό[ς, π]α̣τρίων
τ' οὐκ [ᷣ] ̣ [–––κ]α̣λῶν,

τόσα Παν[θείδαι κλυτό]το-
ξος Ἀπό[λλων ὤπασε]ν,
ἀμφί τ' ἰατο[ρίαι
150   ξείνων τε [φι]λάνορι τ̣[ι]μ̣ᾶι·
ε]ὖ δὲ λαχὼν [Χ]αρίτων
πολλοῖς τε θ[αυ]μασθεὶς βροτῶν

120

after distributing the craggy land to them he sailed
away to the lovely city of Cnossus, that king,
Europa's son[1]; and in the tenth month the fair-
tressed bride gave birth to Euxantius, a ruler for the
glory-winning island ...

9 lines mostly missing

... the daughters (of Damon) fled ... (to settle) a
city steeped in evening sunshine[2]; from his line[3]
came strong-handed Argeius, with a lion's heart (in
his breast?) when need of fighting came his way,
nimble of foot and (no disgrace to?) his father's fine
achievements, all those which the famous archer
Apollo granted to Pantheides[4] because of his
healer's art and his friendly honouring of strangers;
richly gifted by the Graces[5] and admired by many

---

[1] Minos was son of Zeus and Europa.   [2] The reference is
again to the migration to Coresia, the bay of which faces west. B.
may have associated the city's name with *korai*, 'maidens'
(v. 48).   [3] The line of Euxantius.   [4] With reference to
Pythian victories?   [5] As givers of athletic success? See previ-
ous note.

---

123 Blass: Κνωσσον pap.   127 Blass   138 Δάμωνος ἄλ]υξαν
Festa   139 οἰκίσσ]αι vel οἰκισ(σ)α]ν Snell   ἐς νέα]ν Edmonds
140 Edmonds   142 ἔσω τε] Headlam   143 Blass, al.   144
Maehler   145 ἐλα]φρό[ς Nairn, Housman   146 Blass

αἰῶν' ἔλυσεν [π]έντε παῖ-
δας μεγαινή[το]υς λιπών.

155 τ]ῶν ἕνα οἱ Κ[ρο]νίδας
ὑψίζυγος Ἰσ[θ]μιόνικον
θῆκεν ἀντ' [εὐε]ργεσιᾶν, λιπαρῶν τ' ἄλ-
λων στεφάν[ων] ἐπίμοιρον.
φαμὶ καὶ φάσω μέγιστον
160 κῦδος ἔχειν ἀρετάν· πλοῦ-
τος δὲ καὶ δειλοῖσιν ἀνθρώπων ὁμιλεῖ,

ἐθέλει δ' αὔξειν φρένας ἀν-
δρός· ὁ δ' εὖ ἔρδων θεούς
ἐλπίδι κυδροτέραι
165   σαίνει κέαρ. εἰ δ' ὑγιείας
θνατὸς ἐὼν ἔλαχεν
ζώειν τ' ἀπ' οἰκείων ἔχει,
πρώτοις ἐρίζει· παντί τοι
τέρψις ἀνθρώπων βίωι

170 ἕπεται νόσφιν γε νόσων
πενίας τ' ἀμαχάνου.
ἶσον ὅ τ' ἀφνεὸς ἱ-
μείρει μεγάλων ὅ τε μείων
παυροτέρων· τὸ δὲ πάν-
175   των εὐμαρεῖν οὐδὲν γλυκύ
θνατοῖσιν, ἀλλ' αἰεὶ τὰ φεύ-
γοντα δίζηνται κιχεῖν.

170 Blass: νου| . . ν pap.

men he closed his life leaving behind five illustrious sons. One of them the son of Cronus[1] on his high bench has made an Isthmian victor in return for his father's kindnesses, and winner also of other bright garlands.[2]

I say and shall[3] say always that the greatest glory belongs to excellence[4]: wealth may consort even with the worthless and loves to inflate a man's ideas; but he who treats the gods well cheers his heart with hope of greater glory; he is mortal, but if he is blessed with health and is able to live from what is his own,[5] then he rivals the foremost. Joy accompanies any life a man may lead, provided that distress and helpless poverty are absent. With equal longing does the wealthy man yearn for great things, the poorer man for less; but to have ready access to everything brings no pleasure to mortals: they are always seeking to catch what eludes them.

[1] Poseidon, god of the Isthmus.   [2] Won at lesser festivals.
[3] Plutarch, *de aud. poet.* 14. 36c cites the words 'shall say ... worthless' from B.   [4] *Aretē*, with reference in this context to athletic success.   [5] Synesius, *laud. calv.* 13. 77a quotes 'live from what is his own' as Pindar's.

ὅντινα κουφόταται
θυμὸν δονέουσι μέριμναι,
180 ὅσσον ἂν ζώηι †χρόνον, τόνδ᾽ ἔλαχαν† τι-
μάν. ἀρετὰ δ᾽ ἐπίμοχθος
μέν, τ]ελευταθεῖσα δ᾽ ὀρθῶς
ἀνδρὶ κ]αὶ εὖτε θάνηι λεί-
184 π[ει πολυ]ζήλωτον εὐκλείας ἄ[γαλ]μα.

180 λάχε τόνδε χρόνον Housman, Headlam   182 Blass

2

ΤΩΙ ΑΥΤΩΙ

ἄ[ιξον, ὦ] σεμνοδότειρα Φήμα,
ἐς Κ[έον ἱ]εράν, χαριτώ-
νυμ[ον] φέρουσ᾽ ἀγγελίαν,
ὅτι μ[ά]χας θρασύχειρ<ος> Ἀρ-
5   γεῖο[ς ἄ]ρατο νίκαν,

καλῶν δ᾽ ἀνέμνασεν, ὅσ᾽ ἐν κλε[εν]νῶι
αὐχένι Ἰσθμοῦ ζαθέαν
λιπόντες Εὐξαντίδα νᾶ-
σον ἐπεδείξαμεν ἑβδομή-
10   κοντα [σὺ]ν στεφάνοισιν.

καλεῖ δὲ Μοῦσ᾽ αὐθιγενής
γλυκεῖαν αὐλῶν καναχάν,
γεραίρουσ᾽ ἐπινικίοις
14 Πανθείδα φίλον υἱόν.

4 em. Jebb

124

The man whose heart is buffeted by lightweight ambitions wins honour for the duration of his life only: excellence is toilsome, but when rightly brought to its end it leaves a man even when he dies an enviable adornment of glory.

2 [1]

FOR THE SAME VICTOR

Speed to holy Ceos, Report, you giver of majesty, and carry the message of gracious name,[2] that Argeius won the victory in the bold-handed fight and reminded us of all the fine achievements we had displayed at the famous neck of the Isthmus when we left the sacred island of Euxantius[3] and won seventy garlands[4]; and the locally born Muse[5] summons the sweet skirl of pipes as she honours with victory-songs the dear son of Pantheides.

[1] This brief song seems to have been performed at the Isthmus, the elaborate poem 1 at a later celebration on Ceos. [2] The epithet suggests the athletic success given by the Graces. [3] Ceos: see 1. 125 ff. [4] For the recording of Cean victories see 1 n. 2. [5] Since B. is composing at the site of the games; but perhaps 'the compatriot Muse' with reference to the Cean origin of B. and the victor.

3

ΙΕΡΩΝΙ ΣΥΡΑΚΟΣΙΩΙ
ΙΠΠΟΙΣ [ΟΛΥ]ΜΠΙΑ

ἀριστο[κ]άρπου Σικελίας κρέουσαν
Δ[ά]ματρα ἰοστέφανόν τε Κούραν
ὕμνει, γλυκύδωρε Κλεοῖ, θοάς τ' Ὀ-
λυμ]πιοδρόμους Ἱέρωνος ἵππ[ο]υς.

5 σεύον]το γὰρ σὺν ὑπερόχωι τε Νίκαι
σὺν Ἀγ]λαΐαι τε παρ' εὐρυδίναν
Ἀλφεόν, τόθι] Δεινομένεος ἔθηκαν
ὄλβιον τ[έκος στεφάνω]ν κυρῆσαι·

θρόησε δὲ λ[αὸς ⏑ – – .
10   ἁ̈ τρισευδαίμ[ων ἀνήρ,
ὃς παρὰ Ζηνὸς λαχὼν
πλείσταρχον Ἑλλάνων γέρας
οἶδε πυργωθέντα πλοῦτον μὴ μελαμ-
φαρέϊ κρύπτειν σκότωι.

15 βρύει μὲν ἱερὰ βουθύτοις ἑορταῖς,
βρύουσι φιλοξενίας ἀγυιαί·
λάμπει δ' ὑπὸ μαρμαρυγαῖς ὁ χρυσός,
ὑψιδαιδάλτων τριπόδων σταθέντων

3 Blass: Κλειοι pap.   7 τόθι Palmer   8 τ[έκος Edmonds   9 λ.
ἀπείρων Blass

126

3

Of Demeter, ruler of corn-rich Sicily, and of the
violet-garlanded Maid[2] sing, Clio, giver of sweet-
ness, and of Hiero's swift horses, Olympic runners:
they sped in the company of pre-eminent Victory
and Glory by the wide-eddying Alpheus, where they
made Deinomenes' son[3] prosperous in the winning
of garlands; and the (immense) crowd shouted. Ah,
thrice-fortunate man, who got from Zeus the
privilege of ruling over the greatest number of
Greeks and knows how not to hide his towering
wealth in black-cloaked darkness. The temples
abound in feasts where cattle are sacrificed, the
streets abound in hospitality; and gold shines with
flashing light from the high elaborate tripods[4]

[1] In 468 B.C. P.Oxy. 2367 frr. 1–4 has scraps of commentary on
vv. 63–87.   [2] Persephone, daughter of Demeter.   [3] Hiero.
[4] Hiero's brother Gelo dedicated a tripod at Delphi after his victory
over Carthage in 480, Hiero after defeating the Etruscan fleet at
Cumae in 474.

πάροιθε ναοῦ, τόθι μέγιστον ἄλσος
20 Φοίβου παρὰ Κασταλίας ῥεέθροις
Δελφοὶ διέπουσι. θεὸν θ[εό]ν τις
ἀγλαϊζέθὼ γὰρ ἄριστος ὄλβων·

ἐπεί ποτε καὶ δαμασίππου
Λυδίας ἀρχαγέταν,
25 εὖτε τὰν πεπ[ρωμέναν
Ζηνὸς τελέ[σσαντος κρί]σιν
Σάρδιες Περσᾶ[ν ἁλίσκοντο στρ]ατῶι,
Κροῖσον ὁ χρυσά[ορος

φύλαξ' Ἀπόλλων. [ὁ δ' ἐς] ἄελπτον ἆμαρ
30 μ[ο]λὼν πολυδ[άκρυο]ν οὐκ ἔμελλε
μίμνειν ἔτι δ[ουλοσύ]ναν· πυρὰν δὲ
χαλκ[ο]τειχέος π[ροπάροι]θεν αὐ[λᾶς

ναήσατ', ἔνθα σὺ[ν ἀλόχωι] τε κεδ[νᾶι
σὺν εὐπλοκάμοι[ς τ'] ἐπέβαιν' ἄλα[στον
35 θ]υ[γ]ατράσι δυρομέναις· χέρας δ' [ἐς
αἰ]πὺν αἰθέρα σφετέρας ἀείρας

γέ]γωνεν· ὑπέρ[βι]ε δαῖμον,
πο]ῦ θεῶν ἐστιν χάρις;
πο]ῦ δὲ Λατοίδας ἄναξ;
40 ἔρρουσ]ιν Ἀλυά[τ]τα δόμοι
−∪−⏛−∪−⏛] μυρίων
−∪−⏛−∪−]ν·

standing in front of the temple where the Delphians tend the great sanctuary of Phoebus by the waters of Castalia. Let God, God, be glorified: that is the best of prosperities.

For once upon a time the commander[1] of horse-taming Lydia, after Zeus had brought about the fated issue and Sardis had fallen to the Persian army, was protected by Apollo of the golden lyre: Croesus, having reached the day he had hoped to avoid, had no intention of waiting for tearful slavery also: he had a pyre heaped in front of his bronze-walled courtyard and mounted it together with his beloved wife and fair-tressed daughters, who wailed inconsolably. Raising his hands to the lofty heavens he shouted, 'Almighty Spirit,[2] where is the gratitude of the gods? Where is lord Apollo, Leto's son? The palace of Alyattes[3] is in ruins. (There is no recompense for my) countless (gifts to Delphi: the

---

[1] Croesus, king of Lydia c. 560–546. For Herodotus' account of his capture by Cyrus see 1. 86 ff.   [2] I.e. Zeus.   [3] Croesus' father, king of Lydia c. 610–560.

21, 25 Palmer   26 τελέ[σσαντος Wackernagel   κρί]σιν Weil   27 ἁλίσκοντο Wackernagel   ἐπόρθηθεν Maas   28 χρυσά[ορος Palmer   31 Jebb   34 τ' post εὐπλ. Platt   37 ὑπέρ[βι]ε Blass   40 ἔρρουσ]ιν Frick   41ss. τίς δὲ νῦν δώρων ἀμοιβὰ] μυρίων | φαίνεται Πυθωνόθε]ν; | πέρθουσι Μῆδοι δοριάλωτο]ν ἄστυ e.g. Jebb

⏑–⏑ ⏑⏑ ⏑ ⏑⏑ ⏑ –⏑]ν ἄστυ,
ἐρεύθεται αἵματι χρυσο]δίνας
45 Πακτωλός, ἀεικελίως γυναῖκες
   ἐξ ἐϋκτίτων μεγάρων ἄγονται·

τὰ πρόσθεν [ἐχ]θρὰ φίλα· θανεῖν γλύκιστον.'
τόσ' εἶπε, καὶ ἁβ[ρο]βάταν κ[έλε]υσεν
ἅπτειν ξύλινον δόμον. ἔκ[λα]γον δὲ
50   παρθένοι, φίλας τ' ἀνὰ ματρὶ χεῖρας

ἔβαλλον· ὁ γὰρ προφανὴς θνα-
   τοῖσιν ἔχθιστος φόνων·
ἀλλ' ἐπεὶ δεινοῦ πυρὸς
   λαμπρὸν διάϊ[σσεν μέ]νος,
55 Ζεὺς ἐπιστάσας [μελαγκευ]θὲς νέφος
   σβέννυεν ξανθὰ[ν φλόγα.

ἄπιστον οὐδέν, ὅ τι θ[εῶν μέ]ριμνα
τεύχει· τότε Δαλογενὴ[ς Ἀπό]λλων
φέρων ἐς Ὑπερβορέο[υς γ]έροντα
60   σὺν τανισφύροις κατ[έν]ασσε κούραις

δι' εὐσέβειαν, ὅτι μέ[γιστα] θνατῶν
ἐς ἀγαθέαν <ἀν>έπεμψε Π[υθ]ώ.
ὅσο[ι] <γε> μὲν Ἑλλάδ' ἔχουσιν, [ο]ὔτι[ς,
   ὦ μεγαίνητε Ἱέρων, θελήσει

Persians are sacking my) city, the gold-swirling Pactolus is reddened with blood, the women are shamefully carried off from the well-built halls. What once was hateful is welcome: to die is sweetest.' These were his words, and he ordered his soft-stepping attendant to light the wooden building. The girls shrieked and threw up their hands to their mother: the death that is seen coming is the most hateful to mortals. But when the bright strength of the grim fire was darting through the pyre, Zeus set the black cover of a cloud overhead and quenced the yellow flame. Nothing that the planning of the gods brings about is past belief: Delos-born Apollo carried the old man then to the Hyperboreans and settled him there with his slim-ankled daughters by reason of his piety, since he had sent up to holy Pytho greater gifts than any other mortal.

But of all men who dwell in Greece there is none, illustrious Hiero, who will be ready to claim that he

---

47 Fraccaroli: -θεν δ' pap.   ἐχθρὰ Palmer   56 Palmer   62, 63 corr. Blass, alii

65 φάμ]εν σέο πλείονα χρυσὸν
      Λοξί]αι πέμψαι βροτῶν.
   εὖ λέγειν πάρεστιν, ὅσ-
      τις μ]ὴ φθόνωι πιαίνεται,
   ....]λη φίλιππον ἄνδρ’ ἀρήϊον
70 ....]ίου σκᾶπτρον Διός

   ἰοπλό]κων τε μέρο[ς ἔχοντ]α Μουσᾶν·
   ....]μαλέαι ποτ[ὲ .....]′ ιων
   ....]νος ἐφάμερον α[.....]·
   ....]α σκοπεῖς· βραχ[ύς ἐστιν αἰών·

75 πτε[ρ]όεσσα δ’ ἐλπὶς ὑπ[ολύει ν]όημα
   ἐφαμ]ερίων· ὁ δ’ ἄναξ [’Απόλλων
   .....]′ λος εἶπε Φέρη[τος υἱ·
   ’θνατὸν εὖντα χρὴ διδύμους ἀέξειν

   γνώμας, ὅτι τ’ αὔριον ὄψεαι
80   μοῦνον ἀλίου φάος,
   χὤτι πεντήκοντ’ ἔτεα
      ζωὰν βαθύπλουτον τελεῖς.
   ὅσια δρῶν εὔφραινε θυμόν· τοῦτο γὰρ
      κερδέων ὑπέρτατον.’

85 φρονέοντι συνετὰ γαρύω· βαθὺς μὲν
   αἰθὴρ ἀμίαντος· ὕδωρ δὲ πόντου
   οὐ σάπεται· εὐφροσύνα δ’ ὁ χρυσός·
      ἀνδρὶ δ’ οὐ θέμις, πολιὸν π[αρ]έντα

sent more gold to Loxias[1] than you. Anyone who does not fatten himself on envy may praise this (flourishing?), horse-loving warrior who holds the sceptre of Zeus, (god of hospitality?), and has his share in the violet-haired Muses: once ... you look ... of the day.[2] (Life is) brief, and winged hope undoes the thinking of mortals. Lord Apollo (the far-shooter?) said to the son of Pheres[3]: 'Since you are mortal, you must foster two thoughts: that tomorrow will be the only day on which you see the sun's light, and that for fifty years you will live out a life steeped in wealth. Gladden your heart by doing righteous deeds: this is the highest of gains.' I utter words which the wise man may understand: the deep heavens are unsoiled, and the water of the sea does not decay, and gold is a joy; but a man may not throw aside grey old age and retrieve again his

---

[1] Apollo at Delphi. [2] Perhaps instead of 'you look' 'look out for what is appropriate'; see Lloyd-Jones, *C.R.* 72 (1958) 18.
[3] Admetus, king of Pherae in Thessaly. Zeus made Apollo his servant for killing the Cyclopes.

---

65 φάμ]εν Blass   σέο Palmer   66 Blass, alii   68 Palmer
69 εὐθαλῆ Sandys   70 ξεω]ίου Nairn   71 Blass
72 δει]μαλέαι Blass   ρω]μαλέαι Schwartz   74 schol. M
(P.Oxy. 2367) fr. 3]-ατα ἐρευνα ... ὅτι ὀλιγοχρό[νιος ὁ βίος?   καί-
ρι]α σκόπει Lloyd-Jones, qui schol. suppl. δυ]νατὰ ἐρεύνα   75 fr. 5
ἡ πτερ[όεσσα ἐλπὶς δι]αφθείρει τὸ [τῶν ἀνθρώπων ν]όημα : πτερ] iam H.
Fränkel   ὑπ[ολύει Snell   76 ἐπαμ]ερίων Jebb, Sandys   77 ἑκα-
β]όλος Jebb   υἷι Platt, Wackernagel   88 Jebb

γῆρας, θάλ[εια]ν αὖτις ἀγκομίσσαι
90 ἥβαν. ἀρετᾶ[ς γε μ]ὲν οὐ μινύθει
βροτῶν ἅμα σ[ώμ]ατι φέγγος, ἀλλὰ
    Μοῦσά νιν τρ[έφει.] Ἱέρων, σὺ δ᾽ ὄλβου

κάλλιστ᾽ ἐπεδ[είξ]αο θνατοῖς
    ἄνθεα· πράξα[ντι] δ᾽ εὖ
95 οὐ φέρει κόσμ[ον σι]ω-
    πά· σὺν δ᾽ ἀλαθ[είαι] καλῶν
καὶ μελιγλώσσου τις ὑμνήσει χάριν
    Κηίας ἀηδόνος.

91 Ingram

134

flourishing youth. The light of man's excellence, however, does not diminish with his body; no, the Muse fosters it. Hiero, you have displayed to mortals the fairest flowers of wealth, and when a man has prospered, adornment is not brought him by silence; and along with the true telling of your fine achievements men will praise also the grace[1] of the honey-tongued Cean nightingale.

[1] Perhaps 'men will also sing the friendship-gift', i.e. the present ode.

4

ΤΩΙ ΑΥΤΩΙ

<ΙΠΠΟΙΣ> ΠΥΘΙΑ

ἔτι Συρακοσίαν φιλεῖ
   πόλιν ὁ χρυσοκόμας Ἀπόλλων,
ἀστύθεμίν θ' Ἱέ[ρω]να γεραίρει·
τρίτον γὰρ παρ' [ὀμφα]λὸν ὑψιδείρου χθονός
5 Πυ[θ]ιόνικος ἀ[εἰδε]ται
      ὠ[κυ]πόδων ἀρ[ετᾶι] σὺν ἵππων.
ἔ[λακε δ'] ἁδυεπὴς ἀ[να-
      ξιφόρ]μιγγος Οὐρ[αν]ίας ἀλέκτωρ
ποτὲ μ]έν· ἀλλ' ἐκ[όν]τι νόωι
10 νῦν νέο]υς ἐπέσεισ[εν] ὕμνους.

ἔτι δὲ τέ]τρατον, εἴ τις ὀρ-
      θὰ θεὸς] εἷλκε Δίκας τάλαν[τα,
Δεινομένεός κ' ἐγερα[ίρ]ομεν υἱόν.
πάρεστιν δ' ἐν ἀγχιάλοισι Κ[ί]ρρας μυχοῖς
15 μοῦνον ἐπιχθονίων τάδε
      μησάμενον στεφάνοις ἐρέπτειν
δύο τ' ὀλυμπιονικ<ί>ας
      ἀείδειν. τί φέρτερον ἢ θεοῖσιν
φίλον ἐόντα παντο[δ]απῶν
20 λαγχάνειν ἄπο μοῖρα[ν] ἐσθλῶν;

4–12 fr. Flor. A huc traxit M. Norsa   6 ἀρ[ετᾶι] Blass, alii   7 ἔ[λακε δ'] Snell   7s. Maas   9 ποτὲ μ]έν Maehler   ἐκ[όν]τι Blass   10 νῦν Maehler   νέο]υς Gallavotti   schol. M fr. 5 ὕ]μνους ἐπέ[σεισεν ... ἐ]πέσεισεν (suppl. Lobel) ... [ἡ δὲ μ]εταφο[ρὰ ἀπὸ τῆς φυλλοβολίας (e.g. suppl. Snell)   11 ἔτι δὲ Pfeiffer   τέ]τρα-τον Gallavotti   12 Snell   14 Maehler: παρεστίαν ἀγχ. pap.   Κ[ί]ρρας Blass   17 em. Maas

4

FOR THE SAME VICTOR
CHARIOT RACE, PYTHIAN GAMES[1]

Gold-haired Apollo still loves the Syracusan city
and honours its righteous ruler, Hiero, since for the
third time he is hymned by the navel of the high-
ridged land[2] as a Pythian victor, thanks to the excel-
lence of his swift-footed horses; and the sweet-voiced
cock of lyre-ruling Urania[3] (cried out once before?),
but (now) with willing mind he has showered on him
(new) songs of praise. (Moreover), if some (god) had
been holding level the balance of Justice, we should
be honouring Deinomenes' son[4] for a fourth time;
but we may crown with garlands the only mortal
who has accomplished this[5] in the seaside glens of
Cirrha[6] and sing also of two Olympic victories.[7]
What better than to be dear to the gods and win a
full share in all manner of blessings?

[1] Hiero's victory in the chariot-race at Delphi (470 B.C.) was com-
memorated also by Pindar in *Pythian* 1. B.'s short song may have
been sung at Delphi.   [2] I.e. at Delphi; the 'navel' was the
stone believed to mark the centre of the earth. Hiero had won the
horse-race at the Pythian games of 482 and 478.   [3] One of the
Muses: her cock is the poet. Following words uncertain, but may
refer to B.'s composition of poem 5 for Hiero's horse-race victory at
Olympia in 476.   [4] Hiero, who may have narrowly missed a
fourth victory at Delphi.   [5] A third Pythian victory.   [6] Town
in the plain below Delphi where the horse-racing, wrestling and
similar events were held.   [7] In the horse-race of 476 and 472.

5

<ΤΩΙ ΑΥΤΩΙ
ΚΕΛΗΤΙ ΟΛΥΜΠΙΑ>

εὔμοιρε [Σ]υρακ[οσίω]ν
ἱπποδινήτων στρατα[γ]έ,
γνώσηι μὲν [ἰ]οστεφάνων
    Μοισᾶν γλυκ[ύ]δωρον ἄγαλμα, τῶν γε νῦν
5 αἴ τις ἐπιχθονίων,
ὀρθῶς· φρένα δ᾽ εὐθύδικ[ο]ν
ἀτρέμ᾽ ἀμπαύσας μεριμνᾶν
    δεῦρ᾽ <ἄγ᾽> ἄθρησον νόωι·
ἦ σὺν Χαρίτεσσι βαθυζώνοις ὑφάνας
10 ὕμνον ἀπὸ ζαθέας
νάσου ξένος ὑμετέραν
ἐς κλυτὰν πέμπει πόλιν,
    χρυσάμπυκος Οὐρανίας
    κλεινὸς θεράπων· ἐθέλει [δὲ]
15 γᾶρυν ἐκ στηθέων χέων

αἰνεῖν Ἱέρωνα. βαθὺν
δ᾽ αἰθέρα ξουθαῖσι τάμνων
ὑψοῦ πτερύγεσσι ταχεί-
    αις ἀετὸς εὐρυάνακτος ἄγγελος
20 Ζηνὸς ἐρισφαράγου
θαρσεῖ κρατερᾶι πίσυνος
ἰσχύϊ, πτάσσοντι δ᾽ ὄρνι-
    χες λιγύφθογγοι φόβωι·
οὔ νιν κορυφαὶ μεγάλας ἴσχουσι γαίας,

BACCHYLIDES

5

FOR THE SAME VICTOR
HORSE RACE, OLYMPIC GAMES[1]

Blessed war-lord of chariot-whirling Syracusans,
you if any mortal now alive will rightly assess the
sweet gift of the violet-crowned Muses sent for your
adornment: rest your righteous mind in ease from
its cares and come! turn your thoughts this way:
with the help of the slim-waisted Graces your
guest-friend, the famous servant of Urania[2] with
her golden headband, has woven a song of praise
and sends it from the sacred island[3] to your[4] dis-
tinguished city: he wishes to pour a flood of speech
from his heart in praise of Hiero.

Cleaving the deep heavens with tawny swift
wings on high the eagle, messenger of wide-ruling
loud-thundering Zeus, is confident, trusting in his
mighty strength, and clear-voiced birds cower in
fear: the peaks of the great earth do not bar his way,

---

[1] Hiero's victory (476 B.C.) was commemorated also by Pindar in
Olympian 1.   [2] One of the Muses.   [3] Ceos.   [4] Plural,
with reference to Hiero and his brothers.

---

8 Maehler   11s. Maas: ν. ξ. ὑ. πέμ | πει κλεεννὰν ἐς πόλιν pap.
14 Walker, Maas

25   οὐδ' ἁλὸς ἀκαμάτας
    δυσπαίπαλα κύματα· νω-
       μᾶι δ' ἐν ἀτρύτωι χάει
    λεπτότριχα σὺν ζεφύρου πνοι-
       αῖσιν ἔθειραν ἀρίγνω-
30   τος ⟦μετ'⟧ ἀνθρώποις ἰδεῖν·

    τὼς νῦν καὶ <ἐ>μοὶ μυρία πάνται κέλευθος
       ὑμετέραν ἀρετάν
    ὑμνεῖν, κυανοπλοκάμου θ' ἕκατι Νίκας
       χαλκεοστέρνου τ' Ἄρηος,
35   Δεινομένευς ἀγέρωχοι
       παῖδες· εὖ ἔρδων δὲ μὴ κάμοι θεός.
    ξανθότριχα μὲν Φερένικον
    Ἀλφεὸν παρ' εὐρυδίναν
    πῶλον ἀελλοδρόμαν
40   εἶδε νικάσαντα χρυσόπαχυς Ἀώς,

    Πυθῶνί τ' ἐν ἀγαθέαι·
       γᾶι δ' ἐπισκήπτων πιφαύσκω·
    οὔπω νιν ὑπὸ προτέ[ρω]ν
    ἵππων ἐν ἀγῶνι κατέχρανεν κόνις
45   πρὸς τέλος ὀρνύμενον·
       ῥιπᾶι γὰρ ἴσος βορέα
    ὃν κυβερνήταν φυλάσσων
       ἵεται νεόκροτον
    νίκαν Ἱέρωνι φιλοξείνωι τιτύσκων.
50   ὄλβιος ᾧτινι θεός
       μοῖράν τε καλῶν ἔπορεν

nor the rugged waves of the untiring sea: in the
limitless void he plies his fine-feathered plumage
before the blasts of the west wind, a conspicuous
sight for men. Even so I have countless paths in all
directions for singing the praises of your excel-
lence, noble sons of Deinomenes, thanks both to
dark-haired Victory and to bronze-breasted Ares.[1]
May God not weary of treating you well. Chestnut-
maned Pherenicus, storm-paced horse, was seen
winning at the wide-eddying Alpheus by gold-armed
Dawn, and in holy Pytho too[2]; and resting my hand
on the earth I make my proclamation: never yet in a
contest was he dirtied by the dust of horses ahead of
him as he raced to the finish, for he speeds like the
rush of the north wind, heeding his steersman as he
gains for hospitable Hiero a victory which brings
new applause.

Blessed the man to whom God has granted fine

[1] Gelo and his brothers defeated the Carthaginians at Himera in
480.   [2] At the Pythian games of 478.

26s. Walker: νωμαι|ται pap., νωμα|ται post corr.   cf. schol. Hes.
Theog. 116, Ibyc. S223(b)   28 πνο- pap.   30 Walker   31 Blass
33 Palmer: υμνει pap.   37–40 cit. schol. Pind. *Ol.* 1 argum.
49 -ξενωι pap.   50ss. cit. Stob. 4. 39. 2, 4. 34. 25, Apostol. 12. 65e

σύν τ᾽ ἐπιζήλωι τύχαι
ἀφνεὸν βιοτὰν διάγειν· οὐ
γά[ρ τις] ἐπιχθονίων
55 π[άντ]α γ᾽ εὐδαίμων ἔφυ.

τ[οιγάρ π]οτ᾽ ἐρειψιπύλαν
παῖδ᾽ ἀνίκ]ατον λέγουσιν
δῦναι Διὸς] ἀργικεραύ-
νου δώματα Φερσεφόνας τανισφύρου,
60 καρχαρόδοντα κύν᾽ ἄ-
ξοντ᾽ ἐς φάος ἐξ Ἀΐδα,
υἱὸν ἀπλάτοι᾽ Ἐχίδνας·
ἔνθα δυστάνων βροτῶν
ψυχὰς ἐδάη παρὰ Κωκυτοῦ ῥεέθροις,
65 οἷά τε φύλλ᾽ ἄνεμος
Ἴδας ἀνὰ μηλοβότους
πρῶνας ἀργηστὰς δονεῖ.
ταῖσιν δὲ μετέπρεπεν εἴδω-
λον θρασυμέμνονος ἐγ-
70 χεσπάλου Πορθανίδα·

τὸν δ᾽ ὡς ἴδεν Ἀλκμή<ν>ιος θαυμαστὸς ἥρως
τ[ε]ύχεσι λαμπόμενον,
νευρὰν ἐπέβασε λιγυκλαγγῆ κορώνας,
χαλκεόκρανον δ᾽ ἔπειτ᾽ ἐξ
75 εἵλετο ἰὸν ἀναπτύ-
ξας φαρέτρας πῶμα· τῶι δ᾽ ἐναντία
ψυχὰ προφάνη Μελεάγρου,
καί νιν εὖ εἰδὼς προσεῖπεν·

142

achievements as his portion and the passing of a life
of affluence with enviable fortune; for no mortal is
fortunate in all things. Once, they say, the gate-
wrecking, unconquerable son[1] of thunder-flashing
Zeus went down to the house of slender-ankled
Persephone to fetch up to the light from Hades
the jagged-toothed dog,[2] son of unapproachable
Echidna. There he perceived the spirits of wretched
mortals by the waters of Cocytus, like the leaves
buffeted by the wind over the bright sheep-grazed
headlands of Ida. Among them stood out the ghost
of bold-hearted, spear-brandishing Porthanides[3];
and when the wonderful hero, Alcmena's son,[1] saw
him shining in armour, he put the clear-twanging
string on his bow-hook, then opened the lid of his
quiver and took out a bronze-headed arrow. But
Meleager's spirit confronted him, face to face, and in
his full experience addressed him: 'Son of great

[1] Heracles, sacker of cities.   [2] Cerberus; his mother, Echid-
na, is Snake.   [3] Meleager, son of Oeneus and Althaea and
grandson of Porthaon.

---

53 αφνειον pap., Stob., Apostol.   56 Maehler   58 δῦναι Palmer
78 -εειπεν pap.

ὑὲ Διὸς μεγάλου,
80   στᾶθί τ᾽ ἐν χώραι, γελανώσας τε θυμόν

μὴ ταύσιον προΐει
    τραχὺν ἐκ χειρῶν ὀϊστόν
ψυχαῖσιν ἔπι φθιμένων·
    οὔ τοι δέος.᾽ ὣς φάτο· θάμβησεν δ᾽ ἄναξ
85 ᾽Αμφιτρυωνιάδας,
    εἶπέν τε· ᾽τίς ἀθανάτων
ἢ βροτῶν τοιοῦτον ἔρνος
    θρέψεν ἐν ποίαι χθονί;
τίς δ᾽ ἔκτανεν; ἦ τάχα καλλίζωνος ῞Ηρα
90   κεῖνον ἐφ᾽ ἁμετέραι
πέμψει κεφαλᾶι· τὰ δέ που
    Παλλάδι ξανθᾶι μέλει.᾽
τὸν δὲ προσέφα Μελέαγρος
    δακρυόεις· ᾽χαλεπὸν
95   θεῶν παρατρέψαι νόον

ἄνδρεσσιν ἐπιχθονίοις.
    καὶ γὰρ ἂν πλάξιππος Οἰνεύς
παῦσεν καλυκοστεφάνου
    σεμνᾶς χόλον ᾽Αρτέμιδος λευκωλένου
100 λισσόμενος πολέων
    τ᾽ αἰγῶν θυσίαισι πατήρ
καὶ βοῶν φοινικωτάτων·
    ἀλλ᾽ ἀνίκατον θεά
ἔσχεν χόλον· εὐρυβίαν δ᾽ ἔσσευε κούρα
105   κάπρον ἀναιδομάχαν

Zeus, stay where you are! Calm your heart, and do not send a fierce arrow in vain from your hands against the spirits of the dead. You have nothing to fear.' So he spoke, and lordly Amphitryoniades[1] marvelled and said, 'What god or mortal nurtured such an offshoot, and in what land? Who killed you? Fair-belted Hera[2] will send him soon to take my life; but that, I suppose, is the concern of blonde Pallas.'[3]

Meleager answered him in tears: 'It is hard for mortal men to turn aside the purpose of the gods; for otherwise my father, horse-smiting Oeneus, would have checked the anger of august Artemis,[4] white-armed, bud-garlanded, when he entreated her with sacrifices of many goats and red-backed cattle. But no, the maiden goddess had conceived an unconquerable anger, and she sent a boar of vast strength,

[1] Heracles, son of Alcmena and Amphitryon.   [2] Jealous of Heracles as illegitimate son of Zeus.   [3] Athena, Heracles' protectress.   [4] Oeneus had neglected her in his harvest thanksgiving to the gods (*Il.* 9. 534 f.).

ἐς καλλίχορον Καλυδῶ-
ν᾽, ἔνθα πλημύρων σθένει
ὄρχους ἐπέκειρεν ὀδόντι,
σφάζε τε μῆλα, βροτῶν
110 θ᾽ ὅστις εἰσάνταν μόλοι.

τῶι δὲ στυγερὰν δῆριν Ἑλλάνων ἄριστοι
στασάμεθ᾽ ἐνδυκέως
ἓξ ἄματα συνεχέως· ἐπεὶ δὲ δαίμων
κάρτος Αἰτωλοῖς ὄρεξεν,
115 θάπτομεν οὓς κατέπεφνεν
σῦς ἐριβρύχας ἐπαΐσσων βίαι,
Ἀ[γκ]αῖον ἐμῶν τ᾽ Ἀγέλαον
φ[έρτ]ατον κεδνῶν ἀδελφεῶν,
οὓς τέ]κεν ἐν μεγάροις
120 παῖδα]ς Ἀλθαία περικλειτοῖσιν Οἰνέος·

τῶν δ᾽ ὤ]λεσε μοῖρ᾽ ὀλοὰ
πλεῦνα]ς· οὐ γάρ πω δαΐφρων
παῦσεν] χόλον ἀγροτέρα
Λατοῦς θυγάτηρ· περὶ δ᾽ αἴθωνος δορᾶς
125 μαρνάμεθ᾽ ἐνδυκέως
Κουρῆσι μενεπτολέμοις·
ἔνθ᾽ ἐγὼ πολλοῖς σὺν ἄλλοις
Ἴφικλον κατέκτανον
ἐσθλόν τ᾽ Ἀφάρητα, θοοὺς μάτρωας· οὐ γὰρ
130 καρτερόθυμος Ἄρης
κρίνει φίλον ἐν πολέμωι,

a ruthless fighter, rushing on Calydon[1] with its
beautiful plains, where in the floodtide of his might
he hacked down the vine-rows with his tusks and
slaughtered sheep and any mortal who confronted
him. We, the best of the Greeks, persistently waged
hateful war on him for six days on end; and when
God granted victory to the Aetolians, we buried
those whom the loud-squealing boar had killed with
his violent charging, Ancaeus and Agelaus, the
finest of my dear brothers, (sons) whom Althaea
bore in the famous palace of Oeneus; but deadly fate
destroyed (more than these): for the fierce goddess of
the hunt, Leto's daughter, had still not put a stop to
her anger, and we fought persistently for the red-
brown hide against the Curetes,[2] staunch in battle;
then I killed among many others Iphiclus and good
Aphares, swift brothers of my mother—for hard-
hearted Ares does not distinguish a friend in battle,

[1] The Aetolian city of Oeneus. [2] An Aetolian clan from Pleu-
ron to which Althaea's family belonged.

106 Palmer: ος pap. 115 τους κατεπεφνε pap. 117 αγγελον pap.
120 Schadewaldt 121 Jebb: σύν τ᾿ (vel σὺν δ᾿)
Edmonds τοὺς δ᾿ Kenyon 122 Housman: πάντας Ludwich

τυφλὰ δ' ἐκ χειρῶν βέλη
ψυχαῖς ἔπι δυσμενέων φοι-
τᾶι θάνατόν τε φέρει
135 τοῖσιν ἂν δαίμων θέληι.

ταῦτ' οὐκ ἐπιλεξαμένα
Θεστίου κούρα δαΐφρων
μάτηρ κακόποτμος ἐμοὶ
βούλευσεν ὄλεθρον ἀτάρβακτος γυνά,
140 καῖέ τε δαιδαλέας
ἐκ λάρνακος ὠκύμορον
φιτρὸν ἐξαύσασα· τὸν δὴ
μοῖρ' ἐπέκλωσεν τότε
ζωᾶς ὅρον ἁμετέρας ἔμμεν. τύχον μὲν
145 Δαϊπύλου Κλύμενον
παῖδ' ἄλκιμον ἐξεναρί-
ζων ἀμώμητον δέμας,
πύργων προπάροιθε κιχήσας·
τοὶ δὲ πρὸς εὐκτιμέναν
150 φεῦγον ἀρχαίαν πόλιν

Πλευρῶνα· μίνυθεν δέ μοι ψυχὰ γλυκεῖα·
γνῶν δ' ὀλιγοσθενέων,
αἰαῖ· πύματον δὲ πνέων δάκρυσα τλά[μων,
ἀγλαὰν ἥβαν προλείπων.'
155 φασὶν ἀδεισιβόαν
Ἀμφιτρύωνος παῖδα μοῦνον δὴ τότε
τέγξαι βλέφαρον, ταλαπενθέος
πότμον οἰκτίροντα φωτός·

and missiles go blindly from our hands against the lives of the enemy and bring death to those for whom it is God's wish.

'The fierce daughter of Thestius, my ill-fated mother, gave no thought to that and, unflinching woman, planned my destruction; and she set fire to the swift-dooming log,[1] taking it from the elaborate chest, and fate then decreed that that be the limit of my life. I happened to be slaying Clymenus, Daïpylus' son, valiant, faultless in body, having caught him in front of the towers—for they were fleeing to well-built Pleuron, that ancient city; and my sweet life was diminished within me, and I realised that I had little strength left, alas! And as I breathed my last I wept in misery at leaving behind my glorious youth.'

They say that Amphitryon's son, fearless of the battle-cry, shed tears then and only then, pitying the fate of the grief-suffering man, and in answer to

---

[1] Althaea, told by the Fates that her son would live until a log on the hearth was completely burned, kept it in a box.

---

137 κορα pap.   142 Wackernagel: εγκλαυσασα pap.   146 εξαναρ-
pap.   151 Wilamowitz: μινυνθα pap.   154 -λιπων pap.

καί νιν ἀμειβόμενος
160 τᾶδ᾽ ἔφα· 'θνατοῖσι μὴ φῦναι φέριστον

μηδ᾽ ἀελίου προσιδεῖν
    φέγγος· ἀλλ᾽ οὐ γάρ τίς ἐστιν
πρᾶξις τάδε μυρομένοις,
    χρὴ κεῖνο λέγειν ὅτι καὶ μέλλει τελεῖν.
165 ἠρά τις ἐν μεγάροις
    Οἰνῆος ἀρηϊφίλου
ἔστιν ἀδμήτα θυγάτρων,
    σοὶ φυὰν ἀλιγκία;
τάν κεν λιπαρὰν <ἐ>θέλων θείμαν ἄκοιτιν.'
170 τὸν δὲ μενεπτολέμου
    ψυχὰ προσέφα Μελεά-
    γρου· 'λίπον χλωραύχενα
ἐν δώμασι Δαϊάνειραν,
    νῆϊν ἔτι χρυσέας
175 Κύπριδος θελξιμβρότου.'

λευκώλενε Καλλιόπα,
    στᾶσον εὐποίητον ἅρμα
αὐτοῦ· Δία τε Κρονίδαν
    ὕμνησον Ὀλύμπιον ἀρχαγὸν θεῶν,
180 τόν τ᾽ ἀκαμαντορόαν
    Ἀλφεόν, Πέλοπός τε βίαν,
καὶ Πίσαν, ἔνθ᾽ ὁ κλεεννὸς
    πο]σσὶ νικάσας δρόμωι

him spoke thus: 'Best for mortals never to be born, never to set eyes on the sun's light. But since there is nothing to be achieved by weeping over it, one should speak rather of what he means to accomplish. Is there in the palace of Oeneus, dear to Ares, an unwedded daughter, like you in her stature? I should willingly make her my radiant wife.' The spirit of Meleager, staunch in battle, addressed him: 'I left in my home Deianeira, the bloom of youth on her neck, still without experience of golden Cypris,[1] that enchantress of men.'

White-armed Calliope,[2] halt your well-made chariot here: sing in praise of Zeus, son of Cronus, Olympian, ruler of gods, and of Alpheus, tireless stream, and of the might of Pelops,[3] and of Pisa,[4] where famous Pherenicus sped to victory in the race

[1] Aphrodite.   [2] One of the Muses.   [3] Buried and honoured at Olympia.   [4] Olympia.

160–162 cit. Stob. 4.34.26, Heph. Ptol. ap. Phot. *Bibl.* 153a
161 μητ pap. μηδ' Stob.

ἦλθ]εν Φερένικος <ἐς> εὐπύργους Συρακόσ-
185   σας Ἱέρωνι φέρων
   εὐδ]αιμονίας πέταλον.
     χρὴ] δ' ἀλαθείας χάριν
   αἰνεῖν, φθόνον ἀμφ[οτέραισιν
   χερσὶν ἀπωσάμενον,
190   εἴ τις εὖ πράσσοι βροτῶ[ν.

   Βοιωτὸς ἀνὴρ τᾶδε φών[ησεν, γλυκειᾶν
     Ἡσίοδος πρόπολος
   Μουσᾶν, ὃν <ἂν> ἀθάνατοι τι[μῶσι, τούτωι
   καὶ βροτῶν φήμαν ἔπ[εσθαι.
195 πείθομαι εὐμαρέως
     εὐκλέα κελεύθου γλῶσσαν οὐ[κ ἐκτὸς δίκας
   πέμπειν Ἱέρωνι· τόθεν γὰ[ρ
     πυθμένες θάλλουσιν ἐσθλ[ῶν,
   τοὺς ὁ μεγιστοπάτωρ
200   Ζεὺς ἀκινήτους ἐν εἰρήν[αι φυλάσσοι.

184 Blass, Housman   184s. -κουσ]|σας pap.   191 γλ. suppl.
Bruhn   193s. Housman   196 Jebb

and so returned to well-towered Syracuse bringing Hiero the leaves of good fortune.[1] For the sake of the truth one must thrust envy aside with both hands and praise any mortal who is successful. A man of Boeotia, Hesiod, minister of the (sweet) Muses, spoke thus[2]: 'He whom the immortals honour is attended also by the good report of men.' I am easily persuaded to send Hiero speech to bring him glory, without (straying from) the path (of justice); for such speech makes the tree-stocks of blessings flourish: may Zeus, the greatest father, (preserve) them unshaken in peace.

[1] The victor's olive wreath.　　[2] Fr. 344 M.-W.; see also Theognis 169.

6

ΛΑΧΩΝΙ ΚΕΙΩΙ
<ΠΑΙΔΙ> ΣΤΑΔΙΕΙ ΟΛΥΜΠ[ΙΑ

Λάχων Διὸς μεγίστου
λάχε φέρτατον πόδεσσι
κῦδος ἐπ᾽ Ἀλφεοῦ προχοαῖς [∪ – –
δι᾽ ὅσσα πάροιθεν
5 ἀμπελοτρόφον Κέον
ἄεισάν ποτ᾽ Ὀλυμπίαι
     πύξ τε καὶ στάδιον κρατεῦ[σαν
στεφάνοις ἐθείρας

νεανίαι βρύοντες.
10 σὲ δὲ νῦν ἀναξιμόλπου
Οὐρανίας ὕμνος ἕκατι Νίκ[ας,
Ἀριστομένειον
ὦ ποδάνεμον τέκος,
γεραίρει προδόμοις ἀοι-
15   δαῖς, ὅτι στάδιον κρατήσας
Κέον εὐκλέϊξας.

3 Αλφειου pap.   [κάλ᾽ αὔξων Jebb   [ἀέθλων Housman

BACCHYLIDES

6

FOR LACHON OF CEOS
BOYS' SPRINT, OLYMPIC GAMES[1]

Lachon by the speed of his feet latched on[2] to the highest glory from great Zeus at the mouth of the Alpheus,[3] (adding to the fine achievements?) for which in earlier days young men, their hair luxuriant with garlands, sang at Olympia of vine-nurturing Ceos as the winner in sprint and boxing; and now to you, wind-footed son of Aristomenes, thanks to Victory the hymn of song-ruling Urania[4] gives praise in an ode sung before your house, since by winning the sprint you brought fame to Ceos.

[1] In 452 B.C., according to the list of Olympic victors in P.Oxy. 222, where he is called Lacon; in the Cean list, *I.G.* XII 5.608 (see 1 n. 2), which mentions two Nemean victories in the boys' sprint, he is Lachon. [2] B. puns on the boy's name. [3] Olympia was some eight miles from the coast. [4] One of the Muses.

7

ΤΩΙ ΑΥΤΩΙ

ὦ λιπαρὰ θύγατερ Χρόνου τε κ[αί
Νυκτός, σὲ πεντήκοντα μηνῶν ἁμέραν
ἑκκαιδεκάταν ἐν Ὀλυμπ[ίαι ◡ –
Διὸς] βαρυβρ[έντα Κρονίδαο] ἕκατι
5 . . .]ι τοσαιμα[
κρίνειν τα[χυτᾶτά τε] λαιψηρῶν ποδῶν
Ἕλλασι καὶ γυ[ίων ἀ]ρισταλκὲς σθένος·
ὧι δὲ σὺ πρεσβύ[τατο]ν νείμηις γέρας
νίκας, ἐπ' ἀνθρ[ώπ]οισιν εὔδοξος κέκλη-
10 ται καὶ πολυζή[λωτ]ος. Ἀρι[στομ]έν[ε]ιον
παῖδ]' ἐκόσμη[σας στε]φάν[οισι Λάχω]να

12

]χε Χαιρόλαν[
μ]ενον εὐσεβ[ ]ομωι
15]τωι θαν[άτωι]ι δ[
]ι πατρίδος·[
]νεοκρίτου[
]ν ἄτεκνον[

2s. πεντ. –έκκαι. cit. Favorin.   π. φυγῆς col. 4. 49   3ss. Πέλοψ | . . .
ἔθηκε Snell   4 Snell   6 τα[χυ<τᾶ>τά τε] Jurenka   10 Blass
11 Maas: εὖτ'] Edmonds   14 εὐσεβ[εῖ ν]όμωι Maas

BACCHYLIDES

7

FOR THE SAME VICTOR[1]

Radiant daughter[2] of Time and Night, you, the sixteenth day of the fiftieth month,[3] (were established by Pelops?) in Olympia by the will of loud-thundering (Zeus, son of Cronus) ... to judge for the Greeks the speed of swift feet and the power of strongest limbs; and he to whom you grant the most venerable prize of victory is called glorious and much-envied among men. You adorned with garlands Lachon, son of Aristomenes, ... Chaerolas[4] ... (by holy law?) ... death ... native land ... new-judged ... childless ...

[1] Lachon of Ceos, victor in the boys' sprint at Olympia in 452 B.C. The first strophe is pieced together from various fragments; the second is almost wholly lost. [2] Day. [3] Alternating periods of 49 and 50 months separated the Olympic Games, which ended with the award of prizes on the 16th day of the month. The phrase, literally 'the sixteenth day of fifty months', is cited (as Pindar's) by Favorinus. [4] An ancestor of Lachon?

8

[ΛΙΠΑΡΙΩΝΙ ΚΕΙΩΙ ?]

desunt vv. vii

8 . . .]ιοι᾿ ἀγων[– – (?)
. . . .]ταν λιπα[ρ – –
10 . . .]ναισεπα[– – ⏑⏑ – ⏑⏑ – –
π]αῖδας Ἑλλά[νων ⏑⏑ – ⏑⏑ – –
ὁ πο]λυαμπελ[– ⏑⏑ – ⏑⏑ – –
. . .]τον ὑμν[– ⏑ –
. .]ηνος ἐν Κ[έωι
15 . .]ιπερ ἄνιπ[πος ⏑ –
. . .]π[

Πυθῶνά τε μηλοθύταν
ὑμνέων Νεμέαν τε καὶ ᾿Ισθ[μ]όν·
γᾶι δ᾿ ἐπισκήπτων χέρα
20 κομπάσομαι· σὺν ἀλα-
θείαι δὲ πᾶν λάμπει χρέος·
οὔτις ἀνθρώπων κ[αθ᾿ Ἕλλα-
νας σὺν ἅλικι χρόνω[ι
παῖς ἐὼν ἀνήρ τε π[λεῦ-
25 νας ἐδέξατο νίκας.
ὦ Ζεῦ κ[ε]ραυνεγχές, κα[ὶ ἐπ᾿ ἀργυ]ροδίνα

8]ιου pap. ut vid., sed hiatus obstat   ἀγῶν[ος (?) Körte   9 Λι-
πά[ρου παῖς Maas   10 Κλεω]ναῖς vel Κλεω]ναί σε tent. Maehler
11 Blass   12 Maas (-πέλου?)   14 Maas   15 κα]ίπερ ἄνιπ[πος
ἐοῦσ᾿ (?) Körte   22 Blass   23 σὺν Headlam: ἐν pap.   24 Blass
π]οσσὶ πλεῦ- Sandys   26 fin.–28 fin. = fr. 17 Kenyon

BACCHYLIDES

8

(FOR LIPARION OF CEOS?)[1]

... of the ... contest ... (the son of Liparus?) ... (Cleonae?) ... the sons of the Greeks ... vine-rich ... (song of praise?) ... in (Ceos?) ... although horseless ... as I sing in praise of Pytho where sheep are sacrificed and of Nemea and of the Isthmus[2]; and resting my hand on the earth I shall make my vaunt—for with the help of truth any matter shines forth: no one among the Greeks, as boy or as man, won more victories in equal time. Zeus of the thunderbolt spear, on the banks of

[1] The title and most of the first strophe (= fr. 7 Kenyon) are lost, but the epithets 'vine-rich' and 'horseless' point to Ceos (cf. 6. 5, Pind. Pae. 4. 25–27), and the letters Lipa[to Liparion, son of Liparus, who according to the Cean inscription (see 1 n. 2) won thrice at the Isthmus and once at Nemea. The event is not known; if 'Cleonae', a long shot in v. 10, is correct, the games were the Nemean.   [2] The scenes of the athlete's victories.

ὄχθαισιν Ἀλφειοῦ τελέσ[αις μεγ]αλοκλέας
θεοδότους εὐχάς, περὶ κ[ρατί τ᾽ ὀ]πά[σσαι]ς
γλαυκὸν Αἰτωλίδος
30 ἄνδημ᾽ ἐλαίας
ἐν Πέλοπος Φρυγίου
κλεινοῖς ἀέθλοις.

27 Maas: τέλεσ[ας Blass   τέλεσ[σον Kenyon   28 κ[ρατί τ᾽
ὀ]πασσας Blass   ὀ]πάσσαις Maas

9

AYTOMHΔEI ΦΛEIAΣIΩI
ΠΕΝΤΑΘΛΩΙ NEMEA

δόξαν, ὦ χρυσαλάκατοι Χάρι[τ]ες,
πεισίμβροτον δοίητ᾽, ἐπεί
Μουσᾶν γε ἰοβλεφάρων θεῖος προφ[άτ]ας
εὔτυκος Φλειοῦντά τε καὶ Νεμεαίου
5 Ζηνὸς εὐθαλὲς πέδον
ὑμνεῖν, ὅθι μηλοδαΐκταν
θρέψεν ἁ λευκώλε[νο]ς
Ἥρα περι[κλει]τῶν ἀέθλων
πρῶτον [Ἡ]ρ[α]κλεῖ βαρύφθογγον λέοντα.

10 κε[ῖθι φοι]νικάσπιδες ἡμίθεοι
πρ[ώτιστ]ον Ἀργείων κριτοί

3 Blass: τε pap.   6 οτι pap.   10 φοι]νικ. Housman, Wilamowitz

160

silver-eddying Alpheus also may you fulfil his
prayers for great fame, god-given, and grant that he
bind about his head the grey wreath of Aetolian[1]
olive in the famous contests of Phrygian Pelops.[2]

[1] I.e. Elean, as in Pind. *Ol.* 3. 12; Elis was founded by the Aetolian
Oxylus.   [2] Pelops, son of the Lydian Tantalus, could be
regarded as the first Olympic victor because he won his bride by
defeating Oenomaus, king of Pisa, in a chariot-race; see also 5. 181
with n. 3 on p. 151.

9

FOR AUTOMEDES OF PHLIUS

PENTATHLON, NEMEAN GAMES[1]

Graces of the golden distaff, grant the fame that
convinces mortals; for the god-inspired spokesman[2]
of the violet-eyed Muses is ready to sing the praises
of Phlius and the luxuriant ground of Nemean Zeus,
where white-armed Hera nurtured the sheep-killing
deep-voiced lion, first of Heracles' glorious contests.

There demigods with red shields, distinguished
Argives,[3] held contests for the very first time in

[1] Date unknown. Phlius is in the N.E. Peloponnese in the valley
west of Nemea; its river, the Asopus, flows past Sicyon to the
Corinthian Gulf.   [2] The poet himself.   [3] Adrastus, king
of Argos, led the Seven against Thebes to restore Polyneices; among
them was the seer Amphiaraus, son of Oïcles. When the warriors
halted at Nemea, the nurse of Archemorus, infant son of the
Nemean king, left the child untended while she guided them to a
spring. The warriors instituted the Nemean Games in his memory.
Cf. Simon. 553.

ἄθλησαν <ἐ>π᾽ Ἀρχεμόρωι, τὸν ξανθοδερκής
πέφν᾽ ἀωτεύοντα δράκων ὑπέροπλος,
σᾶμα μέλλοντος φόνου.
15 ὦ μοῖρα πολυκρατές· οὔ νιν
πεῖθ᾽ Ὀικλείδας πάλιν
στείχειν ἐς εὐάνδρους ἀγ[υιάς.
ἐλπὶς ἀνθρώπων ὑφαιρ[εῖται νόημ]α·

ἃ καὶ τότ᾽ Ἄδραστον Ταλ[αϊονίδαν
20 πέμπεν ἐς Θήβας Πολυνείκεϊ πλαξί[ππωι φίλον.
κείνων ἀπ᾽ εὐδόξων ἀγώνων
ἐν Νεμέαι κλεινο[ὶ β]ροτῶν,
οἳ τριετεῖ στεφάνωι
ξανθὰν ἐρέψωνται κόμαν·
25 Αὐτομήδει νῦν γε νικά-
σαντί νιν δαίμων ἔ[δ]ωκεν,

πενταέθλοισιν γὰρ ἐνέπρεπεν ὡς
ἄστρων διακρίνει φάη
νυκτὸς διχομηνίδο[ς] εὐφεγγὴς σελάνα·
30 τοῖος Ἑλλάνων δι᾽ ἀπ[εί]ρονα κύκλον
φαῖνε θαυμ[α]στὸν δέμας
δίσκον τροχοειδέα ῥίπτων,
καὶ μελαμφύλλου κλάδον
ἀκτέας ἐς αἰπεινὰν προπέμπων
35 αἰθέρ᾽ ἐκ χειρὸς βοὰν ὤτρυνε λαῶν,

ἢ τε[λε]υτάσας ἀμάρυγμα πάλας·
τοιῶ[ιδ᾽ ὑπερθ]ύμωι σ[θένε]ι

162

honour of Archemorus, whom a monstrous fiery-
eyed serpent killed as he slept, an omen of
bloodshed to come.[1] Ah, powerful fate! The son of
Oïcles could not persuade them to go back again to
the city streets, rich in heroes. Hope steals away
men's (thinking)—she who even then was sending
Adrastus, son of Talaus, to Thebes (as friend) to
horse-smiting Polyneices.

Renowned are the mortals who in those famous
games at Nemea crown their auburn hair with the
triennial[2] garland. Now God has granted it to
Automedes on his victory; for he was conspicuous
among the pentathletes, as the bright moon out-
shines the light of the stars in the midmonth night:
even so in the immense circle of the Greeks did he
display his wonderful form as he threw the wheel-
shaped discus, and hurling from his hand the shaft
of the dark-leaved elder into the sheer heaven
aroused the shout of the people, or when he com-
pleted the flashing moves of the wrestling.

With such proud strength did he bring strong-

---

[1] Arche-morus means 'beginning of doom'; only Adrastus returned
from the attack on Thebes.   [2] Inclusive counting: the Games
were held in alternate years, odd-numbered in our reckoning.

---

13 Neil: ασαγένοντα post corr. pap.   18 νόημ]α Blass   20 Her-
werden: πλα[ξίππωι πέλας Kenyon   36 ἦ Maehler   Hense:
τε[. .]υταιας post corr. pap.   37 τοίω[ι θ' Maehler

γυια[λκέα σώ]ματα [πρὸς γ]αίαι πελάσσα[ς
ἵκετ’ [’Ασωπὸ]ν πάρα πορφυροδίναν·
40 τοῦ κ[λέος π]ᾶσαν χθόνα
ἦλθε[ν καὶ] ἐπ’ ἔσχατα Νείλου,
ταί τ’ ἐπ’ εὐναεῖ πόρωι
οἰκεῦσι Θερμώδον[τος, ἐ]γχέων
ἵστορες κοῦραι διωξίπποι· ῎Αρηος,

45 σῶν, ὦ πολυζήλωτε ἄναξ ποταμῶν,
ἐγγόνων γεύσαντο, καὶ ὑψιπύλου Τροίας ἔδος.
στείχει δι’ εὐρείας κελε[ύ]θου
μυρία πάνται φάτις
σᾶς γενεᾶς λιπαρο-
50 ζώνων θυγατρῶν, ἃς θε[ο]ί
σὺν τύχαις ὤικισσαν ἀρχα-
γοὺς ἀπορθήτων ἀγυιᾶν.

τίς γὰρ οὐκ οἶδεν κυανοπλοκάμου
Θήβας ἔϋδμα[τον πόλι]ν,
55 ἢ τὰν μεγαλώνυ]μον Αἴγιναν, μεγ[ίστ]ου
Ζην]ὸς [ἃ πλαθεῖσα λ]έχει τέκεν ἥρω
   ]δὲ σω[. . . . .]ον,
ὃς γ]ᾶς βασά[νοισιν ’Αχ]αιῶν
   ]υ[   ]α
60 τ[– – ◡ – – – ◡ – –
α[. . . . . .]ω[. . . . . . ἐ]ϋπεπλον [. .]́[

39 Blass, alii   42 εὐναεῖ Jebb   44 κοραι pap.   45 Platt, alii:
-ζηλωτ’ αναξ pap.   46 Weil, alii: εγγονοι pap.   55 Blass   56
Wilamowitz   58 Blass

164

limbed bodies to the ground before returning to dark-eddying Asopus,[1] whose fame has reached every land, even the furthest regions of the Nile[2]; and those maidens who live by the fair-flowing stream of Thermodon,[3] skilled spearswomen, daughters of horse-driving Ares, tasted the valour of your descendants,[4] you much-envied lord of rivers, as did the city of Troy with its high gates.[5] On a wide path travel in all directions the countless reports of your family, the bright-belted daughters whom gods settled with happy fortunes as founders of inviolate cities. Who does not know of the well-built town of dark-haired Thebe or of renowned Aegina, who (came to) the bed of great Zeus and bore the hero[6] ..., who of the land of the Achaeans by the tests ...[7]? ... fair-robed[8] ... and (Peirene,[9]

[1] The river of Phlius; the main river of Boeotia had the same name. [2] Perhaps with reference to the Ethiopian Memnon, killed by Achilles at Troy; see n. 4. [3] River flowing N. into the E. Black Sea; the Amazons lived in the plain near its mouth. [4] Asopus' daughter, Aegina, was mother (by Zeus) of Aeacus, whose sons Telamon and Peleus attacked the Amazons. Peleus' son Achilles killed Penthesilea, queen of the Amazons at Troy. [5] Telamon's son Ajax and Achilles with his son Neoptolemus fought against Troy. [6] Aeacus: see n. 4. The columns containing vv. 55–104 are fragmentary. For the daughters of Asopus see Corinna 654 coll. ii–iv, Paus. 5. 22. 6. [7] There may have been reference to Aeacus' upright character. [8] Epithet of another daughter, perhaps Sinope or Cleone; Corcyra may have been named in the previous line. [9] The fountain of Corinth.

ἠ[δὲ Πειράν]αν ἑλικοστέφα[νον
  κ[ούραν, ὅ]σαι τ᾽ ἄλλαι θεῶν
ε[ὐναῖς ἐδ]άμησαν ἀριγνώτ[ο]ις π[α]λαι[οῦ
65 παῖδες αἰ[δο[ῖ]αι ποταμοῦ κε[λ]άδοντος·
  –⏑– –]αν πόλιν
  – –⏑⏑–]σί τε νικα[
  –⏑– αὐ]λῶν βοαί
  – –⏑– ο]υσαι· μερ[μιν– –
70 –⏑– – –⏑– – –⏑–]αν·

  – –⏑– – –⏑⏑–⏑]νεος
χρ]υσέα[ν προσ]θέντα ἰόπλοκον εὖ εἰπεῖν [Κύπριν,
  τὰν μ]ατ[έρ᾽ ἀκ]νάμ[π]των Ἐρώτων
  –⏑– κλε]ινὰν βροτο[ῖς
75 –⏑⏑–⏑]λέων
  – –⏑– –]προξεν[–
  –⏑– – –]ειώταν
  –⏑– – –⏑]ν ὕμνον,

  ὅς κε – – –] καὶ ἀποφθιμένωι
80 – –⏑ ἄτ]ρυτον χρόνον,
καὶ τοῖς ἐ]πιγεινομένοις αἰεὶ πιφαύσκοι
σὰν Νε]μέαι νίκαν· τό γέ τοι καλὸν ἔργον
γνησίων ὕμνων τυχόν
ὑψοῦ παρὰ δαίμοσι κεῖται.

85 σὺν δ᾽ ἀλαθείαι βροτῶν
κάλλιστον, εἴπ[ερ καὶ θάνηι τις,
λε[ί]πεται Μουσ[ᾶν βαθυζώνων ἄθ]υρμα.

166

the maiden) of the twining garland, and all those others who won glory when bedded by gods, venerable daughters of the ancient noisy river.

... the city[1] ... and (of?) victory ... the shouts of pipes ... (thoughts?) ... (adding?)[2] golden violet-crowned Cypris, to praise her, mother of the inflexible Loves and famous among mortals ... (guest-friend?) ... a song of praise, which ... even when you are dead ... for limitless ages, and may tell all future generations of your victory at Nemea: the fine deed, if it wins authentic songs of praise, is stored on high among the gods; and with the help of men's truthfulness a most fine plaything[3] of the (slim-waisted?) Muses is left behind even when one dies.

[1] Phlius?   [2] B. may have named other gods.   [3] The celebratory poem.

62s. Jebb   64 Blass   65 Jebb   72, 73 (τὰν) Blass   79 Jebb
81s. Kenyon, Blass:]μέα pap.   87 Blass

εἰ[σ]ὶ δ' ἀνθρώ[πων ∪∪–∪∪–
   πολλαί· δι[α]κρίν[ε]ι δὲ θεῶν
90 β]ουλὰ [τὸ καλυπτό]μενον νυκτὸς [δνοφοῖσιν
  .] . . . [∪–––∪]γε καὶ τὸν ἀρείω
–∪–––∪]που·
––∪∪–∪∪]ευσων
–∪–––∪–]
95 ––∪–––∪ π]αύροις
   ἀν]δρ[άσιν ––∪–––]ι τὸ μέλλον·

ἦ τ]ιμίῳ[ι ––∪∪]δῶκε χάριν
κ]αὶ Διων[υσ–∪∪–] θεοτίματ[ο]ν πόλιν
ν]αίειν ἀπο[––∪]ευντας
100 χ]ρυσεοσκάπτρ[–∪–
  ὅς] τι καλὸν φέ[ρεται,
    πᾶς] αἰνέοι· Τιμοξ[ένου
    παιδὶ σὺν κώ[μοις νέων ὑμ-
    νέ]οιτε πεντ[άθλοισι νίκαν.

88 ἀνθρώ[πων ἀρεταῖσιν ὁδοὶ Jebb   89s. Jebb   96 τεκμαίρεσθα]ι
Jebb   97 Snell   100 -σκάπτρ[ου Διὸς Jebb   101 Jebb   102
init. Jebb, fin. Blass   103s. Schadewaldt

There are many (paths for the excellences?) of men, but it is the plan of the gods that decides what is (now concealed in the gloom) of night[1]; ... the better man ... to few men (have the Fates granted the gift of conjecturing) the future; (to the worthy man?) ... (God) has granted glory, and that they inhabit the god-honoured city (of?) Dionysus[2] ... (from?) gold-sceptred (Zeus when a man wins) a fine (prize), let (everyone) praise him: for Timoxenus' son (sing) with the revel-bands (of young men) the praises of his pentathlon (victory).

[1] I.e. the future.   [2] Phlias, son of Dionysus, was eponymous hero of Phlius.

10

[ΑΘΗΝΑΙΩΙ]
[ΔΡΟΜΕΙ (?) ΙΣΘΜΙΑ]

Φή]μα, σὺ γ[ὰ]ρ ἀ[ἐ]ποιχνεῖς
φῦ]λα, καὶ πα . [
        ]μελαμει[
        ]πο κευ[
5   ]νωνται [
        ]ᾁ . ωι ξ[. .]ον, ὅτι χρυ[σ
ο[. . .]ν ὀφθαλμοῖσιν [
    π[αῦλ]αν ἀπράκταν . . [.] . . [
ἀ[. .]ᾳ οἱ καὶ νῦν κασιγνήτας ἀκοίτας
10 νασιῶτιν ἐκίνησεν λιγύφθογγον μέλισσαν,

ἐγχειρὲς ἵν᾽ ἀθάνατον Μουσᾶν ἄγαλμα
ξυνὸν ἀνθρώποισιν εἴη
χάρμα, τεὰν ἀρετὰν
    μανῦον ἐπιχθονίοισιν,
15 ὅσσο<ν αὖ> Νίκας ἕκατι
ἄνθεσιν ξανθὰν ἀναδησάμενος κεφαλάν
κῦδος εὐρείαις Ἀθάναις
    θῆκας Οἰνείδαις τε δόξαν,
ἐν Ποσειδᾶνος περικλείτοις ἀέθλοις
20 ἁνίκ᾽ ἄμφαν]ας Ἕλλασιν ποδῶν ταχεῖαν ὁρμάν.

1–4 suppl. fr. 23 K.   ἀ[θανάτων θνατῶν τ᾽ Headlam   ἀ[μφ᾽ ἀρετᾶι
θνατῶν Blass   2 Wilamowitz   πᾶσ[ιν Blass   6ss. ὅ τι χρυ[σέαν
ἴδον εὖ|ο[λβο]ν ὀφθαλμοῖσι Ν[ίκαν | π[αῦλ]αν ἀπράκταν [τε μόχθων e.g.
Jebb   9 ἀ[λλ]ά οἱ tent. Maehler   11 ἐγχειρὲς Snell
15 Richards: ὅσσα Ν. pap.   20 Barrett

170

10

Report,[2] you visit the tribes (. . . of mortals?) and
(to all?) . . . because with their eyes (they have
looked on) golden (blessed Victory) and leisured
relaxation (from their toils); (but) now his sister's
husband has bestirred for him the clear-voiced
island bee,[3] so that an undying ornament of the
Muses might be at hand, a common joy for mankind,
informing mortals of your prowess—what great
renown you brought once again to wide Athens,
what glory to the Oeneidae,[4] as by the grace of Vic-
tory you bound your blond head with flowers, when
in the far-famed contests of Poseidon you displayed
to the Greeks the swift dash of your feet.

1 Victor's name (perhaps given in v. 6) and date unknown.
2 Personified as in 2. 1.   3 I.e., has commissioned B. to com-
pose a victory-song for him.   4 Members of the Attic tribe to
which the runner's family belonged.

εὖτ[ε γὰρ τέ<ρ>θ]ροισιν ἔπι σταδίου
θερμ[ὰν ἀπο]πνε<ί>ων ἄελλαν
ἔστα[, δίανε]ν δ' αὖτε θατήρων ἐλαίωι
φάρε[' ἐς ἀθρόο]ν ἐμπίτνων ὅμιλον
25 τετρ[αέλικτο]ν ἐπεί
κάμψ[εν δρό]μον, 'Ισθμιονίκαν
δίς ν[ιν ἀγκ]άρυξαν εὐβού-
       λων [ἀεθλάρχ]ων προφᾶται·

δὶς δ' ἐ[ν Νεμέ]αι Κρονίδα Ζηνὸς παρ' ἁγνόν
30 βωμό[ν· ἁ κλει]νά τε Θήβα
δέκτ[ο νιν ε]ὐρύχορον
       τ' Ἄργο[ς Σικυώ]ν τε κατ' αἶσαν·
οἵ τε Π[ελλάν]αν νέμονται,
ἀμφί τ' Εὔβοιαν πολ[υλάϊο]ν, οἵ θ' ἱεράν
35 νᾶσον [Αἴγιν]αν. ματεύει
       δ' ἄλλ[ος ἀλλοί]αν κέλευθον,
ἄντι[να στείχ]ων ἀριγνώτοιο δόξας
τεύξεται. μυρίαι δ' ἀνδρῶν ἐπιστᾶμαι πέλονται·

21 Barrett   22 Platt (πνε<ί>- Barrett)   23 Jebb   24 Bar-
rett   25 Jurenka, Platt   26s. Jebb   28 Platt   30 Jebb
37 Blass

172

For when he had come to a halt at the finishing-line of the sprint, panting out a hot storm of breath, and again when he had wet with his oil the cloaks of the spectators as he tumbled into the packed crowd after rounding the course with its four turns,[1] the spokesmen of the wise judges twice proclaimed him Isthmian victor; twice also in Nemea by the holy altar of Zeus, son of Cronus; and famous Thebes welcomed him and spacious Argos and Sicyon, as was his due; also the inhabitants of Pellene and the rich cornland of Euboea and the sacred island of Aegina.

Men seek various paths to tread in their quest for conspicuous glory, and human knowledge is of

[1] His second race was over four lengths of the stadion, 720–800 metres.

ἦ γὰρ σ[ο]φὸς ἢ Χαρίτων τιμὰν λελογχώς
40 ἐλπίδι χρυσέαι τέθαλεν
ἤ τινα θευπροπίαν
    εἰδώς· ἕτερος δ᾽ ἐπὶ παισί
ποικίλον τόξον τιταίνει·
οἱ δ᾽ ἐπ᾽ ἔργοισίν τε καὶ ἀμφὶ βοῶν ἀ[γ]έλαις
45 θυμὸν αὔξουσιν. τὸ μέλλον
    δ᾽ ἀκρίτους τίκτει τελευτάς,
πᾶ τύχα βρίσει. τὸ μὲν κάλλιστον, ἐσθλόν
ἄνδρα πολλῶν ὑπ᾽ ἀνθρώπων πολυζήλωτον εἶμεν·

οἶδα καὶ πλούτου μεγάλαν δύνασιν,
50 ἃ καὶ τ[ὸ]ν ἀχρεῖον τί[θησ]ι
χρηστόν. τί μακρὰν γ[λ]ῶ[σ]σαν ἰθύσας ἐλαύνω
ἐκτὸς ὁδοῦ; πέφαται θνατοῖσι νίκας
ὕστε]ρον εὐφροσύνα,
αὐλῶν [
55 μείγνυ[ντ
    χρή τιν[

39 ἦ (non ἤ) Snell   τιμᾶν pap.   47 Wilamowitz: εσελων pap.,
ἐσθλῶν Kenyon   51 Blass, Housman, alii

countless kinds: truly the skilled man prospers in golden hope, whether he has won honour from the Graces or understands some prophetic art; another aims his cunning bow at boys; others build up their self-esteem with farmlands and herds or cattle; but it is the future that gives birth to the outcomes, and there is no predicting how Fortune will tip the scales. This is the finest thing: to be a noble man much envied by many. I know also wealth's great power, which makes even the useless man useful. But why do I guide my tongue straight ahead and drive far off course?[1] After the victory festivity is appointed for mortals, . . . pipes . . . blend (-?) . . . one must[2] . . .

[1] By missing the turning-post in the chariot-race. B. reverts from gnomic material to his celebration of the victory.   [2] The poem ends two or three words later.

11

ΑΛΕΞΙΔΑΜΩΙ ΜΕΤΑΠΟΝΤΙΝΩΙ
ΠΑΙΔΙ ΠΑΛΑΙΣΤΗΙ ΠΥΘΙΑ

Νίκα γ[λυκύδωρε· κλυτὰν γὰρ
σοὶ πατ[ὴρ τιμὰν ἔδωκεν
ὑψίζυ[γος Οὐρανίδας
ἐν πολυχρύσωι <τ'> 'Ολύμπωι
5 Ζηνὶ παρισταμένα
κρίνεις τέλος ἀθανάτοι-
σίν τε καὶ θνατοῖς ἀρετᾶς·
ἔλλαθι, [βαθυ]πλοκάμου
κούρα Σ[τυγὸς ὀρ]θοδίκου· σέθεν δ' ἔκατι
10 καὶ νῦ[ν Μετ]απόντιον εὐ-
γυίων κ[ατέ]χουσι νέων
κῶμοί τε καὶ εὐφροσύναι θεότιμον ἄστυ·
ὑμνεῦσι δὲ Πυθιόνικον
παῖδα θαητ[ὸ]ν Φαΐσκου.

15 ἵλεώι νιν ὁ Δα[λ]ογενὴς υἱ-
ὸς βαθυζώνο[ιο] Λατοῦς
δέκτ[ο] βλεφά[ρω]ι· πολέες
δ' ἀμφ' 'Αλεξ[ίδα]μον ἀνθέων
ἐν πεδίωι στέφανοι
20 Κίρρας ἔπεσον κρατερᾶς
ἦρα παννίκοι<ο> πάλας·
οὐκ ε[ἶ]δέ νιν ἀέλιος

1 γλ. Ursinus ex Stob. 3. 3. 66 (iii 219 Hense) B. δὲ τὴν Νίκην
γλυκύδωρόν φησι κτλ   κλυτὰν γὰρ Snell   2 Hense   3 Οὐρ.
Snell   4 <τ'> Snell   8 Jebb   9 Blass   11 Blass, alii
176

11

FOR ALEXIDAMUS OF METAPONTION
BOYS' WRESTLING, PYTHIAN GAMES

Victory, giver of sweetness, to you the father
(, son of Uranus,) on his high bench (has granted
glorious honour), so that in gold-rich Olympus you
stand beside Zeus and judge the outcome of prowess
for immortals and mortals: be gracious, daughter of
thick-tressed, right-judging Styx; it is thanks to you
that Metapontion, the god-honoured city, is now
filled with the celebrations and festivities of strong-
limbed youths, and they sing the praises of the
Pythian victor, the marvellous son of Phaiscus.
With gracious eye the Delos-born son of slim-
waisted Leto welcomed him[1]; and many garlands
of flowers fell about Alexidamus in Cirrha's plain[2]
on account of his invincible strong wrestling:
throughout that day at any rate the sun never saw

[1] I.e., Apollo granted him victory at Delphi.   [2] See p. 137 n. 6.

κείνωι γε σὺν ἅματι πρὸς γαίαι πεσόντα.
φάσω δὲ καὶ ἐν ζαθέοις
25   ἁγνοῦ Πέλοπος δαπέδοις
Ἀλφεὸν πάρα καλλιρόαν, δίκας κέλευθον
εἰ μή τις ἀπέτραπεν ὀρθᾶς,
    παγξένωι χαίταν ἐλαίαι

γλαυκᾶι στεφανωσάμενον
30 πορτιτρόφον [. . . .]ί[. . . . .]ραν θ' ἱκέσθαι·
    [   ]
παῖδ' ἐν χθονὶ καλλιχόρωι
    ποικίλαις τέχναις πέλασσεν·
ἀ]λλ' ἢ θεὸς αἴτιος, ἢ
35   γ]νῶμαι πολύπλαγκ<τ>οι βροτῶν
ἄ]μερσαν ὑπέρτατον ἐκ χειρῶν γέρας.
νῦν δ' Ἄρτεμις ἀγροτέρα
χρυσαλάκατος λιπαράν
Ἡμ]έρα τοξόκλυτος νίκαν ἔδωκε.
40 τ]ᾶι ποτ' Ἀβαντιάδας
    β]ωμὸν κατένασσε πολύλ-
    λ[ι]στον εὔπεπλοί τε κοῦραι·

τὰς ἐξ ἐρατῶν ἐφόβησε<ν>
    παγκρατὴς Ἥρα μελάθρων
45 Προίτου, παραπλῆγι φρένας
    καρτερᾶι ζεύξασ' ἀνάγκαι·
παρθενίαι γὰρ ἔτι
    ψυχᾶι κίον ἐς τέμενος

him fallen on the earth. Indeed I shall assert that in the sacred ground of holy Pelops also, by the fair-flowing Alpheus,[1] had not someone twisted the course of upright justice, he would have garlanded his hair with the grey olive that is there for all comers before returning to (his home in) calf-breeding (Italy?); (for) in the fair precincts of Olympia he brought (many a?) boy (to the ground) by his cunning skills; but either a god was responsible, or the judgements of mortals which often go astray snatched the finest prize from his hands. But now Artemis[2] of the golden distaff, the huntress, the Gentle,[3] famed for her bow, has given him gleaming victory.

For her the son of Abas[4] once established an altar[5] at which many prayers would be made, he and his fair-robed daughters whom all-powerful Hera had sent fleeing from Proetus' lovely palace, yoking their minds to a strong necessity that deranged them; for when they were still virgins they had gone into the sanctuary of the purple-belted

---

[1] I.e., at Olympia, presumably two years earlier. [2] Patron goddess of Metapontion. [3] Her title at Lusi in Arcadia (v. 96). [4] Proetus, king of Tiryns. [5] At Lusi; see v. 110.

---

30 [ʼΙταλ]ί[αν πάτ]ραν Platt 31 [ἤ τινα γὰρ ποτὶ γᾶι] e.g. Maehler 36 Palmer 39, 43 Blass

πορφυροζώνοιο θεᾶς·
50 φάσκον δὲ πολὺ σφέτερον
πλούτωι προφέρειν πατέρα ξανθᾶς παρέδρου
σεμνοῦ Διὸς εὐρυβία.
    ταῖσιν δὲ χολωσαμένα
στήθεσ<σ>ι παλίντροπον ἔμβαλεν νόημα·
55 φεῦγον δ' ὄρος ἐς τανίφυλλον
    σμερδαλέαν φωνὰν ἱεῖσαι,

Τιρύνθιον ἄστυ λιποῦσαι
    καὶ θεοδμάτους ἀγυιάς.
ἤδη γὰρ ἔτος δέκατον
60   θεοφιλὲς λιπόντες Ἄργος
ναῖον ἀδεισιβόαι
    χαλκάσπιδες ἡμίθεοι
σὺν πολυζήλωι βασιλεῖ.
νεῖκος γὰρ ἀμαιμάκετον
65 βληχρᾶς ἀνέπαλτο κασιγνήτοις ἀπ' ἀρχᾶς
Προίτωι τε καὶ Ἀκρισίωι·
    λαούς τε διχοστασίαις
ἦρ<ε>ιπον ἀμετροδίκοις μάχαις τε λυγραῖς,
λίσσοντο δὲ παῖδας Ἄβαντος
70   γᾶν πολύκριθον λαχόντας

Τίρυνθα τὸν ὁπλότερον
κτίζειν, πρὶν ἐς ἀργαλέαν πεσεῖν ἀνάγκαν·
Ζεύς τ' ἔθελεν Κρονίδας
τιμῶν Δαναοῦ γενεὰν
75   καὶ διωξίπποιο Λυγκέος
παῦσαι στυγερῶν ἀχέων.

goddess and declared that their father was far superior in wealth to the fair-haired consort of august wide-powered Zeus. In a fit of rage she had put into their hearts thoughts that turned them about, so that they fled to the leafy mountain uttering terrible cries, leaving behind the city of Tiryns and its god-built streets.

For it was now ten years since the bronze-shielded demigods, fearless of the battle-cry, had left god-loved Argos with their much-envied king and made their home there: overmastering strife had sprung up from a feeble beginning between the brothers Proetus and Acrisius, and they were wrecking their people with their unrighteous quarrels and miserable battles; so they begged those sons of Abas, possessors of the barley-rich land, that the younger of the two should establish a city in Tiryns before they all fell into a grievous plight; besides, Zeus, son of Cronus, was willing to honour the race of Danaus[1] and horse-driving Lynceus by relieving them from their hateful distress. The

---

[1] Danaus was descended from Zeus; Lynceus, his nephew and son-in-law, succeeded him as king of Argos and was father of Abas.

---

52 -βιαι pap.   54 εμβαλεν ομμα pap.

τεῖχος δὲ Κύκλωπες κάμον
ἐλθόντες ὑπερφίαλοι κλεινᾶι π[όλ]ει
κάλλιστον, ἵν᾽ ἀντίθεοι
80 ναῖον κλυτὸν ἱππόβοτον
Ἄργος ἥρωες περικλειτοὶ λιπόντες,
ἔνθεν ἀπεσσύμεναι
Προίτου κυανοπλόκαμοι
φεῦγον ἄδματοι θύγατρες.

85 τὸν δ᾽ εἷλεν ἄχος κραδίαν, ξεί-
να τέ νιν πλᾶξεν μέριμνα·
δοίαξε δὲ φάσγανον ἄμ-
φακες ἐν στέρνοισι πᾶξαι.
ἀλλά νιν αἰχμοφόροι
90 μύθοισί τε μειλιχίοις
καὶ βίαι χειρῶν κάτεχον.
τρισκαίδεκα μὲν τελέους
μῆνας κατὰ δάσκιον ἠλύκταζον ὕλαν
φεῦγόν τε καὶ Ἀρκαδίαν
95 μηλοτρόφον· ἀλλ᾽ ὅτε δή
Λοῦσον ποτὶ καλλιρόαν πατὴρ ἵκανεν,
ἔνθεν χρόα νιψάμενος φοι-
νικοκ[ραδέμνο]ιο Λατοῦς

κίκλη[ισκε θύγατρ]α βοῶπιν,
100 χεῖρας ἀντείνων πρὸς αὐγάς
ἱππώκεος ἀελίου,
τέκνα δυστάνοιο λύσσας
πάρφρονος ἐξαγαγεῖν·

BACCHYLIDES

Cyclopes came in their might and toiled to build a most beautiful wall for the famous city, where the godlike glorious heroes made their home on leaving famed horse-grazing Argos; and it was from there that the dark-haired virgin daughters of Proetus rushed in flight.

Grief seized their father's heart, and a strange thought smote him, for he resolved to plant his two-edged sword in his breast; but his spear-bearers restrained him with soothing words and with the strength of their hands. Now for thirteen whole months they roamed in the shadowy forest and fled all through sheep-grazing Arcadia; but when their father at last reached the fair-flowing Lusus, he washed[1] his body in its water and called on the ox-eyed daughter[2] of Leto of the crimson headdress, stretching his hands up to the rays of the horse-sped sun, that she deliver his children from the wretched frenzy that deranged them; 'and', he said, 'I shall

[1] The name Lusus (Λοῦσος) suggests 'washing'.   [2] Artemis.

94 Palmer: κατα καρδίαν pap.

‘θύσω δέ τοι εἴκοσι βοῦς
105 ἄζυγας φοινικότριχας.’
τοῦ δ’ ἔκλυ’ ἀριστοπάτρα
θηροσκόπος εὐχομένου· πιθοῦσα δ’ Ἥραν
παῦσεν καλυκοστεφάνους
κούρας μανιᾶν ἀθέων·
110 ταὶ δ’ αὐτίκα οἱ τέμενος βωμόν τε τεῦχον,
χραῖνόν τέ μιν αἵματι μήλων
καὶ χοροὺς ἵσταν γυναικῶν.

ἔνθεν καὶ ἀρηϊφίλοις
ἄνδρεσσιν <ἐς> ἱπποτρόφον πόλιν Ἀχαιοῖς
115 ἕσπεο· σὺν δὲ τύχαι
ναίεις Μεταπόντιον, ὦ
χρυσέα δέσποινα λαῶν·
ἄλσος δέ τοι ἱμερόεν
Κάσαν παρ’ εὔυδρον †πρόγο-
120 νοι ἑσσάμενοι† Πρίαμοι’ ἐπεὶ χρόνωι
βουλαῖσι θεῶν μακάρων
πέρσαν πόλιν εὐκτιμέναν
χαλκοθωράκων μετ’ Ἀτρειδᾶν. δικαίας
ὅστις ἔχει φρένας, εὑ-
125 ρήσει σὺν ἅπαντι χρόνωι
μυρίας ἀλκὰς Ἀχαιῶν.

110 Blass, alii: γαι pap.

184

sacrifice to you twenty red-haired oxen, never yoked.' The huntress of animals, daughter of the noblest father, heard his prayer, and persuading Hera she put an end to the god-forsaken frenzies of the bud-garlanded girls; and they at once built a sanctuary and altar for her and drenched it with sheep's blood and established choruses of women.

From there you accompanied war-loving Achaean men to their horse-rearing city,[1] and with happy fortune, golden queen of the people, you have your home in Metapontion; and (they established ...) a delightful grove for you by the fair waters of the Casas[2] when finally by the plans of the blessed gods they had sacked Priam's well-built city with the bronze-corsleted Atreidae. He whose mind is just will find throughout all time countless deeds of valour on the part of these Achaeans.

[1] Metapontion, an Achaean colony; see p. 179 n. 2.   [2] The river to the west of Metapontion, the Casuentus of Pliny, *N.H.* 3. 15. 3, now the Basento.

12

Τ<Ε>ΙΣΙΑΙ ΑΙΓΙΝΗΤΗΙ
ΠΑΛΑΙΣΤΗΙ ΝΕΜΕΑ

ὡσεὶ κυβερνήτας σοφός, ὑμνοάνασ-
σ’ εὔθυνε Κλειοῖ
νῦν φρένας ἁμετέρας,
εἰ δή ποτε καὶ πάρος · ἐς γὰρ ὀλβίαν
5 ξείνοισί με πότνια Νίκα
νᾶσον Αἰγίνας ἀπάρχει
ἐλθόντα κοσμῆσαι θεόδματον πόλιν

τάν τ’ ἐν Νεμέαι γυιαλκέα μουνοπάλαν

desunt vv. 9–32

]‚[   ]πιδ[
ξεινου [. . .]νιοι αστ[
35 ἀμφικ[τιόν]ων ἐν ἀέθλοι[ς ·
σὺν τρι[άκο]ντ’ ἀγλααῖσιν
νίκαις [ἐκ]ωμάσθησαν οἱ μὲν [Πυθόϊ,

οἱ δ’ ἐν Πέλοπος ζαθέας
νάσου π[ι]τυώδεϊ δείραι,
40 οἱ δὲ φοινικοστερόπα τεμένει
Ζηνὸς Νεμεαίου ·
. . . .] ταύτας καὶ ἐπ’ ἀργυροδίνα

desunt vv. 43–69

33–42 = *P.S.I.* xii 1278B   35 M. Norsa   36 Snell   37 M. Norsa
[Πυθόϊ Snell, [Πυθίαις Maas   39 Snell   43 ὄχθαισιν ’Αλφειοῦ e.g.
Snell

12

FOR TEISIAS OF AEGINA

WRESTLING, NEMEAN GAMES

Like a skilled helmsman, Clio, queen of song, steer my thoughts straight now, if ever before; for lady Victory orders me to go to Aegina's blessed island and adorn its god-built city for my friends[1] and (sing of) the strong-limbed wrestling[2] ...

24 lines missing

... (foreigner ... city?) ... in the contests of the neighbours[3]; for thirty glorious victories they[4] were feted, some as winners (in Pytho), others at the pine-rich neck of Pelops' holy island,[5] others in the precinct of Nemean Zeus of the red lightning; ... these (victories?) also (on the banks of) the silver-eddying (Alpheus)[6] ...

27 lines missing

[1] Or 'hosts': the word implies that B. had previously gone there. [2] Literally 'single wrestling', as opposed to wrestling in the pentathlon or pancration. [3] I.e., at regional or local games. [4] The Aeginetans, or only the family of Teisias? [5] I.e., at the Isthmian Games. [6] I.e., at Olympia.

13

[ΠΥΘΕΑΙ ΑΙΓΙΝΗΤΗΙ]
[ΠΑΓΚΡΑΤΙΑΣΤΗΙ ΝΕΜΕΑ]

desunt vv. 1–8

10
               ] Κλειώ
               ]τρ̣[α]ι̣
               ]
                  ]δαν ·

desunt vv. 13–39

40
               ] . ις

desunt vv. 41–43

ὕβριος ὑψινόου
45 παύσει δίκας θνατοῖσι κραίνων,

οἵαν τινὰ δύσλοφον ὠ-
  μηστᾶι λέοντι
Περσείδας ἐφίησι
χεῖρα παντοίαισι τέχναις ·
50 οὐ γὰρ] δαμασίμβροτος αἴθων
χαλ]κὸς ἀπλάτου θέλει
χωρε]ῖν διὰ σώματος, ἐ-
  γνά]μφθη δ' ὀπίσσω
φάσγα]νον · ἦ ποτέ φαμι
55 τᾶιδε] περὶ στεφάνοισι
παγκ]ρατίου πόνον Ἑλ-
  λάνεσσι]ν ἱδρώεντ' ἔσεσθαι.'

---

10 Barrett   40 fr. 30 K.   52 Blass   53 Blass, Tyrrell
55, 57 Blass

BACCHYLIDES

13

FOR PYTHEAS OF AEGINA
PANCRATION,[1] NEMEAN GAMES

8 lines missing

. . . Clio . . .

34 lines almost entirely missing

'. . . he[2] shall make (the wrongdoer) desist from haughty violence by carrying out judgements on mortals: see the neck-breaking hand that Perseus' descendant[3] lays with all manner of skill on the flesh-eating lion[4]; for the gleaming man-mastering bronze refuses to pierce its unapproachable body: his sword was bent back. Truly I declare that one day the Greeks will know sweat and toil here for the garlands of the pancration.'

---

[1] Pytheas seems to have competed as a youth (ἀγένειος, about 17–20 years old): see Pindar, *Nem.* 5. 4 ff., written to honour the same victory. The date was probably 485 or 483. Pindar also commemorated victories of Pytheas' younger brother, Phylacidas, in *Isthm.* 5 and 6.   [2] A prophecy about Heracles, spoken perhaps by Athena or the nymph Nemea.   [3] The line is Perseus-Electryon-Alcmena-Heracles.   [4] The speaker is watching Heracles throttle the Nemean lion, his first labour.

ὡς νῦν παρ]ὰ βωμὸν ἀριστάρχου Διός
Νίκας] φ[ε]ρ[ε]κυδέος ἀν-
60   θρώπο]ισιν ἄ[ν]θεα
χρυσέ]αν δόξαν πολύφαντον ἐν αἰ-
    ῶνι] τρέφει παύροις βροτῶν
α]ἰεί, καὶ ὅταν θανάτοιο
    κυάνεον νέφος καλύψηι, λείπεται
65 ἀθάνατον κλέος εὖ ἐρ-
    χθέντος ἀσφαλεῖ σὺν αἴσαι.

τῶν κα[ὶ σ]ὺ τυχὼν Νεμέαι,
    Λάμπωνος υἱέ,
πανθαλέων στεφάνοισιν
70 ἀνθ]έ[ων] χαίταν [ἐρ]εφθείς
αὔξων] πόλιν ὑψιάγυιαν
ἤλυθες, τε]ρψιμ[β]ρότων
    ὥ[στε βρύεν] ἀβ[ροθρ]όων
    κώμω[ν] πατρ[ώια]ν
75 νᾶσο[ν], ὑπέρβι[ον] ἰσχύν
παμμαχίαν ἄνα φαίνων.
ὦ ποταμοῦ θύγατερ
    δινᾶντος Αἴγιν᾽ ἠπιόφρον,

ἦ τοι μεγάλαν [Κρονίδας
80 ἔδωκε τιμάν
ἐν πάντεσσι ν[εορτόν
πυρσὸν ὡς Ἕλλ[ασι νίκαν
φαίνων· τό γε σὸν [κράτος ὑμ]νεῖ
καί τις ὑψαυχὴς κό[ρα

(So now) by the altar of Zeus, best ruler, the
flowers of glory-bringing Victory nourish for men—a
few mortals—a golden reputation conspicuous in
their life-time always; and when the dark blue cloud
of death covers them there is left behind undying
fame for the deed well done together with a secure
destiny. You,[1] son of Lampon, have won all this at
Nemea, and, your hair crowned with garlands of
luxuriant flowers, you (have come bringing distinc-
tion to) the city[2] with its lofty streets, (so that) your
native island (is rich in) soft-voiced revels that give
joy to men, thanks to your display of overpowering
might in the pancration fighting.

Daughter of the eddying river,[3] gentle-hearted
Aegina, truly (the son of Cronus) has given you
great honour, displaying among all the Greeks (a
new victory) like a beacon; and some high-vaunting
girl sings in praise of your (power), often springing

---

[1] Text and translation of the rest of this paragraph are insecure.
[2] Aegina.   [3] Asopus.

---

58 ὡς νῦν Maehler   59 Νίκας Jebb   φερεκ. Wilamowitz
60 Blass   61 Richards   62 init. Jebb   Platt, al.: παύροισι
pap.   71 Jebb: στείχεις] Herwerden   72 Jebb: Αἰακοῦ Blass
73 init. e.g. Snell   ἀβ[ροθρ]όων Barrett   76 -χίᾱν (gen. pl.)
pap.   ἀναφ. Kenyon   79 Blass   81s. Maehler   83 Barrett
84s. κο[. . . . .]ρᾱν pap., duobus vv. in unum contractis

85   ]ραν

πόδεσσι ταρφέως
ἠΰτε νεβρὸς ἀπεν[θής
ἀνθεμόεντας ἐπ[' ὄχθους
κοῦφα σὺν ἀγχιδόμ[οις
90   θρώισκουσ' ἀγακλειτα[ῖς ἑταίρα]ις·

ταὶ δὲ στεφανωσάμε[ναι φοιν]ικέων
ἀνθέων δόνακός τ' ἐ[πιχω-
ρίαν ἄθυρσιν
παρθένοι μέλπουσι τ[εὸν τέκο]ς, ὦ
95   δέσποινα παγξε[ίνου χθονός,
Ἐν]δαΐδα τε ῥοδό[παχυν,
ἃ τὸ[ν ἰσ]ό[θε]ον ἔτι[κτε Πηλέα
καὶ Τελαμ[ῶ]να [κο]ρυ[στὰν
Αἰακῶι μειχθεῖσ' ἐν εὐ[ναι·

100   τῶν υἶας ἀερσιμάχ[ας
ταχύν τ' Ἀχιλλέα
εὐειδέος τ' Ἐριβοίας
παῖδ' ὑπέρθυμον βοά[σω
Αἴαντα σακεσφόρον ἥ[ρω,
105   ὅστ' ἐπὶ πρύμναι σταθ[εὶς
ἔσχεν θρασυκάρδιον [ὁρ-
μαίνοντα ν[ᾶας
θεσπεσίωι πυ[ρὶ καῦσαι
Ἕκτορα χαλ[κοκορυστά]ν,
110   ὁππότε Πη[λείδας
τρα[χ]εῖαν [ἐν στήθεσσι μ]ᾶνιν

lightly on (white?) feet (over your sacred soil?), as a carefree fawn towards the flowery (hills), with her illustrious near-dwelling (companions); and garlanded with the local adornment of crimson flowers and reeds those maidens sing, queen of a hospitable land, of your (child)[1] and of rose-armed Endais, who bore godlike Peleus and the warrior Telamon after her union with Aeacus.

Of their battle-shouldering sons I shall shout aloud, swift Achilles and the high-spirited child of fair Eriboea, Ajax, shield-bearing hero,[2] who stood on the stern and kept off bold-hearted bronze-helmeted Hector as he strove to burn the ships with awful fire, after Peleus' son had stirred up fierce

---

[1] Aeacus, son of Aegina and husband of Endais.   [2] See *Iliad* 15. 415–746; for the shield 7. 219 ff.

---

85 init. λευκοῖς Jebb, στείχουσ' Blass ἀνὰ γᾶν ἱε]ράν Blass   89 Jebb   91 Headlam   92 Jebb   94 Housman: λέχο]ς Barrett   95 Housman   96 Palmer,   Jebb   97 ἰσ]ό[θε]ον Barrett   fin. Jebb   98 Jebb   99 Sitzler   100 Christ: υἱέας pap.   103 Housman   108 fin. Blass   109–114 fin. suppl. fr. 18 K.   109 Blass   111 Desrousseaux

ὠρίνατ[ο, Δαρδανίδας
   τ᾽ ἔλυσεν ἄ[τας·
οἲ πρὶν μὲν [πολύπυργο]ν
115 ᾽Ι]λίου θαητὸν ἄστυ
οὐ λεῖπον, ἀτυζόμενοι [δέ
πτᾶσσον ὀξεῖαν μάχα[ν,
   εὖτ᾽ ἐν πεδίωι κλονέω[ν
   μαίνοιτ᾽ Ἀχιλλεύς,
120 λαοφόνον δόρυ σείων·
ἀλλ᾽ ὅτε δὴ πολέμοι[ο
λῆξεν ἰοστεφάνο[υ
   Νηρῆιδος ἀτρόμητο[ς υἱός,

ὥστ᾽ ἐν κυανανθέϊ θ[υμὸν ἀνέρων
125 πόντωι Βορέας ὑπὸ κύ-
   μασιν δαΐζει,
νυκτὸς ἀντάσας ἀνατε[λλομένας,
λῆξεν δὲ σὺν φαεσιμ[βρότωι
᾽Αοῖ, στόρεσεν δέ τε πό[ντον
130 οὐρία· Νότου δὲ κόλπ[ωσαν πνοᾶι
ἱστίον ἁρπαλέως <τ᾽> ἄ-
   ελπτον ἐξί[κ]οντο χέ[ρσον·

ὣς Τρῶες, ἐπ[εὶ] κλύον [αἰ-
   χματὰν Ἀχιλλέα
135 μίμνο[ντ᾽] ἐν κλισίαισιν
εἵνεκ[ε]ν ξανθᾶς γυναικός,
Β]ρ[ι]σηΐδος ἱμερογυίου,

anger (in his breast) and freed the Dardanids from
their bewilderment: previously they would not leave
the marvellous (many-towered) city of Ilium, but in
bewilderment cowered in fear of the keen fighting,
whenever Achilles went on his furious rampage in
the plain, brandishing his murderous spear; but
when the fearless son of the violet-crowned Nereid[1]
ceased from the fight,—as on a dark-blossoming sea
Boreas rends men's hearts with the billows, coming
face to face with them as night rises up, but ceases
on the arrival of Dawn who gives light to mortals,
and a gentle breeze levels the sea, and they belly out
their sail before the south wind's breath and eagerly
reach the dry land which they had despaired of see-
ing again; so when the Trojans heard that the spear-
man Achilles was remaining in his tent on account
of the blonde woman, lovely-limbed Briseis, they

[1] Thetis, mother of Achilles; see test. 11 n. 2.

112s. Desrousseaux   114 Blass   116 οὐ Blass   124 Schwartz
127 Blass   130 ουρανια in ουριαι corr. pap.   κόλπ[ωσαν Blass
πνοᾶι Housman   131 τ' Blass   135 Smyth: -σίηισιν
pap.

θεοῖσιν ἄντειναν χέρας,
    φοιβὰν ἐσιδόντες ὑπαὶ
140 χειμῶνος αἴγλαν·
πασσυδίαι δὲ λιπόντες
τείχεα Λαομέδοντος
ἐ]ς πεδίον κρατερὰν
    ἄιξαν ὑ[σ]μίναν φέροντες·

145 ὦρσάν τ[ε] φόβον Δαναοῖς·
    ὤτρυνε δ' Ἄρης
ε]ὐεγχής, Λυκίων τε
Λοξίας ἄναξ Ἀπόλλων·
ἷξόν τ' ἐπὶ θῖνα θαλάσσας·
150 ν]αυσὶ δ' εὐπρύμνοις παρα<ὶ>
    μάρναντ', ἐναριζ[ο]μ[έν]ων
    δ' ἔρ]ευθε φώτων
αἵμα]τι γαῖα μέλα[ινα
Ἑκτορ]έας ὑπὸ χει[ρός,
155 ἦν <δὲ> μ]έγ' ἡμιθέοις
    ὄνααρ] ἰσόθεον δι' ὁρμάν.

ἆ δύσφ]ρονες, ἦ μεγάλαισιν ἐλπίσιν
πνε<ί>]οντες ὑπερφ[ία]λόν
    θ' ἱέντες] αὐ[δὰ]ν
160 Τ[ρῶε]ς ἱππευταὶ κυανώπιδας ἐκ-
    πέρσαντες ὤισθεν] νέας
νεῖσθαι πάλιν εἰλα]πίνας τ' ἐν
    λαοφό]ροις ἕξειν θ[εόδ]ματον πόλιν.
μ]έλλον ἄρα πρότε[ρο]ν δι-
165 ν]ᾶντα φοινίξει[ν Σκ]άμανδρ[ον,

196

stretched up their hands to the gods, since they saw
the bright gleam under the stormcloud; leaving
Laomedon's walls[1] with all speed they rushed into
the plain bringing violent battle, and they roused
fear in the Danaans: Ares of the mighty spear urged
them on, and Loxias Apollo, lord of the Lycians, and
they reached the shore of the sea; and by the
strong-sterned ships they fought, and the black
earth grew red with the blood of men slain by
Hector's hand, for he was a great (boon) to the demi-
gods[2] in his godlike charge. Misguided ones! High-
spirited in their great hopes and uttering arrogant
shouts those Trojan horsemen (thought that they
would lay waste) the dark-eyed ships (and return
home again) and that their god-built city would hold
feasts in (its streets?). In truth they were destined
first to crimson the eddying Scamander as they died

---

[1] Troy: L. was Priam's father.   [2] The Trojan heroes; but the
supplement and emendation of vv. 155 f. are uncertain.

---

150 fin. Housman   155s. Barrett   156 ἰσόθεον Tyrrell: -θέων
pap.   157 Blass   158 Barrett post Blass   159 Barrett   161
πέρσ. Blass   ἄμοθεν Barrett   162s. Barrett

θ]νάισκοντες ὑπ[' Ἀλα]κίδαις
    ἐρειψ[ι]πύ[ργοις·
τῶν εἰ καὶ τ[
ἢ βαθυξύλῳ[ι πυρᾶι
        desunt vv. 170–174

175 οὐ γὰρ ἀλαμπέϊ νυκ[τός
πασιφανὴς Ἀρετ[ὰ
    κρυφθεῖσ' ἀμαυρο[ῦται καλύπτραι,

ἀλλ' ἔμπεδον ἀκ[αμάται
    βρύουσα δόξαι
180 στρωφᾶται κατὰ γᾶν [τε
καὶ πολύπλαγκτον θ[άλασσαν.
καὶ μὰν φερεκυδέα ν[ᾶσον
Αἰακοῦ τιμᾶι, σὺν Εὐ-
    κλείαι δὲ φιλοστεφ[άνωι
185   πόλιν κυβερνᾶι,
Εὐνομία τε σαόφρων,
ἃ θαλίας τε λέλογχεν
ἄστεά τ' εὐσεβέων
    ἀνδρῶν ἐν εἰ[ρ]ήναι φυλάσσει·

190 νίκαν ἐρικυ[δέα] μέλπετ', ὦ νέοι,
Π]υθέα, μελέτα[ν τε] βροτω-
    φ[ε]λέα Μενάνδρου,
τὰν ἐπ' Ἀλφειοῦ τε ρο[αῖς] θαμὰ δὴ
    τίμασεν ἁ χρυσάρματος
195 σεμνὰ μεγάθυμος Ἀθάνα,
    μυρίων τ' ἤδη μίτραισιν ἀνέρων

at the hands of the tower-wrecking Aeacidae.[1]

If their (bodies have perished) either on a high-timbered pyre [or under a mound of earth, their fame still lives]; for Excellence, shining among all men, is not dimmed, hidden by the lightless (veil) of night: flourishing constantly with undying fame she ranges over the land and the sea that drives many from their course. Look, now she honours the glory-winning island of Aeacus and with garland-loving Eucleia[2] steers the city, she and wise Eunomia,[3] who has festivities as her portion and guards in peace the cities of pious men: sing, youths, of the glorious victory of Pytheas and of Menander's helpful care, which by the waters of the Alpheus august stout-hearted Athena[4] of the golden chariot has often honoured, when she garlanded with head-

---

[1] Achilles and Ajax.   [2] Good Fame.   [3] Good Order in civic government. In Hesiod *Theog.* 901 ff. Eunomia, Justice and Peace are the three Seasons.   [4] Menander, Pytheas' trainer, was Athenian.

---

167 Tucker, Barrett   169 Blass   177 καλ. Barrett   178 Blass, Platt   190 Barrett: νίκαν τ' ἐρ. pap.   193 θαμὰ Nairn, al.

ἐστεφάνωσεν ἐθείρας
  ἐν Πανελλάνων ἀέθλοις.

    εἰ μή τινα θερσι[ε]πὴς
200   φθόνος βιᾶται,
    αἰνείτω σοφὸν ἄνδρα
    σὺν δίκαι. βροτῶν δὲ μῶμος
    πάντεσσι μέν ἐστιν ἐπ' ἔργοις·
    ἀ δ' ἀλαθεία φιλεῖ
205   νικᾶν, ὅ τε πανδ[α]μάτωρ
    χρόνος τὸ καλῶς
    ἐ]ργμένον αἰὲν ἀ[έξει·
    δυσμενέων δὲ μα[ταία
    γλῶσσ' ἀϊδ]ὴς μιν[ύθει
        desunt vv. 210–219
220 ἐλπίδι θυμὸν ἰαίν[ει·
    τᾶι καὶ ἐγὼ πίσυνο[ς
      φοινικοκραδέμνοις [τε Μούσαις

    ὕμνων τινὰ τάνδε ν[εόπλοκον δόσιν
    φαίνω, ξενίαν τε [φιλά-
225   γλαον γεραίρω,
    τὰν ἐμοί, Λάμπων, σ[ὺ πορὼν τίσιν οὐ
    βληχρὰν ἐπαθρήσαις τ[έκει·
    τὰν εἰκ ἐτύμως ἄρα Κλειὼ
    πανθαλὴς ἐμαῖς ἐνέσταξ[εν φρασίν,
230 τερψιεπεῖς νιν ἀ̣ο̣ι̣δαὶ
      παντὶ καρύξοντι λα[ῶ]ι.

200

bands the hair of countless men in the contests of all Greeks.

Let those who are not mastered by bold-tongued envy praise the skilled man as is his due. Fault is found by mortals in all achievements; but truth loves to prevail, and all-conquering time always (fosters) the deed that is well done, while the foolish speech of enemies dwindles out of sight . . .

10 lines missing

. . . warms his heart with hope: trusting in it and in the Muses of the crimson headdress I for my part display this (gift) of songs, (new-woven) as it were, and so do honour to the splendour-loving hospitality which you, Lampon, (have shown) me; may[1] you now look favourably upon (a recompense for your son) that is no slight one; if it was indeed flowering Clio[2] who made it drip into my (heart), there will be delight in the words of the songs that proclaim him to all the people.

[1] Supplement and interpretation of the last nine lines are uncertain: the 'recompense' will be B.'s song, which proclaims Pytheas; in other versions it is Lampon or his hospitality that is proclaimed.   [2] See v. 9.

207 ἀ[νίσχει Maehler   208s. Blass ex *Anecd. Oxon.* i 65 (Cramer) δυσμενέων δ' ἀϊδὴς λέγει Βακχυλίδης   222 Nairn   223 ν[εοπλ. Jebb   δόσιν Blass   226s. Barrett   229 Jebb (φρεσίν: φρασίν Blass, Housman)

14

ΚΛΕΟΠΤΟΛΕΜΩΙ ΘΕΣΣΑΛΩΙ
ΙΠΠΟΙΣ ΠΕΤΡΑΙΑ

εὖ μὲν εἱμάρθαι παρὰ δαίμ[ονος ἀν-
θρώποις ἄριστον·
σ]υμφορὰ δ' ἐσθλόν <τ'> ἀμαλδύ-
νει β]αρύτλα[α]τος μολοῦσα
5 καὶ τ]ὸν κακ[ὸν] ὑψιφανῆ τεύ-
χει κ]ατορθωθεῖσα· τιμὰν
δ' ἄλ]λος ἀλλοίαν ἔχει·

μυρί]αι δ' ἀνδρῶν ἀρετ[αί,] μία δ' ἐ[κ
πασᾶ]ν πρόκειται,
10 ὃς τὰ] πὰρ χειρὸς κυβέρνα-
σεν δι]καίαισι φρένεσσιν.
οὔτ' ἐ]ν βαρυπενθέσιν ἁρμό-
ζει μ]άχαις φόρμιγγος ὀμφὰ
καὶ λι]γυκλαγγεῖς χοροί,

15 οὔτ' ἐ]ν θαλίαις καναχά
χαλκ]όκτυπος· ἀλλ' ἐφ' ἑκάστωι
καιρὸς] ἀνδρῶν ἔργματι κάλ-

1 Blass, alii: δαίμοσιν Kenyon   3 <τ'> Jebb   5 init. Suess,
Wilamowitz   ]ον ἤδη ὑψιφ., ἤδη del. et και[superscr. pap.: κακ[ὸν
Schwartz   8s. ἐ[κ πασᾶ]ν Jurenka   10 Wilamowitz, Bruhn
11 -σεν Wilamowitz   12, 15 οὔτ' Platt   13 μ]άχαις Jebb   17 Jebb

BACCHYLIDES

14

FOR CLEOPTOLEMUS OF THESSALY

CHARIOT-RACE, PETRAEAN GAMES[1]

To have a good portion from God is the best thing for men; but if Fortune comes with a load of suffering, she ruins a fine man, while if set on a prosperous course she makes even a base man shine on high. Men have honours of different kinds, and their excellences are countless, but one stands out from them all—that man's who with justice in his heart manages the task at hand.

In battles with their load of sorrow the note of the lyre and clear-voiced choirs are not fitting, nor in festivities the clang of clashing bronze: for each of men's activities the appropriate moment is best; and

---

[1] Games (equestrian only?) held in Thessaly, perhaps near Tempe, in honour of Poseidon 'Petraios' (v. 20 f.), so called either because he split the rocks (πέτραι) at Tempe so as to allow the river Peneus a passage to the sea, or because he created the first horse by striking a rock (πέτρα) with his trident.

λιστος· [ε]ὖ ἔρδοντα δὲ καὶ θεὸς ὀ[ρθοῖ.
Κλεοπτολέμωι δὲ χάριν
20 νῦν χρὴ Ποσειδᾶνός τε Πετρ[αί-
ου τέμενος κελαδῆσαι
Πυρρίχου τ' εὔδοξον ἱππόνικ[ον υἱόν,

ὃς φιλοξείνου τε καὶ ὀρθοδίκου

desunt ceteri vv.

18 ὀ[ρθοῖ Jebb   ὀ[μβρεῖ Maehler   22 Blass   (24) πατρὸς πεφυκώς
Herwerden

P.Oxy. 2363 vv. 4–6

14A

```
                          ]μνατοῖσιν ἄστρο[
5   . αι . [              ]ϊκας Διωνύσου τε[
    μου . [              ] . τι .
```

5s. τε [καὶ] Μουσ[ᾶν ἕκα]τι Snell

the successful man is prospered by God too. So now
in tribute to Cleoptolemus we must sing of the sanc-
tuary of Poseidon of the Rock and of Pyrrhichus'
glorious chariot-victor (son), who, (offspring?) of a
hospitable and right-judging (father?) . . .[1]

1 At least 21 lines are lost, considerably more if a myth was told.

Oxyrhynchus papyrus (c. 200 A.D.)

14A

. . . star(s) . . . (thanks to) Dionysus and the
Muses.[1]

1 The last lines of a poem.

P.Oxy. 2363 vv. 7–17 + frr. 11, 22 Kenyon

14в

[ΑΡΙΣΤΟΤΕΛΕΙ Λ]Α[ΡΙΣΑΙΩΙ
]ΠΑ[

Ἑστία χρυσόθρον᾽, εὐ-
    δόξων Ἀγαθοκλεαδᾶν ἅτ᾽ ἀφνε[ῶν
ἀνδρῶν μέγαν ὄλβον ἀέξεις
ἡμένα μέσαις ἀγυιαῖς
5 Πηνειὸν ἀμφ᾽ εὐώδεα Θεσσαλία[ς
μηλοτρόφου ἐν γυάλοις·
κεῖθεν καὶ Ἀριστοτέλης Κίρ-
    ραν πρὸς εὐθαλέα μολών
δὶς στεφανώσατο Λα-
10   ρίσα[ς ἀ]ναξίππου χάριν [
κλυ . [   ] . ος
        desunt ceteri vv.

suppl. ed. pr. (Lobel)   inscr.]α,]πα : v. Maehler ii 302s.   4 schol.
marg. [ ] τὴν ἑστίαν λέγ[ει   οὐ] μό(νον) τὸ πῦρ τοῦτο ἀ[λλὰ καὶ
7 schol. marg. Πηνιο

BACCHYLIDES

Same papyrus, overlapping with frr. of the British Museum papyrus

14B

FOR ARISTOTELES OF LARISSA[1]

Gold-throned Hestia,[2] you who increase the great prosperity of the glorious Agathocleadae,[3] those men of wealth, as you sit in mid-city by the fragrant Peneus in the glens of sheep-rearing Thessaly: from there Aristoteles went to luxuriant Cirrha[4] and garlanded himself twice, joy for horse-ruling Larissa . . .

---

[1] The wording of the inscription, only three letters of which remain, is uncertain: that the poem is epinician was deduced from the reference to the Pythian Games (v. 7 f.), and the epithet 'horse-ruling' (v. 10) might (but need not) point to a chariot-victory; C. Carey suggests that the victor was a wrestler (πα/[λαιστῆι: *J.H.S.* 103, 1983, 165). Maehler, however, argues that the poem, like Pindar's *Nemean* 11, which also begins with an invocation to Hestia, commemorates not an athletic success but entry into a local magistracy.   [2] Goddess of the hearth, here the public hearth 'in mid-city' of Larissa. This may be the point of the marginal note.   [3] The family of Aristoteles.   [4] See p. 137 n. 6.

ΒΑΚΧΥΛΙΔΟΥ ΔΙΘΥΡΑΜΒΟΙ

15

ΑΝΤΗΝΟΡΙΔΑΙ
Η ΕΛΕΝΗΣ ΑΠΑΙΤΗΣΙΣ

  Ἀντή]νορος ἀντιθέου
. . . . . .]ρακοιτις Ἀθάνας πρόσπολος
    ] Παλλάδος ὀρσιμάχου
    ]χρυσέας
5   ]ν Ἀργείων Ὀδυσσεῖ
Λαρτιάδαι Μενελ]άωι τ' Ἀτρεῖδαι βασιλεῖ
  βαθύ]ζωνος Θεανώ

    ]ον
    ]ν προσήνεπεν·
10   ἐ]ϋκτιμέναν
    ]
    ]δων τυχόντες
     ]ς σὺν θεοῖς†
14   ]δους
   desunt vv. viii
23   μεσονύ]κτιος κέαρ
   desunt vv. xiii
37 ἆγον, πατὴρ δ' εὔβουλος ἥρως

2 κεδνὰ πα]ράκοιτις? Snell-Maehler 3s. ὤιξεν ἁγνὸν] Π. ὁ./ναὸν πύλας τε] χρ. Crusius 5 ἀγγέλοις δισσοῖσι]ν Jebb 6 Nairn, Crusius, Wilamowitz 7 ὥς ποτ' ἤντησεν e.g. Körte 13 γε vel τε vel δὲ post σὺν add. Jebb 23 fr. 9 Kenyon (hic coll. Blass)

BACCHYLIDES

DITHYRAMBS

15

THE SONS OF ANTENOR
or THE REQUEST FOR THE RETURN OF HELEN

Godlike Antenor's ... wife, the priestess of
Athena,[1] ... (of) battle-rousing Pallas ... golden ...
to (the two envoys) of the Greeks, Odysseus, (son of
Laertes,) and king Menelaus, son of Atreus ...
slim-waisted Theano ... addressed them: '... well-
built (city of Troy) ... having obtained ... with the
help of the gods ...'

9 lines mostly lost

... midnight ... the heart ...

13 lines lost

... (the sons of Antenor)[2] brought (the envoys into
the agora), while their father, the wise-counselling

---

[1] Theano, for whom see *Il.* 6. 297 ff. B. may have said that she
opened the temple doors to the two Greeks and then addressed
them; Odysseus may have replied in the missing lines. For her
husband Antenor, who gave the Greeks hospitality, see *Il.* 3. 203 ff.
The story of the embassy was told in the *Cypria*; see also *Il.* 11.
138 ff.   [2] Acc. to schol. *Il.* 24. 496 B. said that Theano bore
fifty sons to Antenor. Ten are named in the *Iliad*.

209

πάντα σάμαινεν Πριάμωι βασιλεῖ
παίδεσσί τε μῦθον Ἀχαιῶν.
40   ἔνθα κάρυκες δι᾽ εὐ-
ρεῖαν πόλιν ὀρνύμενοι
Τρώων ἀόλλιζον φάλαγγας

δεξίστρατον εἰς ἀγοράν.
πάνται δὲ διέδραμεν αὐδάεις λόγος·
45 θεοῖσ<ιν> δ᾽ ἀνίσχοντες χέρας ἀθανάτοις
εὔχοντο παύσασθαι δυᾶν.
Μοῦσα, τίς πρῶτος λόγων ἄρχεν δικαίων;
Πλεισθενίδας Μενέλαος γάρυϊ θελξιεπεῖ
φθέγξατ᾽, εὐπέπλοισι κοινώσας Χάρισσιν·

50 ᾽ὦ Τρῶες ἀρηΐφιλοι,
Ζεὺς ὑψ[ιμέδων ὃ]ς ἅπαντα δέρκεται
οὐκ αἴτιος θνατοῖς μεγάλων ἀχέων,
ἀλλ᾽ ἐν [μέσ]ωι κεῖται κιχεῖν
πᾶσιν ἀνθρώποις Δίκαν ἰθεῖαν, ἁγνᾶς
55 Εὐνομίας ἀκόλουθον καὶ πινυτᾶς Θέμιτος·
ὀλβίων π[αῖδές] νιν αἱρεῦνται σύνοικον.

ἁ δ᾽ αἰόλοις κέρδεσσι καὶ ἀφροσύναις
ἐξαισίοις θάλλουσ᾽ ἀθαμβής
῾Ύβρις, ἃ πλοῦτ[ο]ν δύναμίν τε θοῶς
60 ἀλλότριον ὤπασεν, αὖτις
δ᾽ ἐς βαθὺν πέμπει φθόρον,
κε]ίνα καὶ ὑπερφιάλους
Γᾶς] παῖδας ὤλεσ<σ>εν Γίγαντας.᾽

45 Barrett   47 Purser: ἄρχεν λόγων pap.   51–56 ex Clem. Alex.
Strom. 5. 136. 5 suppl. (54 -ποισι Δ. ὁσίαν ἁγνάν, 55 Θέμιδος, 56 παῖδες
ὦ νιν εὑρόντες Clem.)

210

hero, told king Priam and his sons the whole proposal of the Greeks. Then heralds, speeding through the wide city, gathered the ranks of Trojans into the agora where the army musters, and their loud summons raced everywhere; and raising their hands to the immortal gods they prayed for an end to their griefs.[1]

Muse, who first began the righteous plea? Pleisthenes' son[2] Menelaus spoke with spell-binding words, making partners of the fair-robed Graces: 'Trojans dear to Ares, high-ruling Zeus, who sees all things, is not the author of great woes for mortals: rather it is open to all men to reach unswerving Justice, the attendant of holy Eunomia and wise Themis[3]; blessed are they whose sons choose her to share their home; but that other, shameless Insolence,[4] luxuriating in shifty tricks and lawless follies, who swiftly gives a man another's wealth and power only to bring him into deep ruin—it was she who destroyed those arrogant sons of Earth, the Giants.'[5]

---

[1] The *Cypria* told how the Trojans fought two battles against the Greeks before the embassy came. The siege followed.
[2] Pleisthenes was in some versions the son of Atreus and father of Agamemnon and Menelaus: see Stes. 209 n. 7, 219, Ibyc. 282(a) n. 2; 'son of Atreus' above (v. 6) will mean 'descendant of Atreus'.   [3] See p. 199 n. 3; the Seasons, Eunomia, Justice and Peace, were daughters of Zeus and Themis (Right Order): Hesiod, *Theog.* 901 f. Clement of Alexandria quoted from 'the lyric poet' the passage about Zeus and Justice.   [4] Menelaus has in mind the outrageous behaviour of Paris.   [5] When they fought against the Olympian gods.

16

[ΗΡΑΚΛΗΣ ΕΙΣ ΔΕΛΦΟΥΣ]

   ]ιου ιο ἐπεί
ὁλκ]άδ' ἔπεμψεν ἐμοὶ χρυσέαν
Πιερ]ίαθεν ἐ[ύθ]ρονος [Ο]ὐρανία,
  πολυφ]άτων γέμουσαν ὕμνων
5 . . . . .]νειτις ἐπ' ἀνθεμόεντι Ἕβρωι
 . . . . ἀ]γάλλεται ἢ δολιχαύχενι κύ[κνωι
 . . . .]δεϊαν φρένα τερπόμενος
  . . . . .]δ' ἵκηι παιηόνων
ἄνθεα πεδοιχνεῖν,
10 Πύθι' Ἄπολλον,
τόσ[[σ]]α χοροὶ Δελφῶν
σὸν κελάδησαν παρ' ἀγακλέα ναόν.

πρίν γε κλέομεν λιπεῖν
Οἰχαλίαν πυρὶ δαπτομέναν
15 Ἀμφιτρυωνιάδαν θρασυμηδέα φῶ-
 θ', ἵκετο δ' ἀμφικύμον' ἀκτάν·
ἔνθ' ἀπὸ λαΐδος εὐρυνεφεῖ Κηναίωι
Ζηνὶ θύεν βαρυαχέας ἐννέα ταύρους
δύο τ' ὀρσιάλωι δαμασίχθονι μέ[λ-
20 λε κόραι τ' ὀβριμοδερκεῖ ἄζυγα
παρθένωι Ἀθάναι
ὑψικέραν βοῦν.
τότ' ἄμαχος δαίμων

1 φαί]νου [Δ]ιὸ[ς υἷ'] Milne 2 Sandys 3 Blass 5 εἴ τις
Milne 6 θηροῖν ἀ]γ. Jebb 7 θαλίαις ἁ]δινὰ Milne 8 init. cor-
ruptum esse vid.

212

16

HERACLES; FOR DELPHI

..., since[1] fine-throned Urania[2] has sent me from Pieria a golden cargo-boat laden with glorious songs, ... by the flowery Hebrus[3] takes his pleasure (in beasts?) or in the long-necked swan ... gladdening his heart ... you come, Pythian Apollo, to seek the flowers of paeans—all those which the choirs of Delphians cry aloud by your far-famed temple.

Until then we sing how Amphitryon's son,[4] bold-planning hero, left behind Oechalia[5] consumed in fire; and he came to the sea-washed headland, where he was about to sacrifice from his booty nine deep-bellowing bulls to wide-clouded Cenaean Zeus[6] and two to the sea-rouser and earth-subduer[7] and a high-horned ox, never yoked, to the maiden with might in her glance, the virgin Athena.

At that moment the irresistible god[8] wove for

[1] Supplement of the few words missing in vv. 1–8 is difficult. B. seems to offer a dithyramb for performance at Delphi during the three winter months when Apollo is absent on a visit to his favourites, the Hyperboreans.   [2] One of the Muses, born in Pieria in Macedonia.   [3] Thracian river, which Apollo would pass on his northern journey.   [4] Heracles.   [5] A city in the east of Euboea; Heracles destroyed it, killed its king Eurytus and carried off his daughter, Iole.   [6] Worshipped on the promontory of Cenaeum in N.W. Euboea.   [7] Poseidon, god of sea and earthquakes.   [8] Fate, as in the 'godsent' gift of 35.

Δαϊανείραι πολύδακρυν ὕφα[νε

25 μῆτιν ἐπίφρον' ἐπεὶ
    πύθετ' ἀγγελίαν ταλαπενθέα,
    Ἰόλαν ὅτι λευκώλενον
    Διὸς υἱὸς ἀταρβομάχας
    ἄλοχον λιπαρὸ[ν] ποτὶ δόμον πέμ[π]οι.
30 ἆ δύσμορος, ἆ τάλ[αι]ν', οἷον ἐμήσατ[ο·
    φθόνος εὐρυβίας νιν ἀπώλεσεν,
    δνόφεόν τε κάλυμμα τῶν
    ὕστερον ἐρχομένων,
    ὅτ' ἐπὶ [ποταμῶι] ῥοδόεντι Λυκόρμαι
35 δέξατο Νέσσου πάρα δαιμόνιον τέρ[ας.

34 Ludwich, Wilamowitz

Deianeira a tear-filled shrewd plan, when she
learned the sorrowful news that Zeus' battle-
dauntless son[1] was sending to his gleaming home
white-armed Iole to be his wife. Ah, ill-starred,
unhappy woman to devise such a plan![2] Wide-
mighted jealousy destroyed her, together with the
murky veil that hid the future when at the rosy
Lycormas she received from Nessus the godsent
miraculous gift.

---

[1] Heracles, her husband.   [2] As Heracles took his bride
Deianeira from Calydon (see 5. 173), the centaur Nessus assaulted
her at the river Lycormas, and H. shot him with an arrow poisoned
with the Hydra's venom. As he died, Nessus told D. to keep the
clotted blood from his wound as a charm to retain H.'s love. Now,
on hearing of a rival in Iole, D. smeared a garment with the blood
and sent it to H., who suffered agonising pain when he put it on and
died soon after. Sophocles used the myth in *Trachiniae* (date
unknown, but not necessarily later than B.'s dithyramb); see also
fr. 64 (dub.).

17

ΗΙΘΕΟΙ Η ΘΗΣΕΥΣ
[ΚΗΙΟΙΣ ΕΙΣ ΔΗΛΟΝ]

κυανόπρωιρα μὲν ναῦς μενέκτυ[πον
   Θησέα δὶς ἑπτ[ά] τ' ἀγλαοὺς ἄγουσα
   κούρους 'Ιαόνω[ν
   Κρητικὸν τάμνε[[ν]] πέλαγος·
5 τηλαυγέϊ γὰρ [ἐν] φάρεϊ
   βορήϊαι πίτνο[ν] αὖραι
   κλυτᾶς ἕκατι π[ε]λεμαίγιδος 'Αθάν[ας·
   κνίσεν τε Μίνω<ϊ> κέαρ
   ἱμεράμπυκος θεᾶς
10 Κύπριδος [α]ϊνὰ δῶρα·
   χεῖρα δ' οὐ[κέτι] παρθενικᾶς
   ἄτερθ' ἐράτυεν, θίγεν
   δὲ λευκᾶν παρηΐδων·
   βόασ' 'Ερίβοια χαλκο-
15 θώρα[κα Π]ανδίονος
   ἔκγ[ο]νον· ἴδεν δὲ Θησεύς,
   μέλαν δ' ὑπ' ὀφρύων
   δίνα[σ]εν ὄμμα, καρδίαν τέ οἱ
   σχέτλιον ἄμυξεν ἄλγος,

de metro iambico et textu v. R. Führer, *Nachr. . . . Gött., phil.-hist.
Kl.* 5 (1976) 167–234, M. L. West, *Z.P.E.* 37 (1980) 137–142   7
Wackernagel, Housman, al.: πολεμ- Kenyon   8 Jebb   10 [ἀ]γνὰ
Blass   14 Führer: βόασέ τ' 'Ερ. pap. (Blass)

17

THE YOUNG ATHENIANS *or* THESEUS

FOR THE CEANS TO PERFORM IN DELOS

The ship with the blue-black prow, as it carried
Theseus, steadfast in the battle din, and the twice
seven splendid youths and maidens of the Ionians,[1]
was cleaving the Cretan sea, for northerly breezes
fell on the far-shining sail thanks to glorious
Athena, the aegis-shaker[2]; but Minos' heart was
chafed by the dread gifts of the Cyprian goddess
with desire in her headband, and he could no longer
keep his hand from the girl but touched her white
cheeks. Eriboea shouted for the bronze-corsleted
descendant of Pandion,[3] and Theseus saw it and
rolled his eyes darkly beneath his brows as cruel
pain tore his heart, and he spoke: 'Son of peerless

[1] I.e. seven youths and seven maidens from Athens, the tribute
taken by Minos to Crete to feed the Minotaur: cf. Servius on Virgil,
Aen. 6. 21 ('B. in his dithyrambs').   [2] Perhaps 'Athena of the
warlike aegis'.   [3] Father of Aegeus and grandfather of
Theseus.

20 εἶρέν τε· Διὸς υἱὲ φερτάτου,
ὅσιον οὐκέτι τεᾶν
ἔσω κυβερνᾶις φρενῶν
θυμ[όν]· ἴσχε μεγαλοῦχον ἥρως βίαν.

ὅ τι μ[ὲ]ν ἐκ θεῶν μοῖρα παγκρατὴς
25 ἄμμι κατένευσε καὶ Δίκας ῥέπει τά-
λαντον, πεπρωμέν[α]ν
αἶσαν [ἐ]κπλήσομεν, ὅτ[α]ν
ἔλθηι· [σ]ὺ δὲ βαρεῖαν κάτε-
χε μῆτιν. εἰ καί σε κεδνὰ
30 τέκεν λέχει Διὸς ὑπὸ κρόταφον Ἴδας
μιγεῖσα Φοίνικος ἐρα-
τώνυμος κόρα βροτῶν
φέρτατον, ἀλλὰ κἀμὲ
Πιτθ[έ]ος θυγάτηρ ἀφνεοῦ
35 πλαθεῖσα ποντίωι τέκεν
Ποσειδᾶνι, χρύσεόν
τέ οἱ δόσαν ἰόπλο-
κοι κάλυμμα Νηρηῖδες.
τῶ σε, πολέμαρχε Κνωσσίων,
40 κέλομαι πολύστονον
ἐρύκεν ὕβριν· οὐ γὰρ ἂν θέλοι-
μ’ ἀμβρότοι’ ἐραννὸν Ἀο[ῦς
ἰδεῖν φάος, ἐπεί τιν’ ἠϊθέ[ων
σὺ δαμάσειας ἀέκον-
45 τα· πρόσθε χειρῶν βίαν
δε[ί]ξομεν· τὰ δ’ ἐπιόντα δα[ίμω]ν κρινεῖ.’

37 κοι | κάλ. div. pap.

218

Zeus, in your breast you no longer steer thoughts
that are righteous: restrain your arrogant might,
hero. Whatever all-powerful Fate has ordained for
us from the gods and the scales of Justice confirm,
we shall fulfil it as our destined portion when it
comes. But check your disastrous intention. What
if the noble daughter[1] of Phoenix, maiden with love
in her name, bore you, peerless among mortals,
after union with Zeus under the brow of mount Ida?
Why, the daughter of wealthy Pittheus[2] bore me
after drawing close to the sea-god Poseidon, when
the violet-crowned Nereids gave her a golden veil.
Therefore, warlord of the Cnossians, I tell you to
curb an insolence which will bring much sorrow; for
I should not wish to see the lovely light of immortal
Dawn if once you had forcibly assaulted any of this
youthful band; sooner than that we shall display the
might of our hands, and God will decide the out-
come.'

[1] Europa.   [2] King of Troezen and father of Aethra (59).

219

τόσ᾽ εἶπεν ἀρέταιχμος ἥρως·
τ]άφον δὲ ναυβάται
φ]ωτὸς ὑπεράφανον
50 θ]άρσος· Ἀλίου τε γαμβρῶι χόλωσεν ἦτορ,
ὕφαινέ τε ποταινίαν
μῆτιν, εἶπέν τε· 'μεγαλοσθενές
Ζεῦ πάτερ, ἄκουσον· εἴ πέρ με νύμ[φα
Φοίνισσα λευκώλενος σοὶ τέκεν,
55 νῦν πρόπεμπ᾽ ἀπ᾽ οὐρανοῦ θοάν
πυριέθειραν ἀστραπάν
σᾶμ᾽ ἀρίγνωτον· εἰ
    δὲ καὶ σὲ Τροιζηνία σεισίχθονι
    φύτευσεν Αἴθρα Ποσει-
60 δᾶνι, τόνδε χρύσεον
χειρὸς ἀγλαὸν
    ἔνεγκε κόσμον ἐκ βαθείας ἁλός,
δικὼν θράσει σῶμα πατρὸς ἐς δόμους.
εἴσεαι δ᾽ αἴκ᾽ ἐμᾶς κλύηι
65 Κρόνιος εὐχᾶς
ἀναξιβρέντας ὁ πάντω[ν με]δ[έω]ν.᾽

κλύε δ᾽ ἄμεμπτον εὐχὰν μεγασθενὴ[ς
Ζεύς, ὑπέροχόν τε Μίνωι φύτευσε
τιμὰν φίλωι θέλων
70 παιδὶ πανδερκέα θέμεν,
ἄστραψέ θ᾽· ὁ δὲ θυμάρμενον

47–78 pap. O (P.Oxy. 1091)   63 om. O, perperam inter 61 et 62
inser. A   67 ἀμεπτον A   70 πάνταρκέα O

220

So spoke the spear-valiant hero, and the sea-farers were astonished at the man's proud boldness; but the son-in-law[1] of Helius felt anger in his heart and set about weaving a new plan, and he said, 'Mighty father Zeus, hear me: if the white-armed Phoenician maiden[2] indeed bore me as your son, send from heaven now a swift fire-tressed lightning flash, a sign clearly recognisable; as for you, if Troezenian Aethra in fact bore you to earth-shaking Poseidon, fetch from the depths of the sea this splendid gold ornament of my hand, boldly flinging yourself into your father's home. And you will learn whether my prayer is heard by the thunder-lord, Cronus' son, ruler of all.'

Mighty Zeus heard the prayer, found it blameless and fathered a surpassing honour for Minos, wishing to make it visible to all men for the sake of his dear son, and he flashed his lightning; and when the

[1] Minos, whose wife Pasiphaë was daughter of Helius (the Sun).
[2] Europa, daughter of Phoenix.

ἰδὼν τέρας χεῖρας πέτασσε
κλυτὰν ἐς αἰθέρα μενεπτόλεμος ἥρως
εἶρέν τε· 'Θησεῦ, τάδε μὲν <ἐ-
75 μὰ> βλέπεις σαφῆ Διός
δῶρα· σὺ δ' ὄρνυ' ἐς βα-
ρύβρομον πέλαγος· Κρονί[δας
δέ τοι πατὴρ ἄναξ τελεῖ
Ποσειδὰν ὑπέρτατον
80 κλέος χθόνα κατ' εὔδενδρον.'
ὣς εἶπε· τῶι δ' οὐ πάλιν
θυμὸς ἀνεκάμπτετ', ἀλλ' εὐ-
πάκτων ἐπ' ἰκρίων
σταθεὶς ὄρουσε, πόντιόν τέ νιν
85 δέξατο θελημὸν ἄλσος.
τάφεν δὲ Διὸς υἱὸς ἔνδοθεν
κέαρ, κέλευσέ τε κατ' οὖ-
ρον ἴσχε[ι]ν εὐδαίδαλον
νᾶα· Μοῖρα δ' ἑτέραν ἐπόρσυν' ὁδόν.

90 ἵετο δ' ὠκύπομπον δόρυ· σόει
ν[ε]ιν βορεὰς ἐξόπι[θε]ν πνέουσ' ἀήτα·
τρέσσαν δ' Ἀθαναίων
ἠϊθέων <πᾶν> γένος, ἐπεί
ἥρως θόρεν πόντονδε, κα-

74s. West: τάδε | μὲν A   τάδε[| μὲν O   75 βλέπει O   83 πήκτων
pap.   91 νιν Housman, al.   94s. δάκρυ | χέον div. pap.

222

hero, staunch in battle, saw the welcome portent he stretched his hands to the glorious sky and spoke: 'Theseus, you see these clear gifts of mine given by Zeus; so for your part plunge into the deep-roaring sea, and Cronus' son, lord Poseidon, your father, will achieve for you supreme fame throughout the well-wooded earth.'

So he spoke, and the other's heart did not recoil: he took his stance on the well-built sterndeck and leapt, and the precinct of the sea gave him kindly welcome. Zeus' son was astonished in his heart, and he gave orders to keep the cunningly-made ship on course before the wind; but Fate was preparing another course. The swiftly-moving bark raced on, as the northerly breeze blowing astern sped it along; but the whole group of young Athenians had trembled when the hero sprang into the sea, and they

95   τὰ λειρίων τ' ὀμμάτων δά-
κρυ χέον, βαρεῖαν ἐπιδέγμενοι ἀνάγκαν.
φέρον δὲ δελφῖνες ἐναλι-
ναιέται μέγαν θοῶς
Θησέα πατρὸς ἱππί-
100   ου δόμον· ἔμολέν τε θεῶν
μέγαρον. τόθι κλυτὰς ἰδὼν ἔδει-
σε Νηρῆος ὀλβίου
κόρας· ἀπὸ γὰρ ἀγλα-
ῶν λάμπε γυίων σέλας
105   ὧτε πυρός, ἀμφὶ χαίταις
δὲ χρυσεόπλοκοι
δίνηντο ταινίαι· χορῶι δ' ἔτερ-
πον κέαρ ὑγροῖσι⟦ν ἐν⟧ ποσ⟨σ⟩ίν.
εἰδέν τε πατρὸς ἄλοχον φίλαν
110   σεμνὰν βοῶπιν ἐρατοῖ-
σιν Ἀμφιτρίταν δόμοις·
ἅ νιν ἀμφέβαλλεν ἀΐονα πορφυρέαν,

κόμαισί τ' ἐπέθηκεν οὔλαις
ἀμεμφέα πλόκον,
115   τόν ποτέ οἱ ἐν γάμωι
δῶκε δόλιος Ἀφροδίτα ῥόδοις ἐρεμνόν.
ἄπιστον ὅ τι δαίμονες
θέλωσιν οὐδὲν φρενοάραις βροτοῖς·
νᾶα πάρα λεπτόπρυμνον φάνη· φεῦ,
120   οἵαισιν ἐν φροντίσι Κνώσιον
ἔσχασεν στραταγέταν, ἐπεί
μόλ' ἀδίαντος ἐξ ἁλός
θαῦμα πάντεσσι, λάμ-

shed tears from their lily-bright eyes, expecting a
woeful doom. But sea-dwelling dolphins were
swiftly carrying great Theseus to the house of his
father, god of horses, and he reached the hall of the
gods. There he was awe-struck at the glorious
daughters of blessed Nereus, for from their splendid
limbs shone a gleam as of fire, and round their hair
were twirled gold-braided ribbons; and they were
delighting their hearts by dancing with liquid feet.
And he saw his father's dear wife, august ox-eyed
Amphitrite, in the lovely house; she put a purple
cloak about him and set on his thick hair the fault-
less garland which once at her marriage guileful
Aphrodite had given her, dark with roses. Nothing
that the gods wish is beyond the belief of sane mor-
tals: he appeared beside the slender-sterned ship.
Whew, in what thoughts did he check the Cnossian
commander when he came unwet from the sea, a
miracle for all, and the gods' gifts shone on his

101s. West: ἰδὼν | ἔδεισε div. pap.   102 Νηρέος pap.

πε δ' ἀμφὶ γυίοις θεῶν δῶρ', ἀγλ<α>ό-
125 θρονοί τε κοῦραι σὺν εὐ-
θυμίαι νεοκτίτωι
ὠλόλυξαν, ἔ-
κλαγεν δὲ πόντος· ἤίθεοι δ' ἐγγύθεν
νέοι παιάνιξαν ἐρατᾶι ὀπί.
130 Δάλιε, χοροῖσι Κηΐων
φρένα ἰανθείς
ὄπαζε θεόπομπον ἐσθλῶν τύχαν.

18

ΘΗΣΕΥΣ
[ΑΘΗΝΑΙΟΙΣ]

<Χορός>
βασιλεῦ τᾶν ἱερᾶν Ἀθανᾶν,
τῶν ἁβροβίων ἄναξ Ἰώνων,
τί νέον ἔκλαγε χαλκοκώδων
σάλπιγξ πολεμηΐαν ἀοιδάν;
5 ἦ τις ἁμετέρας χθονὸς
δυσμενὴς ὅρι' ἀμφιβάλλει
στραταγέτας ἀνήρ;
ἦ λησταὶ κακομάχανοι
ποιμένων ἀέκατι μήλων
10 σεύοντ' ἀγέλας βίαι;
ἦ τί τοι κραδίαν ἀμύσσει;
φθέγγευ· δοκέω γὰρ εἴ τινι βροτῶν
ἀλκίμων ἐπικουρίαν
καὶ τὶν ἔμμεναι νέων,
15 ὦ Πανδίονος υἱὲ καὶ Κρεούσας.

limbs; and the splendid-throned maidens[1] cried out with new-founded joy, and the sea rang out; and nearby the youths raised a paean with lovely voice.

God of Delos, rejoice in your heart at the choirs of the Ceans and grant a heaven-sent fortune of blessings.

[1] The seven Athenian girls rather than the Nereids: see D. E. Gerber, *Z.P.E.* 49 (1982) 3–5.

18

THESEUS

FOR THE ATHENIANS[1]

Chorus of Athenians[2]

King of holy Athens, lord of the delicately-living Ionians,[3] why did the bronze-belled trumpet sound its war-song just now? Does some hostile army commander surround the borders of our land? Or do evil-planning robbers drive off forcibly the flocks of sheep against the shepherds' will? Or what is it that rends your heart? Speak; for I think that you, if any mortal, son of Pandion and Creusa,[4] have valiant young warriors to help you.

[1] This is deduced from the subject-matter; R. Merkelbach, *Z.P.E.* 12 (1973) 56–62 argues that it was written for an ephebic festival.   [2] The papyrus does not identify the singers.   [3] Cf. 17. 3.   [4] In other versions the mother of Aegeus is Pylia or Pelia, and Creusa, daughter of Erechtheus, is wife of Xuthus and mother (by Apollo) of Ion.

9 Palmer, van Branteghem: δ' ἕκατι pap.   12 Blass, Wackernagel: φθεγγου pap.

\<Αἰγεύς\>
νέον ἦλθε\<ν\> δολιχὰν ἀμείψας
κᾶρυξ ποσὶν Ἰσθμίαν κέλευθον·
ἄφατα δ' ἔργα λέγει κραταιοῦ
φωτός· τὸν ὑπέρβιόν τ' ἔπεφνεν
20 Σίνιν, ὃς ἰσχύϊ φέρτατος
θνατῶν ἦν, Κρονίδα Λυταίου
σεισίχθονος τέκος·
σὺν τ' ἀνδροκτόνον ἐν νάπαις
Κρεμ\<μ\>υῶνος ἀτάσθαλόν τε
25 Σκίρωνα κατέκτανεν·
τάν τε Κερκυόνος παλαίστραν
ἔσχεν, Πολυπήμονός τε καρτερὰν
σφῦραν ἐξέβαλλεν Προκό-
πτας, ἀρείονος τυχών
30 φωτός. ταῦτα δέδοιχ' ὅπαι τελεῖται.

\<Χορός\>
τίνα δ' ἔμμεν πόθεν ἄνδρα τοῦτον
λέγει, τίνα τε στολὰν ἔχοντα;
πότερα σὺν πολεμηΐοις ὅ-
πλοισι στρατιὰν ἄγοντα πολλάν;

Aegeus

A herald came just now, having completed on foot the long journey from the Isthmus, and he tells of indescribable deeds on the part of a strong man[1]: he has slain the mighty Sinis,[2] who was the foremost of mortals in strength, offspring of Cronus' son, the earth-shaker, the loosener[3]; and he has killed the man-killing sow in the glens of Cremmyon, and wicked Sciron[4] too; and he has put an end to the wrestling-school of Cercyon[5]; and Procoptes[6] has dropped the mighty hammer of Polypemon, having met a better man than himself. I am afraid how all this will end.

Chorus

Who does he say that this man is? From where? How equipped? Does he bring a large force armed

---

[1] Aegeus' son, Theseus, making his way from Troezen to seek his father. [2] Known as Pine-bender, because he tied his victims' arms to two bent pines which he then released. [3] Poseidon, who 'loosened' the rocks at Tempe (see 14 n. 1). [4] A robber who kicked his victims over the 'Scironian' cliffs. [5] He forced passersby to wrestle with him and killed the losers. [6] The Cutter, better known as Procrustes, the Crusher, who fitted his victims to the size of his bed by lopping or traction. Polypemon may have been his father.

35 ἢ μοῦνον σὺν ὀπάοσιν
    στ<ε>ίχειν ἔμπορον οἶ' ἀλάταν
    ἐπ' ἀλλοδαμίαν,
    ἰσχυρόν τε καὶ ἄλκιμον
    ὧδε καὶ θρασύν, ὃς τ<οσ>ούτων
40 ἀνδρῶν κρατερὸν σθένος
    ἔσχεν; ἦ θεὸς αὐτὸν ὁρμᾶι,
    δίκας ἀδίκοισιν ὄφρα μήσεται·
    οὐ γὰρ ῥάιδιον αἰὲν ἔρ-
    δοντα μὴ 'ντυχεῖν κακῶι.
45 πάντ' ἐν τῶι δολιχῶι χρόνωι τελεῖται.

<Αἰγεύς>
    δύο οἱ φῶτε μόνους ἁμαρτεῖν
    λέγει, περὶ φαιδίμοισι δ' ὤμοις
    ξίφος ἔχειν <ἐλεφαντόκωπον>,
    ξεστοὺς δὲ δύ' ἐν χέρεσσ' ἄκοντας
50 κηὔτυκτον κυνέαν Λάκαι-
    ναν κρατὸς πέρι πυρσοχαίτου·
    χιτῶνα πορφύρεον
    στέρνοις τ' ἀμφί, καὶ οὖλιον
    Θεσσαλὰν χλαμύδ'· ὀμμάτων δὲ
55 στίλβειν ἄπο Λαμνίαν
    φοίνισσαν φλόγα· παῖδα δ' ἔμ<μ>εν
    πρώθηβον, ἀρηΐων δ' ἀθυρμάτων
    μεμνᾶσθαι πολέμου τε καὶ
    χαλκεοκτύπου μάχας·
60 δίζησθαι δὲ φιλαγλάους Ἀθάνας.

35 Weil, Festa, al.: οπλοισιν pap.   39 Platt: τ<οι>ούτων Kenyon
40 καρτερον pap.   48 Desrousseaux   51 Jebb, Blass: ὑπερ pap.

230

for war or travel alone with his attendants like a wanderer journeying to foreign parts, so strong, valiant and bold that he has overcome the powerful might of such great men? Truly a god must be driving him on to contrive just punishments for the unjust; for it is not easy to perform deed after deed without meeting disaster. All things come to an end in the long course of time.

Aegeus

He says that only two men accompany him; he has a sword with ivory hilt slung from his bright shoulders, two polished spears in his hands, a well-made Laconian cap[1] about his fire-red hair, a purple tunic over his chest and a woolly Thessalian cloak; from his eyes flashes red Lemnian[2] flame; he is a youth in his earliest manhood, and his thoughts are of the pastimes of Ares, war and the clashing bronze of battle; and he seeks splendour-loving Athens.

[1] Or 'sun-hat'.   [2] Like the volcanic fire on Lemnos.

19

ΙΩ

ΑΘΗΝΑΙΟΙΣ

πάρεστι μυρία κέλευθος
 ἀμβροσίων μελέων,
ὃς ἂν παρὰ Πιερίδων λά-
 χῃσι δῶρα Μουσᾶν,
5 ἰοβλέφαροί τε κ<όρ>αι
 φερεστέφανοι Χάριτες
βάλωσιν ἀμφὶ τιμάν
ὕμνοισιν· ὕφαινέ νυν ἐν
 ταῖς πολυηράτοις τι καινὸν
10 ὀλβίαις Ἀθάναις,
εὐαίνετε Κηΐα μέριμνα·
 πρέπει σε φερτάταν ἴμεν
ὁδὸν παρὰ Καλλιόπας λα-
 χοῖσαν ἔξοχον γέρας.
15 †τιην† Ἄργος ὅθ' ἵππιον λιποῦσα
 φεῦγε χρυσέα βοῦς,
εὐρυσθενέος φραδαῖσι φερτάτου Διός,
Ἰνάχου ῥοδοδάκτυλος κόρα,

ὅτ' Ἄργον ὄμμασι βλέποντα
20 πάντοθεν ἀκαμάτοις
μεγιστοάνασσα κέλευσεν
 χρυσόπεπλος Ἥρα
ἄκοιτον ἄϋπνον ἐόν-
 τα καλλικέραν δάμαλιν

19

IO

FOR THE ATHENIANS

Countless paths of ambrosial verses lie open for
him who obtains gifts from the Pierian Muses and
whose songs are clothed with honour by the violet-
eyed maidens, the garland-bearing Graces. Weave,
then, in lovely, blessed Athens a new fabric,
renowned Cean fantasy[1]: you must travel by the
finest road, since you have obtained from Calliope a
superlative prize.

There was a time when by the counsels of wide-
powered Zeus the golden[2] cow had left Argos, land
of horses, and was in flight—the rose-fingered
daughter of Inachus; when Argus,[3] looking from all
sides with tireless eyes, was ordered by the great
queen, gold-robed Hera, to guard unresting and
unsleeping the lovely-horned heifer, and Maia's

---

[1] B. addresses the poetic skill of his island; his uncle Simonides
was also Cean.   [2] I.e. splendid or peerless, as associated with
a god. Io, daughter of the Argive river-god Inachus, had been
transformed into a cow by Hera (or by Zeus himself).   [3] Son
of Earth (v. 31), depicted as having eyes all over his body.

---

4 Blass, Wackernagel   5 Erbse   9 καινὸν: κλεινον pap. corr.
15 ἦεν Headlam   21 Platt

25   φυλάσσεν, οὐδὲ Μαίας
υἱὸς δύνατ᾽ οὔτε κατ᾽ εὐ-
    φεγγέας ἀμέρας λαθεῖν νιν
    οὔτε νύκτας ἀγν[άς.
εἶτ᾽ οὖν γένετ᾽ ε[
30   ποδαρκέ᾽ ἄγγελο[ν Διὸς
κτανεῖν τότε [Γᾶς τέκος αἰνὸν
    ὀβριμοσπόρου λ[ίθωι
Ἄργον· ἦ ῥα καὶ .[
ἄσπετοι μέριμν[αι·
35 ἦ Πιερίδες φύτευ[σαν ἀδύμωι μέλει
καδέων ἀνάπαυσ[ιν . . .

ἐμοὶ μὲν οὖν
ἀσφαλέστατον ἀ πρὸ[ς ἔσχατ᾽ οἶμα,
ἐπεὶ παρ᾽ ἀνθεμώ[δεα
40 Νεῖλον ἀφίκετ᾽ ο[ἰστροπλὰξ
Ἰὼ φέρουσα παῖδ[α γαστρὶ τὸν Διὸς
Ἔπαφον· ἔνθα νι[ν τέκ᾽ Αἰγυπτίων
λινοστόλων πρύτ[ανιν . . .
ὑπερόχωι βρύοντ[α τιμᾶι,
45 μεγίσταν τε θνα[τῶν ἔφανεν γενέθλαν,
ὅθεν καὶ Ἀγανορί[δας
ἐν ἑπταπύλοισ[ι Θήβαις
Κάδμος Σεμέλ[αν φύτευσεν,
ἃ τὸν ὀρσιβάκχα[ν
50 τίκτε<ν> Διόνυσον [. . .
καὶ χορῶν στεφαν[αφόρων ἄνακτα.

234

son[1] could elude him neither in the bright daytime
nor in the holy night. Now whether it came about
that ... Zeus' swift-footed messenger killed Argus
then, (grim child of Earth) of the mighty offspring,
(with a stone), or his endless anxieties (closed his
grim eyes), or the Pierians engendered rest for his
cares (through sweet song)[2]; for me at any rate the
safest course is (the path which leads me to the end):
for Io (driven by the gadfly's sting)[3] reached the
flowery Nile, carrying (in her womb) Epaphus, child
(of Zeus); there (she gave birth to) him, ruler of the
linen-robed (Egyptians), abounding in exceptional
(honour), and (brought to light) the mightiest (line)
among mortals. From it came Agenor's son,
Cadmus, who in seven-gated Thebes (fathered)
Semele; and she gave birth to Dionysus, rouser of
Bacchants ..., (lord of garland-wearing) choirs.[4]

[1] Hermes, messenger of Zeus (v. 30), directed by him to kill Argus.
[2] Ovid *Met.* 1. 673 ff. tells how Hermes sent Argus to sleep by play-
ing a shepherd's syrinx.   [3] On Argus' death Hera sent a
gadfly to torment Io.   [4] The dithyramb ends with mention of
the dithyrambic choirs which competed in Athens.

28 Jebb, Sandys   29 ἐ[ν μάχας ἀγῶνι Jebb   30 Jebb   31 Γᾶς
Jebb   τέκος αἰνὸν Snell   32 Deubner   33 ὄ[μματ' αἰνὰ λῦσαν
Jebb   35 Jebb   36 ἀνάπ. ἐμπέδων Jebb   38 Jebb: ἁ πρὸ[ς
τέρμαθ' ὁρμά Schadewaldt   40 Blass, Festa   41 Jebb   42 νι[ν
τέκ' ἀνδρῶν Blass   Αἰγ. Snell   44 Blass   45 Jebb   46 Blass,
al.   47, 48 Jebb   50 Jurenka   [ἀγλαῶν τε κώμων
Jurenka   51 Wilamowitz

20

ΙΔΑΣ
ΛΑΚΕΔΑΙΜΟΝΙΟΙΣ

Σπάρται ποτ' ἐν ε[ὐρυχόρωι
ξανθαὶ Λακεδα[ιμονίων κόραι
τοιόνδε μέλος κ[ελάδησαν,
ὅτ' ἄγετο καλλιπά[ραιον
5 κόραν θρασυκάρ[διος Ἴδας
Μάρπησσαν ἰοτ[
φυγὼν θανάτου τ[
ἀναξίαλος Ποσ<ε>ι[δὰν
ἵππους τέ οἱ ἴσαν[ἔμους
10 Πλευρῶν' ἐς ἐϋκτ[ιμέναν
χρυσάσπιδος υἱὸ[ν Ἄρηος

desunt cetera

1 Rossbach, al.   2 Λακεδα[ιμόνιαι κ. Headlam   -ίων Wilamowitz,
Jebb   3 Gomperz, Jurenka   4 vel καλλίπα[χυν   6 ἰότ[ριχ] ἐς
οἴκους Jebb   7 τ[έλος αἰπύ Pingel   8 Π. [ὅτε δίφρον ὀπάσσας Jebb
10 vel ἐϋκτ[ιτον   ἐϋκτ. [ἐπόρευσε παραὶ Jebb   11 Sandys, Reinach

21

Schol. Pind. *Ol.* 10. 83a (i 331 Drachmann) + pap. A fr. 2
Kenyon

τὴν Μαντινέαν φησὶν (sc. ὁ Δίδυμος, p. 223 Schmidt) εἶναι
ἱερὰν Ποσειδῶνος, καὶ παρατίθεται τὸν Βακχυλίδην λέγοντα οὕτω·

Ποσει]δάνιον ὡ[ς
Μαντ]ινέες τριό[δοντα χαλκοδαιδάλοισιν ἐν
ἀσπίσι]ν φορεῦν[τες
    ]οφευγε[

236

20

IDAS

FOR THE SPARTANS

Once in (spacious) Sparta the blonde (daughters) of the Lacedaemonians (sang) a song such as this, when bold-hearted (Idas)[1] was bringing home the lovely-cheeked[2] maiden, (violet-haired) Marpessa, having escaped the (fate) of death,[3] when sea-lord Poseidon[4] (had given him a chariot) and wind-swift horses (and sent) him to well-built Pleuron to the son[5] of gold-shielded (Ares) . . .

[1] The Spartan (or Messenian) Idas, son of Aphareus, carried off Marpessa, daughter of king Euenus of Pleuron in Aetolia; see fr. 20A, Simon. 563.   [2] Or 'lovely-armed'.   [3] Euenus competed against his daughter's suitors and roofed Poseidon's temple with their skulls; acc. to schol. Pind. *Isthm.* 4. 92 B. told the story, presumably in this poem.   [4] Said to be Idas' father.
[5] Euenus.

21

Scholiast on Pindar, *Ol.* 10. 69 f. ('Mantinea') + a fragment of the London papyrus.

Didymus[1] says that Mantinea is sacred to Poseidon[2] and adduces this passage of Bacchylides:

. . . how the Mantineans, bearing Poseidon's trident on their shields of finely-worked bronze, . . .

[1] D.'s text of Pindar seemed to refer to Poseidon.   [2] As god of horses.

23

ΚΑΣΣΑΝΔΡΑ

P.Oxy. 2368 col. i

⁷ Ἀθ[ανᾶν (.) . . αν]δρον ἱερᾶν ἄωτο[ν · ταύτην τ]ὴν

ᾠδὴν Ἀρίσταρχ(ος) ¹⁰[μὲν διθ]υραμβικὴν εἶ[ναί φησι]ν διὰ τὸ

παρειλῆ[φθαι ἐν α]ὐτῆι τὰ περὶ Κασ[σάνδρας], ἐπιγράφει δ' αὐτὴν

[... Κασσ]άνδραν, πλανη[θέντα δ' α]ὐτὴν κατατάξαι [ἐν τοῖς

Π]αιᾶσι Καλλίμαχον [διὰ τὸ ἰή], οὐ συνέντα ὅτι [τὸ ἐπί-

φθ]εγ[γ]μα κοινόν ἐ[στι καὶ δ]ιθυράμβου· ὁμοί[ως δὲ ὁ Φ[ασαη-

λίτης Διονύσιο(ς).

]ειον τέμενος · το[   ] . αι τὸ τῆς Ἀθήνας

]α δ' ἀχὼ κτυπεῖ λι[γείαι σὺν] αὐλῶν πνοᾶι ·
αρε[   ]τηι τῶν αὐλῶν

]έλικτον δὲ ἀντὶ [τοῦ . . . .] . . τως

ἐπεὶ δε[   ] . . . . αρχος ἔπειτα

[ἀπὸ τοῦ χ]άρις πρέπει ἕως ³⁰[τοῦ . . . .] . ιονων
νοο[. . .

⁴⁰τανυ[άκης ἀντὶ τοῦ τανυ]ήκης

suppl. ed. pr. (Lobel) praeter 10 μὲν Maehler   8 εὔαν]δρον dub.
Lobel   φίλαν]δρον Snell

238

BACCHYLIDES

23

CASSANDRA

Oxyrhynchus papyrus (2nd c. A.D.): commentary[1] on Bacchylides

The cream of holy (Athens, fine) men[2]: Aristarchus says this song is dithyrambic because the story of Cassandra has been included in it, and he entitles it *Cassandra*; he says that Callimachus classified it among the *Paeans* because he was misled (by the cry iē)[3] and did not realise that it belongs to both the paean and the dithyramb; similarly Dionysius of Phaselis.

precinct . . .: the (sanctuary) of Athena.

the sound rings out with the clear blowing of pipes: . . . of the pipes.

twisted: instead of (the adverb?).

and when[4] . . . : . . . (then?)

from gratitude is fitting to . . . (the mind?) . . .

long-pointed: (with Doric -άκης for -ήκης?)

1 Perhaps by Didymus (see test. 11). 2 The opening words of the poem, which may have been commissioned by the Athenians. 3 The cry must have occurred in B.'s poem. 4 It is not certain that this is text rather than commentary.

Porphyr. in Hor. *Carm.* 1. 15 (p. 23 Holder)

hac ode Bacchylidem imitatur; nam ut ille Casandram facit vaticinari futura belli Troiani, ita hic Proteum.

24

P.Oxy. 2364 fr. 2 (= C) + p. Berol. 16139 + 21209 (= D)

<pre>
        ]αρα[
  . . . .]δαλον χα[
  . . .]μα φαινω[
  . . .] ˙ φρονος λ[
5 . . . .]ηι γυναι[   ]τεκνος
   θυμὸν αἱρείτω[
   οὐ γάρ τις ἀνθρώπ[ωι, τῶι ἂν εὐθύ]δικοι
   Μοῖραι παρὰ χρυσ[αλάκατοι
   στᾶσαι φατίξωσιν [κακά,
10 φύξις, οὐδ' εἰ χαλκέο[ις φράξεν δόμον
   τείχε]σιν, μίμνη[[ση]]ι κε τάδε βρο[τὸς εἴργων ·
   ὄλβος τε καὶ δόξα[

   ταῦτ᾽ ε[ἶ]πε φιλαγλαο[
   παντ[˙]ς · ἄϊξεν δ᾽ ἀπ[
15 ˙ [. . .]πινας ανο
</pre>

2 εὐδαί]δ. Snell   4ss. sec. Snell sententia: μήτε με . . .]ηι γυναι[κεία φιλό]τεκνος θ. αἱ. [μαλακία   7 Lobel (τὸν ἂν) : τῶι ἂν ego   vel ὀρθό]-δικοι   8 e.g. Snell   9 φατίξωσιν C φατίζωσιν D   suppl. Snell 10 φράξεν vel φράξηι δόμον Snell   11 Snell   13 Lobel

BACCHYLIDES

Porphyrio on Horace, *Ode* 1.15

In this ode Horace copies Bacchylides: Bacchylides makes Cassandra prophesy the events of the Trojan War, and Horace makes Proteus[1] do the same.

[1] Nereus in fact.

24

Oxyrhynchus papyrus (150–200 A.D.?) + Berlin papyrus (100–140 A.D.)

'... (cunningly made?) ... (I?) show ... -minded ... woman- ... child- ... let (it) seize the heart[1]; since the man (for whom) the righteous Fates with the golden (distaffs), taking their place by his side,[2] predict (evils) has no escape, not even if (he has fortified his house with) bronze (walls) and stays there (trying to shut them out), a mere mortal: both prosperity and fame ...'

So spoke the splendid (hero) ... and he rushed from ...

[1] Perhaps a hero addresses his mother: 'and let no womanish child-loving softness seize your heart' (Snell).   [2] At his birth; but text and translation of the sentence are insecure.

25

[ΜΕΛΕΑΓΡΟΣ ?]

P. Ashmol. inv. 20

1 θ]έορτον στρατόν[2]ποικίλων   3]ον παιή-
ονα   6 Ἀρτ]έμιδος τεμ[εν-   9]ἀπὸ λευκῶν   10]ισα
γᾶρυν   11 πολυθ]αρσέα θηροδα[ίκταν   12 θελ]ξίμβρο-
τος   13 α]νθέϊ   15 κ]υανάμπυκα Νύ[κτα   16 ἐπι]χθο-
νίοισι δὲ κουφαι   19]Διὸς υἱὸν   20] ι δαμέ[ν]τα
πολύλλισ[το   21] θεοις   22] πυκινὰν   23]ρον
ἀνδρῶν   24 παγ]κρατὴς   25 Ἀ]μφιτρυωνιάδας
27 ἔ]νθ' ἀπὸ τειχέων   28 ἔκλα]γξεν αἰθήρ·
29 Κλ]ύ[τι]ον Προκάωνά τε θε[33 ἐ]ύτ[ρ]οφος (vel
πολ]ύ-) αινα . [

1, 11 (θηρ.), 29 suppl. Lobel, cetera Snell

26

[ΠΑΣΙΦΑΗ ?]

P.Oxy. 2364 fr. 1

φρα . [
Πασι[φ]ά[α
ἐν Κύπ[ρις φύτευσε
πόθον[
5 Εὐπαλά[μοι'] υἱε[ῖ

BACCHYLIDES

25

MELEAGER (?)

Ashmole papyrus (150–200 A.D.?)

... god-sent army ... cunningly made ... paean
... (sanctuary of Artemis?)[1] ... from white ... voice
... bold animal-killer ... man-enchanting ...
(flower?) ... (Night?) of the blue-black headband ...
for mortals light-weight ... son (of Zeus?) ... sub-
dued ... of many prayers ... gods ... shrewd ... of
men ... the all-powerful son[2] of Amphitryon ...
then from the walls ... the sky resounded ...
Clytius and Procaon[3] ... well-nourished (?) ...

[1] Supplement by Snell, who notes that it was Artemis who sent the
boar to ravage Calydon.　　　[2] Heracles, unless the reference is
to H.'s brother Iphicles or to Iphicles' son Iolaus, both reported to
have taken part in the boar-hunt.　　　[3] Brothers of Althaea and
uncles of Meleager: see Stes. 222.

26

PASIPHAE (?)

Oxyrhynchus papyrus (150–200 A.D.?)

... Pasiphaë[1] ... (the Cyprian[2] implanted) desire
in her ... : to Eupalamus' son Daedalus, most

[1] Minos' wife, who mated with a bull and became mother of the
Minotaur.　　　[2] Aphrodite.

τεκτόν[ω]ν σοφω[τάτωι
φράσε Δαιδάλωι ἄς[πετον
νόσον· ὅρκια πίσ[τ᾽ ἔλαβε ξυλίναν
    τ]ε τεύχειν κέλευ[σε βοῦν, ἵνα
10 μείξειε ταυρείωι σ[θένει δέμας,
κρύπτουσα σύννο[μον εὐνὰν
Μίνωα [τ]οξοδάμαν[τα,

Κνωσσίων στρατα[γέταν·
ὁ δ᾽ ἐπεὶ μάθε μῦθο[ν
15 σχέτο φροντίδι· δε[ῖσε γὰρ
. . . .] ἀλόχου[

suppl. ed. pr. (Lobel) praeter 3, 5, 7, 8, 10, 15 Snell   7 ἀω[ρον
Lobel

27

[ΧΙΡΩΝ ?]

P.Oxy. 2364 fr. 3 col. 2 + frr. 9 + 4 + P.Oxy. 661 fr. 2

ξανθᾶς νιν εὔβ[ο]υλ[ο]ς θαμ[ὰ Φ]ιλλυρί[δας
35 ψαύων κεφ[αλ]ᾶς ἐνέπει·
φατί νιν [δινᾶ]ντα φοινίζειν Σκά[μανδρον
κτείνον[τα φιλ]οπτολέμους
Τρῶας· π . [. . . .] ΄ . . . . ΄ · ι . . α[ ]ματ[

suppl. ed. pr. (Lobel) praeter   34 εὔβουλος Snell

244

BACCHYLIDES

skilled of carpenters, she told her (unspeakable?) sickness; (she made him swear) a binding oath and ordered him to build (a wooden cow, so that) she might join (her body[1] to that of the mighty) bull, hiding from Minos, bow-subduer, commander of the Cnossians, the union she shared; but when he got wind of it he was gripped by worry, (for he feared) ... of his wife ...

[1] Concealed in the artefact.

27

CHIRON (?)[1]

Oxyrhynchus papyrus (150–200 A.D.?)

... (when I remember what?) the wise son[2] of Philyra often says of him, touching his blond head: he declares that he will crimson the eddying Scamander as he kills the battle-loving Trojans; ...

[1] Scraps remain of 14 lines, then at least 19 are missing. [2] The centaur Chiron, prophesying about his ward Achilles: cf. Hor. *Epod.* 13. 11ff. Perhaps Achilles' mother Thetis is speaking.

```
       ξείναι τε . [                          ]  .  [
40  ἀλκίμουσ[                              ]τ᾽ ἐπ[
     Μυσῶν τ᾽ α[                           ]      [
     ταῦτ᾽ ἐπέπ[
     καρδίαν π[


     φίλα[ι]ς δεχ[
45        δ᾽ εὔφυλλ[ο
```

39 κ[είσεσθαί νιν ἐν γᾶι vel sim. Snell   44 δὲ χ[ερσίν vel sim. Snell

28

[ΟΡΦΕΥΣ ?]

P.Oxy. 2364 addendum (*Ox. Pap.* 32. 160s.) fr. 1 (b)

```
          ] . [ ]λευ[
              ]χαρ[
          ] . ε ἐπ᾽ ἀη[
          ]ον σοφ . [ ] .
5       .]ωσι γέρας·
          ]οι καὶ δένδρα κ[
          ]ον τ᾽ [ε]ὐαγὲς οἶδ[μα
     εὐαί]νετον Οἰαγρίδα[ν
```

suppl. ed. pr. (Lobel) praeter 10, 12, 16, 20, 21 (Snell)

and (will lie in a) foreign (land) ... valiant ...
Mysians[1] ... That is what he says ... (my?) heart
... (and in my?) loving (hands?) ... leafy ...

[1] Neighbours and allies of the Trojans; at the beginning of the War
Achilles wounded and later healed their king Telephus.

28

ORPHEUS (?)

Oxyrhynchus papyrus (150–200 A.D.?)

... prize[1] ... and trees ... and ... the shining
swell of the sea ... the renowned son[2] of Oeagrus ...

[1] The gift of music given to Orpheus?   [2] Orpheus.

```
          ]ι Μούσας ἐρασιπ[λοκάμου
10   παῖδ' ὃ]ν ὁ τοξοδάμας
          ἑ]κάεργος Ἀπόλλ[ων·
          ὁ ]μὲν κυρεῖ θεῶν[
          ] ὀψιγόνων
          ]μελιτευχέα παγ[άν
15        ]αι πιθεῖν εοθε[
          ] καὶ ἐμ' ἀμ[β]ρ[οσ-
          ]ι κατασπειρ . [
          ]τοριας
          -οι]σι καλύμμα[σι
20        ἰ]θύσας φρένα[
          ]αιω κλυ[τ]οφ[ορμιγ-
          ]θεα καὶ γ[ . ] . [
```

11 τίμας' ἑ]κ. Snell   v. R. Führer, *Maia* 21 (1969) 83–85

29

P.Oxy. 2364

fr. 5(a) 1]αι θεοτ[ιμο vel θεοτ[ευκτο (Snell)   3
]υφαινεσο[4]'.[.]ροβρον[τ   5 σχέ]τλιος

fr. 8   4 ν]εκρόν (? Snell)   6 θ]αρσει·[(? Snell)

fr. 12   1 Π]υθοῖ βρύει[2]ἀγλαῖα[3]ον ξενίαισ[

(child) of the lovely-haired Muse, (whom) Apollo,
bow-subduer, far-worker, (honoured?); ... he meets
with the gods ... late-born (men) ... honey-
fashioned spring[1] ... to persuade ... and me ...
ambrosial ... to sow ... veils ... guiding straight
(his thoughts?) ... (famed lyre-player?) ...

[1] Metaphorically, a fount or source of honey-sweet song.

29

Oxyrhynchus papyrus (150–200 A.D.?)

(a) ... god-honoured (*or* god-made) ... wove ... the
thunderer ... cruel ...

(b) ... (corpse?) ... (bold?) ...

(c) ... at Pytho festivity abounds ... hospitality ...

GREEK LYRIC

FRAGMENTA

ΕΠΙΝΙΚΟΙ

fr. 1 Stob. 3. 10. 14 (iii 411 Hense) (περὶ ἀδικίας)

Βακχυλίδου Ἐπινίκων·

ὡς δ' ἅπαξ εἰπεῖν, φρένα καὶ πυκινάν
κέρδος ἀνθρώπων βιᾶται.

ΥΜΝΟΙ

fr. 1A P.Oxy. 2366. 1s.

[ΕΙΣ ΑΠΟΛΛΩΝΑ]

ὄρνυ[ο
Λοξία[

suppl. Snell

FRAGMENTS

Frr. 1–21 are arranged by genre: epinicians (1), hymns (1A–3), paeans (4–6), dithyrambs (7–10), prosodia (processionals) (11–13), parthenia (maiden-songs), hyporchemata (dance-songs) (14–16), love poetry (17–19), encomia (20–21). Frr. 22–40 give words from Bacchylides without indicating the genre; frr. 41–53 deal with topics mentioned in his poems. These fragments are distinguished from the papyrus texts of epinicians and dithyrambs by the label 'fr.'

EPINICIANS

fr. 1 Stobaeus, *Anthology* (on injustice)

Bacchylides, *Epinicians*:

To say it once for all time, men's minds, even the wise, are mastered by love of gain.

HYMNS

fr. 1A Oxyrhynchus papyrus (2nd or 3rd c. A.D.)

TO APOLLO[1]

. . . hasten, Loxias! . . .

1 From the last two lines of a hymn, perhaps apopemptic.

Men. Rh. π. ἐπιδ. 333, 336 (pp. 6, 12 Russell-Wilson)

ἀποπεμπτικοὶ δὲ (sc. ὕμνοι) ὁποῖοι καὶ παρὰ τῷ Βακχυλίδῃ ἔνιοι εὕρηνται, ἀποπομπὴν ὡς ἀποδημίας τινὸς γινομένης ἔχοντες. . . .

οἱ τοίνυν ἀποπεμπτικοί εἰσιν, ὡς καὶ τοὔνομα δηλοῖ, τοῖς κλητικοῖς ὑπεναντίοι, ἐλάχιστον δὲ τὸ τοιοῦτον εἶδος, καὶ παρὰ τοῖς ποιηταῖς μόνον εὑρίσκεται. ἐπιλέγονται δὲ ἀποδημίαις θεῶν νομιζομέναις ἢ γινομέναις, οἷον Ἀπόλλωνος ἀποδημίαι τινὲς ὀνομάζονται παρὰ Δηλίοις καὶ Μιλησίοις, καὶ Ἀρτέμιδος παρὰ Ἀργείοις. εἰσὶ τοίνυν καὶ τῷ Βακχυλίδῃ ὕμνοι ἀποπεμπτικοί. ἀφορμὴ δ᾽ ὑποβέβληται τοῖς τοιούτοις ὕμνοις ἡ χώρα ἣν καταλείπει, καὶ πόλεις καὶ ἔθνη, καὶ πρὸς ἣν ἄπεισι πόλιν ὁμοίως ἢ χώραν, καὶ διαγραφαὶ τόπων, καὶ ὅσα τοιαῦτα. γινέσθω δὲ δι᾽ ἡδονῆς προϊὼν ὁ λόγος· δεῖ γὰρ μετὰ ἀνειμένης τινὸς ἁρμονίας καὶ εὐμενεστέρας προπέμπεσθαι. διατριβὴν δὲ ἐνδέχεται πλείονα, οὐχ ὥσπερ οἱ κλητικοὶ ἐλάττονα. ἐν μὲν γὰρ τοῖς ὅτι τάχιστα ἡμῖν συνεῖναι τοὺς θεοὺς βουλόμεθα, ἐν δὲ τοῖς ὅτι βραδύτατα ἀπαλλάττεσθαι. ἀνάγκη δὲ εἶναι καὶ εὐχὴν ἐπὶ ἐπανόδῳ καὶ ἐπιδημίᾳ δευτέρᾳ. ταῦτά σοι [καὶ] περὶ ἀποπεμπτικῶν ὕμνων εἰρήσθω.

Schol. Callim. *Hymn.* 4. 28 (ii 67 Pfeiffer) (λίην πολέες σε — sc. Delum — περιτροχόωσιν ἀοιδαί)· αἱ Πινδάρου καὶ Βακχυλίδου.

fr. 1B P.Oxy. 2366. 3–8

ΕΙ[Σ ΕΚΑΤΗΝ

  Ἑκάτα [δαϊδοφόρε
  ταν ἱε[ρ
  Νυκ[τὸς μεγαλοκόλπου θύγατερ,
  σὺ κα[
5 βα . [
  . . .

suppl. ed. pr. (Lobel) e schol. Ap. Rhod.

252

BACCHYLIDES

Menander, *On Display Oratory*

Apopemptic hymns (i.e. hymns of farewell) are like some of those found in Bacchylides and contain a valediction since someone is leaving his country . . .

Apopemptic hymns, as the name shows, are the opposite of hymns of invocation[1]; the type is very rare, found only in the poets. They are performed at the departures, imagined or real,[2] of gods, for example at the so-called departures of Apollo in Delos and Miletus and of Artemis in Argos. Bacchylides has apopemptic hymns. Hymns of this kind have as their basic material the land or cities or peoples which the god is leaving behind, and similarly the city or land to which he is going, descriptions of places and suchlike. The text must run pleasantly along, since one should see travellers off in a relaxed, happy style. One may dwell longer on the topics: in hymns of invocation one spends less time on them, since we want the gods to join us as quickly as possible; but in apopemptic hymns we want them to take as long as possible over their departure. There must be a prayer for a return on a second visit. So much for apopemptic hymns.

[1] See Sa. test. 47, Alcm. 55.   [2] In effigy.

Scholiast on Callimachus, *Hymn to Delos* ('very many songs encompass you'): those of Pindar and Bacchylides.

fr. 1B Oxyrhynchus papyrus (2nd or 3rd c. A.D.)

TO HECATE

Torch-bearing Hecate, . . . holy . . . , daughter of great-bosomed[1] Night, you . . .

[1] Ursinus conjectured 'black-bosomed'.

GREEK LYRIC

Schol. Ap. Rhod. 3. 467 (p. 233 Wendel)

Βακχυλίδης δὲ Νυκτός φησιν αὐτὴν (sc. Hecaten) θυγατέρα·
Ἑκάτα δαϊδοφόρε, Νυκτὸς μεγαλοκόλπου (μελανο- ci. Ursinus)
θύγατερ.

fr. 2 Stob. 4. 54. 1 (v 1113 Hense) (περὶ πένθους)

Βακχυλίδου " Υμνων·

αἰαῖ τέκος ἁμέτερον,
μεῖζον ἢ πενθεῖν ἐφάνη κακόν, ἀφθέγκτοισιν ἶσον.

fr. 3 Schol. Ar. *Ach.* 47 (p. 14 Wilson)

τοῦ δὲ Κελεοῦ μέμνηται Βακχυλίδης διὰ τῶν " Υμνων.

ΠΑΙΑΝΕΣ

fr. 4 Athen. 5. 178b (i 409 Kaibel) (vv. 21–25) + P.Oxy.
426 (vv. 39–70) + Stob. 4. 14. 3 (iv 371s. Hense) (περὶ
εἰρήνης) (vv. 61–80) + Plut. *Num.* 20 (iii 2. 81 Ziegler) (vv.
69–77)

[ΑΠΟΛΛΩΝΙ ΠΥΘΑΙΕΙ ΕΙΣ ΑΣΙΝΗΝ]

21   στᾶ δ' ἐπὶ λάϊνον οὐ-
        δόν, τοὶ δὲ θοίνας ἔντυον, ὧδέ τ' ἔφα·
    ' αὐτόματοι δ' ἀγαθῶν

v. W. S. Barrett, *Hermes* 82 (1954) 421ss.   21–25 B. δὲ περὶ Ἡρα-
κλέους λέγων ὡς ἦλθεν ἐπὶ τὸν τοῦ Κήυκος οἶκον φησίν· ἔστη ... φῶτες
(Athen.)   21 Barrett: ἔστη codd.   22 Neue: ἔντυνον, ἔφασ' codd.

BACCHYLIDES

Scholiast on Apollonius of Rhodes ('daughter of Perses', i.e. Hecate)

Bacchylides calls her Night's daughter: 'Torch-bearing Hecate, daughter of great-bosomed Night'.

fr. 2 Stobaeus, *Anthology* (on mourning)

Bacchylides, *Hymns*:

Alas, my child,[1] an evil has come too great for mourning, like those that cannot be mentioned.

[1] Demeter to Persephone? See fr. 3 n. 1.

fr. 3 Scholiast on Aristophanes, *Acharnians* ('Celeüs')[1]

Celeüs is mentioned by Bacchylides in his *Hymns*.

[1] Mythical king of Eleusis, whose wife welcomed the disguised Demeter; perhaps mentioned in a hymn to Demeter: cf. fr. 47.

PAEANS

fr. 4 Athenaeus, *Scholars at Dinner* (vv. 21–25) + Oxyrhynchus papyrus (3rd c. A.D.) (vv. 39–70) + Stobaeus, *Anthology* (on peace) (vv. 61–80) + Plutarch, *Numa* (vv. 69–77)

FOR APOLLO PYTHAIEUS AT ASINE

. . . he[1] halted at the stone threshold as they were preparing a feast,[2] and he spoke thus: 'Just men

[1] 'B., telling how Heracles went to the house of Ceÿx, says ...' (Athen.). Ceÿx, Heracles' cousin, was king at Trachis. [2] Hesiod composed 'The Wedding feast of Ceÿx' (frr. 263–269 M.-W.).

<ἐς> δαῖτας εὐόχθους ἐπέρχονται δίκαιοι
25 φῶτες.'

desunt vv. xiii aut xliii

        ]τα Πυθω[
40   ]ει τελευτ[

κείνους] κέλευσεν Φοῖβος ['Αλ-
   κμήνας] πολεμαίνετον υ[ίόν
στέλλεν] ἐκ ναοῦ τε καὶ παρ' [ὀμφαλοῦ·
    τᾶ]ιδ' ἐνὶ χώρα<ι>
45   ]χισεν †ταν φυλλο . [
   στ]ρέψας ἐλαίας
   σ]φ' 'Ασινεῖς
   κά]λεσσ'· ἐν δὲ χρόν[ωι
   ]ες ἐξ 'Αλικῶν τε . [
50 μάντι]ς ἐξ "Αργευς Μελάμ[πους

ἦλ]θ' 'Αμυθαονίδας
βω]μόν τε Πυθα<ι>εῖ κτίσε[
καὶ] τέμενος ζάθεον.
κείν]ας ἀπὸ ρίζας τόδε χρ[
55 ἐξό]χως τίμασ' 'Απόλλων
ἄλσο]ς, ἵν' ἀγλαΐαι

24 <ἐς> Barrett   41, 42 init. Barrett   υ[ίόν Edmonds   43 Barrett   44 ἀλλ' ὅ γε τᾶ]ιδ' Snell   46, 47 Barrett   48 Lobel

arrive unbidden at the plentiful banquets of the good.'[1]

13 or 43 lines are missing [2]

... Pytho ... end ... Phoebus ordered the battle-famed (son[3] of Alcmena to convey them) from the temple and (the earth's navel?), (and he settled them?) in (this?) land[4] ... (leaf?) ... when he had twisted olive-trees,[5] (he called them) Asinaeans[6]; and in time ... from the men of Halieis[7] ... (the seer) Melampus, son of Amythaon, (came) from Argos and founded an altar for Pythaieus[8] and a holy sanctuary. From that root (came) this (pre-cinct), and Apollo gave it exceptional honour, a place

---

[1] There were two forms of the proverb: 'good men ... banquets of the good' and 'good men ... banquets of cowards'; see Athen. *loc. cit.*, Zenobius Ath. 1. 15 (Miller, *Mélanges* 350), Cratinus 182 and Eupolis 315 K.-A., Plato, *Symp.* 174b with scholiast.   [2] They will have told how Heracles was entertained by Ceÿx, went south to defeat the Dryopes, a people of central Greece, and dedicated them at Delphi.   [3] Apollo told Heracles to remove the Dryopes from Delphi and settle them at Asine, S.E. of Argos.   [4] Asine.   [5] Or 'an olive-tree'; Pausanias 2. 28. 2 mentions the Twisted Olive, said to have been bent by Heracles to mark the boundary between Asine and Epidaurus.   [6] In popular etymology, 'those who do no harm'.   [7] 20 miles S.E. of Asine.   [8] Cult name of Apollo.

---

50 init. Snell	fin. edd. prr. (Grenfell-Hunt)	51 Edmonds
52 Blass	<ι> Snell 53–55 Blass	56 Snell
57 init. Barrett	fin. Blass	

τ' ἀνθ]εῦσ[ι] καὶ μολπαὶ λίγ[ειαι·
　　]ονες, ὦ ἄνα, τ . . [
　　]τι, σὺ δ' ὄλ[βον ὀπάζοις
60　　]ναιοισιν[

τίκτει δέ τε θνατοῖσιν εἰ-
　　ρήνα μεγαλάνορα πλοῦτον
καὶ μελιγλώσσων ἀοιδᾶν ἄνθεα
δαιδαλέων τ' ἐπὶ βωμῶν
65 θεοῖσιν αἴθεσθαι βοῶν ξανθᾶι φλογί
μηρί' εὐμάλλων τε μήλων
γυμνασίων τε νέοις
αὐλῶν τε καὶ κώμων μέλειν.
ἐν δὲ σιδαροδέτοις πόρπαξιν αἰθᾶν
70 ἀραχνᾶν ἱστοὶ πέλονται,

ἔγχεα τε λογχωτὰ ξίφεα
　　τ' ἀμφάκεα δάμναται εὐρώς.
<
　　　　　　　>
75 χαλκεᾶν δ' οὐκ ἔστι σαλπίγγων κτύπος,
οὐδὲ συλᾶται μελίφρων
ὕπνος ἀπὸ βλεφάρων
ἀῷος ὃς θάλπει κέαρ.
συμποσίων δ' ἐρατῶν βρίθοντ' ἀγυιαί,
80 παιδικοί θ' ὕμνοι φλέγονται.

desunt vv. x

where festivities blossom and clear songs; . . . , lord,
. . . ; grant prosperity (and quiet?) to . . .

Peace gives birth to noble wealth for mortals, to
the flowers of honey-tongued songs, to the burning
for gods of thighs of oxen and fleecy sheep in yellow
flame on elaborate altars, to young men's concern
with the gymnasium, with pipes and revelry. On
iron-pinned shieldgrips are found the spinnings of
red-brown spiders, and sharp-pointed spears and
double-edged swords are subdued by rust.

2 lines are missing

There is no din of bronze trumpets, and sleep, honey
for the mind, still soothing the heart at daybreak, is
not pillaged from men's eyelids. The streets are
laden with lovely feasts, and the songs of boys[1] rise
like flame.[2]

[1] Or 'songs in praise of boys'.   [2] The paean ended after 10
more lines.

58s. τᾶν αἴμ]ονες . . . Τρ[οζηνίων σε κοῦροι | κλείζον]τι tent. Bar-
rett   59 fin. Snell   62 εἰρήνη μεγάλα πλ. Stob.   66 Barrett:
μηρίταν εὐτρίχων Stob.   75 χαλκέων δ' οὐκέτι Stob.   78 Blass:
ἇμος (ἆμος) Stob.

fr. 5 Clem. Alex. *Strom.* 5. 68. 5 (ii 372 Stählin)

ἕτερος ἐξ ἑτέρου σοφός
τό τε πάλαι τό τε νῦν,

φησὶ Βακχυλίδης ἐν τοῖς Παιᾶσιν. οὐδὲ γὰρ ῥᾷστον
ἀρρήτων ἐπέων πύλας
ἐξευρεῖν.

cf. Theodoret. *Gr. Aff.* 1. 78 (p. 23 Raeder) (οὐδὲ . . . ἐξευρεῖν)

1 ἕτερος δὲ ἐξ Clem.

fr. 6 Zenob. *Cent.* 2. 36 (i 42 Leutsch-Schneidewin)

ἄρκτου παρούσης ἴχνη μὴ ζήτει· ἐπὶ τῶν δειλῶν κυνηγῶν
εἴρηται ἡ παροιμία. μέμνηται δὲ αὐτῆς Βακχυλίδης ἐν Παιᾶσιν.

ΔΙΘΥΡΑΜΒΟΙ

fr. 7 Schol. Pind. *Pyth.* 1. 100 (ii 18s. Drachmann)

τῇ ἱστορίᾳ καὶ Βακχυλίδης συμφωνεῖ ἐν τοῖς διθυράμβοις, ὅτι δὴ
οἱ Ἕλληνες ἐκ Λήμνου μετεστείλαντο τὸν Φιλοκτήτην Ἑλένου
μαντευσαμένου. εἵμαρτο γὰρ ἄνευ τῶν Ἡρακλείων τόξων μὴ πορ-
θηθῆναι τὴν Ἴλιον.

fr. 8 Serv. in Verg. *Aen.* 11. 93 (ii 488 Thilo-Hagen)
(versis Arcades armis)

lugentum more mucronem hastae, non cuspidem contra
terram tenentes, quoniam antiqui nostri omnia contraria
in funere faciebant, scuta etiam invertentes propter
numina illic depicta, ne eorum simulacra cadaveris pol-
luerentur aspectu, sicut habuisse Arcades Bacchylides in
dithyrambis dicit.

fr. 5 Clement of Alexandria, *Miscellanies*

One gets his skill[1] from another, now as in days of old,

says Bacchylides in his *Paeans*; for it is no easy matter

to discover the gates of verse unspoken before.

[1] I.e. his poetic skill; B. may be answering Pindar's claim (*Ol.* 2. 86 ff.), 'the skilled man is he who knows much by the gift of nature: those who learned . . . utter idle words.'

fr. 6 Zenobius, *Proverbs*

'Don't look for a bear's tracks when it is nearby.' The proverb is used of cowardly hunters. It is mentioned by Bacchylides in his *Paeans*.

DITHYRAMBS

fr. 7 Scholiast on Pindar, *Pythian* 1. 52

Bacchylides in his *Dithyrambs* agrees with this story, that the Greeks removed Philoctetes from Lemnos in accordance with a prophecy of Helenus, since it was fated that without Heracles' bow[1] Troy would not be sacked.

[1] Which he had bequeathed to Philoctetes.

fr. 8 Servius on Virgil, *Aeneid* ('the Arcadians with arms reversed')

in the manner of mourners, holding the point of the spear, not the butt, to the ground; for at a funeral our ancestors always observed the opposite of their usual practice, reversing their shields also, so that the likenesses of the deities depicted on them would not be polluted by the sight of a corpse; Bacchylides in his *Dithyrambs* says the Arcadians held them like that.

GREEK LYRIC

fr. 9 Serv. in Verg. *Aen.* 2. 201 (ii 377s. edit. Harvard.)

sane Bacchylides de Laocoonte et uxore eius vel de serpentibus a Calydnis insulis venientibus atque in homines conversis dicit.

fr. 10 Schol. AB Hom. *Il.* 12. 292 (i 427, iii 506 Dindorf)

Εὐρώπην τὴν Φοίνικος Ζεὺς θεασάμενος ἔν τινι λειμῶνι μετὰ νυμφῶν ἄνθη ἀναλέγουσαν ἠράσθη, καὶ κατελθὼν ἤλλαξεν ἑαυτὸν εἰς ταῦρον καὶ ἀπὸ τοῦ στόματος κρόκον ἔπνει· οὕτως τε τὴν Εὐρώπην ἀπατήσας ἐβάστασε, καὶ διαπορθμεύσας εἰς Κρήτην ἐμίγη αὐτῇ. εἶθ᾽ οὕτως συνῴκισεν αὐτὴν Ἀστερίωνι τῷ Κρητῶν βασιλεῖ. γενομένη δὲ ἔγκυος ἐκείνη τρεῖς παῖδας ἐγέννησε Μίνωα Σαρπηδόνα καὶ Ῥαδάμανθυν. ἡ ἱστορία παρ᾽ Ἡσιόδῳ (fr. 141 M.-W.) καὶ Βακχυλίδῃ.

ΠΡΟΣΟΔΙΑ

frr. 11 + 12 Stob. 4. 44. 16 + 46 (v 962, 969 Hense) (ὅτι δεῖ γενναίως φέρειν τὰ προσπίπτοντα κτλ)

Βακχυλίδου Προσοδίων·

(11) εἷς ὅρος, μία βροτοῖσίν ἐστιν εὐτυχίας ὁδός,
  θυμὸν εἴ τις ἔχων ἀπενθῆ δύναται
  διατελεῖν βίον· ὃς δὲ μυ-
  ρία μὲν ἀμφιπολεῖ φρενί,
5 τὸ δὲ παρ᾽ ἆμάρ τε <καὶ> νύκτα μελλόντων
  χάριν αἰὲν ἰάπτεται
  κέαρ, ἄκαρπον ἔχει πόνον.

(11) cf. Stob. 3. 1. 12 (iii 6s. Hense), Apostol. 6. 55f (ii 379 Leutsch-Schneidewin) (εἷς ... βίον) 3 Grotius: οἷς codd. 5 Grotius: παρόμαρτε codd. 6 Boeckh: αονι ἄπτεται codd.

BACCHYLIDES

fr. 9 Servius on Virgil ('Laocoon')

Bacchylides certainly speaks of Laocoon and his wife and of the serpents coming from the Calydnae islands and turning into men.

fr. 10 Scholiast on *Iliad* (Sarpedon, son of Zeus)

Zeus caught sight of Europa, daughter of Phoenix, gathering flowers with young girls in a meadow, and fell in love; coming down, he changed himself into a bull and breathed the scent of saffron from his mouth. Tricking Europa by these means he took her on his back, carried her over the sea to Crete and had intercourse with her there. Then he gave her in marriage to Asterion, king of Crete; but she was pregnant and gave birth to three sons, Minos, Sarpedon and Rhadamanthys. The story is in Hesiod[1] and Bacchylides.[2]

[1] Fr. 141 M.-W.   [2] Cf. 17. 29 ff.

PROCESSIONALS

frr. 11 + 12[1] Stobaeus, *Anthology* (on the need to bear our lot nobly)

Bacchylides, *Processionals*

(11) There is one guideline,[2] one path to happiness for mortals: to be able to keep an ungrieving spirit throughout life. The man who busies his mind with a thousand cares, whose heart is hurt day and night for the sake of the future, has fruitless toil.

[1] The two passages are likely to belong to the same poem.
[2] Literally, 'boundary-mark'.

(12) τί γὰρ ἐλαφρὸν ἔτ᾽ ἐστὶν ἄ-
   πρακτ᾽ ὀδυρόμενον δονεῖν
   καρδίαν;

(12) 1 Blass: ἔτ᾽ ἔστ᾽ codd.

fr. 13 Stob. 4. 34. 24 (v 833 Hense) (περὶ τοῦ βίου, ὅτι βραχὺς καὶ εὐτελὴς καὶ φροντίδων ἀνάμεστος)

   Βακχυλίδου Προσοδίων·
   πάντεσσι <γὰρ> θνατοῖσι δαί-
      μων ἐπέταξε πόνους ἄλλοισιν ἄλλους.

1 <γὰρ> vel <δὲ> Snell

ΠΑΡΘΕΝΕΙΑ

[Plut.] *Mus.* 17. 1136f (p. 118 Lasserre, vi 3. 14 Ziegler)

   οὐκ ἠγνόει (sc. Πλάτων) δ᾽ ὅτι πολλὰ Δώρια παρθένεια 〚ἄλλα〛 Ἀλκμᾶνι καὶ Πινδάρῳ καὶ Σιμωνίδῃ καὶ Βακχυλίδῃ πεποίηται, ἀλλὰ μὴν καὶ ὅτι προσόδια καὶ παιᾶνες.

(12) For what relief is there any longer in buffeting one's heart with useless lamentation?

fr. 13 Stobaeus, *Anthology* (that life is short, worthless and full of cares)

Bacchylides, *Processionals*

(since) for all mortals God ordained toils, these for one, those for another.

MAIDEN-SONGS

'Plutarch', *On Music*

Plato was well aware that many maiden-songs in the Dorian mode were composed by Alcman, Pindar, Simonides and Bacchylides, in addition to processionals and paeans.

ΥΠΟΡΧΗΜΑΤΑ

fr. 14 Stob. 3. 11. 19 (iii 432s. Hense) (περὶ ἀληθείας)

Βακχυλίδου Ὑπορχημάτων·
   Λυδία μὲν γὰρ λίθος
   μανύει χρυσόν, ἀν-
      δρῶν δ' ἀρετὰν σοφία τε
   παγκρατής τ' ἐλέγχει
5 ἀλάθεια. . . .

cf. gemmam ap. Caylus, *Rec. d'Ant.* v tab. 50.4   1 μὲν γὰρ om.
gemma   3 σοφίαν codd. L, Br   5 ἀληθ- Stob.   ἀλαθ- gemma

fr. 15 Dion. Hal. *Comp.* 25 (vi 131 Usener-Radermacher)

τοῦτο γὰρ ἔοικεν . . . τῷ παρὰ Βακχυλίδῃ·
   οὐχ ἕδρας ἔργον οὐδ' ἀμβολᾶς,
   ἀλλὰ χρυσαίγιδος Ἰτωνίας
   χρὴ παρ' εὐδαίδαλον ναὸν ἐλ-
      θόντας ἁβρόν τι δεῖξαι <μέλος>.

4 suppl. Blass   ἀδρόν Borthwick

Athen. 14. 631c (iii 393 Kaibel)

   ἡ δ' ὑπορχηματική ἐστιν ἐν ᾗ ᾄδων ὁ χορὸς ὀρχεῖται. φησὶ γοῦν
ὁ Βακχυλίδης· οὐχ ἕδρας ἔργον οὐδ' ἀμβολᾶς.

BACCHYLIDES

DANCE-SONGS

fr. 14 Stobaeus, *Anthology* (on truth)

Bacchylides, *Dance-songs*

For as the Lydian stone[1] indicates gold, so men's excellence is proved by the poet's skill and all-powerful truth.

[1] The touchstone. A slightly shortened version of the lines was inscribed on a touchstone, now lost: see Daremberg-Saglio 1/2.1548 (s.v. *coticula*).

fr. 15 Dionysius of Halicarnassus, *On Literary Composition* (on cretics)[1]

This[2] resembles (in its rhythm) the passage[3] in Bacchylides:

This is no time for sitting or delaying[4]: we must go to the richly-built temple of Itonia[5] of the golden aegis and display a delicate (song? dance?).

[1] A grammarian in Keil, *Anal. Gramm.* 7. 21 says that dance-songs are often in cretic rhythm and quotes v. 1. [2] A passage from the beginning of Demosthenes, *De Corona*. [3] The opening words of the song. [4] The line became proverbial: Aelian, *Hist. Anim.* 6. 1, Lucian, *Scyth.* 11, Achilles Tatius 5. 12. [5] Title of Athena in Thessaly, Boeotia and Amorgos; see fr. 15A, Alc. 325.

Athenaeus, *Scholars at Dinner*

The hyporchematic (i.e. dance-song) is one in which the chorus dances while it sings. Bacchylides at any rate says, 'This is no time for sitting or delaying.'

GREEK LYRIC

fr. 15A Lactant. ad Stat. *Theb.* 7. 330s. (p. 361 Jahnke) (ducit Itonaeos et Alalcomenaea Minervae | agmina)

in qua Itonus regnavit, Herculis filius; haec civitas Boeotiae est. hinc Bacchylides Minervam Itoniam dixit (fr. 15) et Alchomenem ('Ἀλαλκομενίην Snell) significavit.

cf. Steph. Byz. (p. 69 Meineke) 'Ἀλαλκομενία ἡ 'Ἀθηνᾶ ἐκεῖ τιμᾶται.

fr. 16 Heph. *Ench.* 13. 7 (p. 42 Consbruch)

δεδηλώσθω δὲ ὅτι καὶ ὅλα ᾄσματα κρητικὰ συντίθεται, ὥσπερ καὶ παρὰ Βακχυλίδῃ·

> ὦ περίκλειτε Δᾶλ᾽, ἀγνοή-
> σειν μὲν οὔ σ᾽ ἔλπομαι

1 Blass: δ᾽ ἀλλ᾽ codd.   ὦ Π., δῆλ᾽ Wilamowitz   τἀλλ᾽ Bergk

ΕΡΩΤΙΚΑ

Apul. *Apol.* 9 (p. 10 Helm)

fecere tamen et alii talia . . . : apud Graecos Teius quidam et Lacedaemonius et Cius (Bosscha: civis cod., Ceius Helm) cum aliis innumeris, etiam mulier Lesbia . . .

---

1 Anacreon.   2 Alcman.   3 Bacchylides: Simonides is not known to have written love-songs.   4 Sappho test. 48.

268

BACCHYLIDES

fr. 15A Lactantius Placidus on Statius, *Thebaid* ('he leads Itonaeans and the Alalcomenaean ranks of Minerva')

A city in Boeotia, ruled by Itonus, son of Hercules; whence Bacchylides called Minerva (i.e. Athena) Itonia[1] and named her

Alalcomenian.[2]

[1] See fr. 15.　　[2] From the Boeotian town of Alalcomenae; see *Il.* 4. 8, Paus. 9. 33. 4–34. 1, Steph. Byz. s.v. Ἀλαλκομένιον, K. Lehmann, *Hesperia* 28 (1959) 158. Perhaps B.'s poem was for performance at the Pamboeotic festival held in the sanctuary of Athena Itonia at Coroneia.

fr. 16 Hephaestion, *Handbook on Metres*

Let it be clear that whole songs are composed in cretics, as in Bacchylides:

Far-famed Delos, I do not expect that you will be ignorant . . .[1]

[1] Beginning of a poem, assigned to the Dance-songs by Neue because of the metre: see fr. 15 n. 1. Text uncertain: with Wilamowitz's emendation, 'Pericleitus, I do not expect that you will be ignorant of what is clear'; with Bergk's, 'Pericleitus, I do not expect that you will be ignorant of the rest, (but I shall tell you this)'.

LOVE-SONGS

Apuleius, *Apology*

Yet others too have composed such things (i.e. amatory verse) . . . : among the Greeks a Teian,[1] a Lacedaemonian[2] and a Ceian[3] along with countless others, and a woman[4] of Lesbos too . . .

269

fr. 17 Athen. 15. 667c (iii 475 Kaibel)

ἐκάλουν δ' ἀπ' ἀγκύλης τὴν τοῦ κοττάβου πρόεσιν διὰ τὸ ἐπαγκυλοῦν τὴν δεξιὰν χεῖρα ἐν τοῖς ἀποκοτταβισμοῖς. οἱ δὲ ποτηρίου εἶδος τὴν ἀγκύλην φασί. Βακχυλίδης ἐν Ἐρωτικοῖς·

<blockquote>
εὖτε
τὴν ἀπ' ἀγκύλης ἵησι τοῖσδε τοῖς νεανίαις
λευκὸν ἀντείνασα πῆχυν.
</blockquote>

cf. epitom. 11. 782e (iii 20 Kaibel)   2 τοῖσδε om. epitom.   3 ἐντείνουσα epitom.

fr. 18 Heph. *Poem.* 7. 3 (p. 71 Consbruch)

ἔστι δέ τινα καὶ τὰ καλούμενα ἐπιφθεγματικά, ἃ διαφέρει ταύτῃ τῶν ἐφυμνίων, ὅτι τὰ μὲν ⟦ἐφύμνια⟧ καὶ πρὸς νοῦν συντελεῖ τι, τὰ δὲ ⟦ἐπιφθεγματικὰ⟧ ἐκ περιττοῦ ὡς πρὸς τὸ λεγόμενον τῇ στροφῇ πρόσκειται· οἷον τὸ Βακχυλίδου·

<blockquote>
ἦ καλὸς Θεόκριτος·
οὐ μοῦνος ἀνθρώπων ὁρᾷς,
</blockquote>

καὶ πάλιν (v. fr. 19).

2 Wilamowitz: μόνος codd.   ὁρᾷς Ursinus

fr. 19 Heph. *Poem.* 7. 3 (p. 71 Consbruch) + P.Oxy. 2361

. . . καὶ πάλιν (v. fr. 18) παρὰ τῷ αὐτῷ Βακχυλίδῃ· σὺ . . . φεύγεις.

Pap. fr. 1   σὺ δὲ σ]ὺν χιτῶνι μούνωι
παρὰ τ]ὴν φίλην γυναῖκα φεύγ[ε]ις.

1 σὺ δ' ἐν χ. Heph.

BACCHYLIDES

fr. 17 Athenaeus, *Scholars at Dinner*

They used the term ἀπ' ἀγκύλης, 'from bent wrist', of the cottabus throw[1] since they bent the right wrist in the throws[2]; others say that ἀγκύλη is not the bent wrist but a kind of cup. Cf. Bacchylides in his *Love-songs*:

when she[3] makes the throw from bent wrist for these young men, raising her white arm.

[1] Drinkers aimed the last drops of the cup into a dish; see Alc. 322, Anacr. 415.   [2] See E. K. Borthwick, *J.H.S.* 84 (1964) 51 f.
[3] A hetaera or piper at a party.

fr. 18 Hephaestion, *On Poems*

There are also the so-called 'epiphthegmatic' refrains, which differ from the 'ephymnia' in that they make a contribution to the sense, whereas the others are added superfluously to the strophe as far as the meaning goes[1]; there are examples in Bacchylides:

Theocritus is indeed beautiful: you are not the only one to see it;

and again (fr. 19).

[1] E.g. the cry 'O Dithyrambus!'

fr. 19 Hephaestion, *On Poems* (cont.)

. . . and again, also in Bacchylides: 'and you . . . wife'.

Oxyrhynchus papyrus (*c.* 200 A.D.)

. . . ; and you wearing only your tunic run away to your dear wife.

$$]ι\ μάχαις$$
$$]$$
5    $]οι.\ [\ .\ ]ί[$ $]s$
.....$]απατ[η]ς\ καὶ\ ψίθυ[ρος$
   $ἐπ]ίορκος·$
$σὺ\ δὲ\ σὺ]ν\ χιτῶνι\ μούν[ωι$
$παρὰ\ τ]ὴν\ φίλην\ γυ[ναῖκ]α\ φεύγεις.$

6 ξειν]απάτης Lobel 6s. ψίθυρος | τε κἀπίορκος Lobel 8 σὺ δ' ἐν χ. Heph. fr. 2 (schol.) πωδ[

<ΕΓΚΩΜΙΑ> *vel* <ΣΚΟΛΙΑ>?

fr. 20A P.Oxy. 1361 frr. 5 al. + 2081 (e)

     $κ]αθημένη$
5   $]νο[\ .\ ]π[$ $]μας$
    $]καὶ\ ὑπέρ[μορ'\ ἄχθε]ται\ πατρί,$

$ἱκ[ε]τεύει\ δὲ\ κα[μοῦσα$
$χ[θ]ονίας\ τάλαι[ν'\ Ἀρὰς]\ ὀ$-
$ξ[ύ]τερόν\ νιν\ τελ[έσαι$
10 $γῆρας\ καὶ\ κατάρατ[ον,\ ὅστ'\ εἴργει\ κόρη]ν$
$μούνην\ ἔνδον\ ἔχω[ν\ γάμων,$
$λε]υκαὶ\ δ'\ ἐν\ [κ]εφαλ[ῆι\ γενήσονται\ τ]ρίχες.$

5 δέ]μας Snell 6 Snell 7 ἱκετ. H. Fränkel καμ. Snell
8 fin., 9 Maas 10, 11 Kapp 12 init. ed. pr. (Hunt), cet. Snell schol. ὑπὸ πατρὸς ἐν[

. . . in battles . . . deceiver (of host?) and slanderer (and) perjurer; and you wearing only your tunic run away to your dear wife.[1]

[1] Dialect, metre and content point to Anacreon rather than B.; see H. Lloyd-Jones, *C.R.* 72 (1958) 17. The scholiast on the poem seems to refer to Pindar.

ENCOMIA *or* SCOLIA[1]

fr. 20A Oxyrhynchus papyrus (1st c. A.D.)

. . . she, sitting (at home?) . . . and is exceedingly angry with her father, and (in her affliction?) she makes supplication to the nether-world Curses, poor wretch, that he complete a bitter and accursed old age for keeping his daughter alone indoors and (preventing her from marrying), although the hair (will turn) white on her head.

[1] Title of this group (20A–20G) uncertain: encomia are poems in praise of individuals, scolia are drinking-songs; fr. 20A does not seem to be either but rather an attack on a father who refuses to marry off his daughter; see B. Snell, *Hermes* 80 (1952) 156 ff.

Ἄρ]εος χρυσολόφου παῖ-
    δα] λέγουσι χαλκ[[ε]]ομίτραν
15 τα]νυπέπλοιο κόρης
Εὐ]εανὸ[ν] θρασύχειρα καὶ μιαι[φόνο]ν
Μ]αρπήσσης καλυκώπιδος
    τοι]οῦτον πατέρ' ἔμμεν'· ἀλλά ν[ιν] χρόνος

ἐδά]μασσε κρατερά τ' ἔκ-
20 δικος ο]ὐ θέλοντ' ἀνάγκη[[ι]].
        ἀ]ελίου
        ]εν Ποσειδαωνίας
ἵππους ὠκυδρόμ]ας ἐλαύ-
    νων Ἴδας Ἀφάρ]ητος ὄλβιον τέκος.

25 ἐθέλουσαν δ]ὲ κόρην ἥρ-
    πασεν εὐέθει]ραν ἥρως
        ]του
    κ]αλλικρηδέμνου θεᾶς
        ]
30   καλλίσφυρον   ὠ]κὺς ἄγγελος

        ]αν εὖτ' | ἔμολεν

desunt vv. 32–35; vv. 36–42 frr. exigua exstant

13 Snell   13s. παῖδα Maas, Snell   14 χαλκο- Snell   15, 16, 18
Hunt   19 Hunt, Snell   schol. Πτολ(εμαῖος)· καρτε[ρ
]ε̣ι̣ν̣   20 init. Snell   ἀνάγκη H. Fränkel   22 τέλλοντος πέλασ]εν
e.g. Snell   Snell: -δαονίας pap.   23s. Snell   24 Ἀ. Maas
25 ἐθ. Maas   δ]ὲ Snell   25s. ἥρπασε ed. pr.   εὐέθ. Maas
30 καλλ. e schol. κ[α]λλισφύραν Diehl   38 fin.]πόσιν

274

Such a father, they say, was the bronze-belted
son of gold-crested Ares, Euenus,[1] bold of hand and
murderous,[2] to his long-robed daughter, bud-eyed
Marpessa; but time subdued him and strong[3] aveng-
ing necessity against his will: (as the sun rose?)
(came Idas), prosperous son of Aphares, driving the
(swift-racing mares) of Poseidon[4]; and the hero car-
ried off the (beautiful-haired) girl, (as she wished,)
(from the sanctuary?) of the lovely-veiled goddess[5]
...; when a swift messenger came (to report that)
the lovely-ankled (girl had been taken) ... hus-
band(?) band(?)...

[1] See 20 n. 1.   [2] See 20 n. 3.   [3] A marginal note gives
an interpretation by Ptolemaeus: see test. 11 n. 1.   [4] See 20
with n. 4.   [5] Artemis: see schol. D on *Iliad* 9. 557 (Idas car-
ried off the girl as she was dancing in the sanctuary of Artemis).

43 π[ατέρ' ἡ μ]αινόλις ἄκρο[ι'
        ἀπ' ὄ[ρεος   ]ν κατ[ῶσεν
45 θυγατ[   ]νο[
     Μαρ[πησσ   ]ς· ὑπ[
     ξα[νθ   ]σαισ[
      ἐμ[   ]τνο[
          viii versuum vestigia

43–47 Snell

fr. 20B P.Oxy. 1361 frr. 1 al. + Athen. *epitom*. 2. 10
(p. 39ef, i 92 Kaibel) (vv. 6–16)

[ΑΛΕΞΑ]Ν[ΔΡΩΙ ΑΜΥΝΤ]Α

ὦ βάρβιτε, μηκέτι πάσσαλον φυλάς[σων
ἑπτάτονον λ[ι]γυρὰν κάππαυε γᾶρυν·
δεῦρ' ἐς ἐμὰς χέρας· ὁρμαίνω τι πέμπ[ειν
χρύσεον Μουσᾶν 'Αλεξάνδρωι πτερόν

5 καὶ συμποσ[ίαι]σιν ἄγαλμ' [ἐν] εἰκάδεσ[σιν,
εὖτε νέων ἀ[παλὸν γλυκεῖ' ἀ]νάγκα
σευομενᾶν κ[υλίκων θάλπη]σι θυμ[όν,
Κύπριδος τ' ἐλπ[ὶς <δι>αιθύσσηι φρέ]νας,

ἀμμειγνυμέν[α Διονυσίοισι] δώροις·
10 ἀνδράσι δ' ὑψο[τάτω πέμπει] μερίμν[ας·
αὐτίκ[α] μὲν π[ολίων κράδε]μνα λ[ύει,
πᾶσ[ι δ' ἀνθρώποις μοναρ]χῆσ[ειν δοκεῖ·

5 -σ[ίαι]σιν Maas   -σ[ίοι]σιν edd. prr. (Grenfell, Hunt)   fin. edd.
prr.   6 Maas: ἀ[ταλὸν Erbse   7 σευομενα Athen.   -πη]ισι pap.

276

... his furious (anger) thrust her father from the top (of the bank?) (into the river?)[1] ... his daughter Marpessa ... blonde ...[2]

[1] See Simon. 563: Euenus drowned in the river Lycormas, which thereafter took his name.   [2] There are tiny fragments of 8 more lines; length of poem unknown; it may well have begun with v. 1.

fr. 20B Oxyrhynchus papyrus (1st c. A.D.) + Athenaeus, *Scholars at Dinner*[1]

FOR ALEXANDER,[2] SON OF AMYNTAS

My lyre, cling to your peg no longer, silencing your clear voice with its seven notes. Come to my hands! I am eager to send Alexander a golden wing of the Muses, an adornment for banquets at the month's end, when the sweet compulsion of the speeding cups warms the tender hearts of the young men, and hope of the Cyprian, mingling with the gifts of Dionysus, makes their hearts flutter. The wine sends a man's thoughts soaring on high: immediately he is destroying the battlements of cities, and he expects to be monarch over all the

[1] Athenaeus quotes vv. 6–16 to illustrate the ability of wine to change a man's thinking and turn it towards unreality.   [2] King of Macedonia from 498 to 454.

ante corr., Athen.   8 Κυπρ. ἐλπὶς δ' αἰθύσσει Athen.   <δι>
Erfurdt, Barrett   -θύσσῃ Blass   9 Dindorf (ἀμμιγ.): ἆ μειγ. pap.
ἀναμιγ. Athen.   10 ἀνδράσιν ὑψ. pap.   11 αὐτὰς, αὐτὴ Athen.

χρυ[σ]ῶι [δ' ἐλέφαντί τε μαρμ[αίρ]ουσιν οἶκοι,
πυροφ[όροι δὲ κατ' αἰγλάεντ]α πό[ντον
15 νᾶες ἄγο[υσιν ἀπ' Αἰγύπτου μέγιστον
πλοῦτον· ὣς [πίνοντος ὁρμαίνει κέαρ.

ὦ π[α]ῖ μεγαλ[οκλεὲς] ὑ[ψαυχέος Ἀμύντα,
. . .]εουπ[. . . . .]ον[
. . . .]λάχ[ον·] τί γὰρ ἀνθρώ[ποισι μεῖζον
20 κέρδο]ς ἢ θυμῶι χαρίζε[σθα]ι κ[αλά

. . . . .]φρονο[. . . . .]ρά[. .]κα[
. . . . . .]επερ[. .] . . . [.]μ[
. . . . . .]φης σκότος· ὄλβ[ον δ' ἔσχε πάντα
οὔτις] ἀνθρώπων διαισ[. . . .] . . ε[

25 αἰῶ]νος· ἴσας δ' ὁ τυχὼν [τῶ]ν εὖ[
]αταιτοσα[
.]ε[ ]ον θέμεθ[λ
θυ[ ] ποτε τρω[

θα[ ]αν ζαθεο[
30 μν[ ]ατε δη κα[
ἡ]μίθεοι[ ]π[
]νσυνβ[ ]ηκιτ[ ]ου[

15 Musurus: ἐπ' Athen.   17 Snell ('Αμ. Maas)   19, 20 Snell
alterius carm. fin.: 47 δο . . [48 στεφαναφο[ρ   49 τότε νέων ὁμό-
φ[ωνος   50 δ' εὐλύραι τε Φοί[βωι

278

world; his house gleams with gold and ivory, and wheat-bearing ships bring great wealth from Egypt over a dazzling sea. Such are the musings of the drinker's heart. (Glorious) son of (high-vaunting) Amyntas, ... (they) (won?); for what (greater gain) is there for men than to gratify one's heart with (fine deeds)? ... darkness; and no man ever got (complete) prosperity (throughout his life); but he who has obtained an equal (share) of good (and evil) ... foundations ... once ... holy ... heroes ...[1]

---

[1] The poem is complete in 8 strophes. A few words remain from the end of another poem: 'then (a paean rang out) in unison from the garlanded youths; and (they sang) to Phoebus, fine lyre-player, (and to the Muses?)' with Snell's supplements.

fr. 20C P.Oxy. 1361 frr. 4 al.

Ι]ΕΡΩΝΙ [ΣΥ]ΡΑΚΟΣΙΩΙ

μήπω λιγυαχ[έα κοίμα
    βάρβιτον· μέλλ[ω π]ολ[υφθόγγων τι καινόν
ἄνθεμον Μουσᾶ[ν Ἱ]έρων[ι κλυτῶι
    ξανθαῖσιν ἵπποις
5 ἱμ]ερόεν τελέσας
κα]ὶ συμπόταις ἄνδρεσσι π[έμπειν

Αἴ]τναν ἐς ἐΰκτιτον, εἰ κ[αὶ
    πρ]όσθεν ὑμνήσας τὸν [ἐν Δελφοῖς θ᾽ ἑλόντα
πο]σσὶ λαιψ[η]ρο[ῖ]ς Φερ[ένικον ἐπ᾽ Ἀλ-
10 φ[ει]ῶι τε ν[ί]καν
ἀν[δ]ρ[ὶ χ]αριζόμενος
εἰ[. . . . . . .]εανθυ[

᾽. [. . . . . . .] ἐμοὶ τότε κοῦραι[
    τ᾽ ἠΐθεοί θ᾽] ὅσσοι Διὸς πάγχρ[υσον ἄλσος
15 . . . .]μο[ι]ς τίθεσαν μ[
    . . . . .]ερ ειπε[
ὅστι]ς ἐπιχθονίων
. . .]ω τὸ μὴ δειλῶι . υναι[

τέχν]αι γε μέν εἰσ[ι]ν ἅπα[σαι
20 μυρία]ι· σὺν θεῶι δὲ θ[α]ρσή[σας πιφαύσκω·
οὔτι]ν᾽ ἀνθρώπων ἕ[τερον καθορᾶι
λε[ύκι]ππος Ἀώς

1 κοίμα Maas   κρήμνα Edmonds   2 Snell   3 Ἱ]έρων[ί τε καὶ
Maas   8 Snell: ἐξευρόντα Πυθοῖ Barrett   9 schol. Φερέ[νικος . . .]
τ[ο]υσ[. . .   11, 13, 14 Snell   15 aut]μος   17, 19, 20 Maas
21 Schadewaldt

BACCHYLIDES

fr. 20C Oxyrhynchus papyrus (1st c. A.D.)

FOR HIERO OF SYRACUSE

Do not put the clear-sounding lyre (to sleep) yet: I intend, now that I have completed a (new) blossom of the (melodious) Muses, a lovely blossom, to (send) it to Hiero, (glorious in) his bay horses, and his drinking companions in well-built Aetna,[1] if ever before I sang the praises of Pherenicus[2] who (won) the victory with his swift feet (both at Delphi) and by the Alpheus,[3] that I might give pleasure to the man ... (with?) me on that occasion maidens and all (the youths) who made the all-gold (sanctuary) of Zeus (loud with celebration?) ... (whoever) among mortals ... not cowardly.... Skills number ten thousand in all; but with God's help I make bold to (declare): white-horsed Dawn as she brings light to

[1] City founded in 475 by Hiero on the site of Catana. [2] Hiero's race-horse, winner at Olympia in 476: see 5. 37, 184. [3] At Olympia.

τόσσ[ο]ν ἐφ᾽ ἁλικία[ι
φέγγος κατ᾽ ἀνθρώπ[ους φέρουσα

29 χ]αριτε̣[ς   31]θεόπο[μπον ἔ]μελπο[ν   36]ι̣ς καὶ
φύσιν̣   37]ε χαίταν ἐξ[38 π]ολυχρ̣[υσ

23 Maas   24 Snell   cetera edd. prr. (Grenfell, Hunt)

fr. 20D P.Oxy. 2362 fr. 1 col. ii + 1361 fr. 36 (vv. 10–12) +
2081 (e) fr. 2

υ-]

ψόθεν εὐειδὴς ἄλοχος Π[άριος τὰν
λοισθίαν ὥρμασεν Οἰν[ώνα κέλευθον·

οὐδὲ τλαπενθὴς Νιόβα [τόσ᾽ ἔπασχεν,
5   τὰν ὤλεσαν Λατοῦς ἀγ[αυοί
παῖδες δέκα τ᾽ ἠϊθέους δ[έκα τ᾽ εὐπλό]κου̣[ς θ᾽ ἅμα
κο<ύ>ρας τανυάκεσιν ἰοῖς·
τὰ[ν δὲ πατὴρ] ἐσιδών
ὑψίζυγος οὐραν[όθεν
10 Ζεὺς ἐλέησεν ἀνακέστ[οις κατα]τε̣[ι]ρ̣ομέ[ναν
ἄχεσιν, θῆκέν τέ νιν ὀκριόεντ[α
λᾶαν ἄμπαυσέν τε δυστλάτ[ου πάθας.

vii versuum vestigia

1–3 ed. pr. (Lobel), nisi potius Οἰν[ῆος vel Οἰν[ηίς   4 Maas: [γενεάν
Lobel   5 Snell   6–10 Barrett, qui 2081 (e) fr. 2]κ[αμ]ου et
]τε[ι]ρομε[in vv. 6, 10 inserit, pap. colometriam mutans, ubi 7 fin.
τα[8 εἰσιδὼν ὑψ. οὐραν[7 Snell   8 τὰ[ν ed. pr.   δὲ π. Bar-
rett   9 ed. pr.   10 ἀνακέστοις ed. pr.   fin. Barrett   11 ed.
pr.   12 Maas

men (looks down at no other) man who is so great[4]
at his time of life[5] ... Graces ... they (or 'I') sang of
the heaven-sent ... nature ...

[4] As Hiero.   [5] The scraps which follow are from the last two
strophes of the poem. The words 'hair' and 'gold-rich' are preserved
from the beginning of the next poem.

fr. 20D Oxyrhynchus papyrus (c. 200 A.D.)

... from high above[1] the comely wife of (Paris),
Oen(one), hastened along her final (path)[2]; not even
grieving Niobe (suffered so much), she whom Leto's
(august) children destroyed[3] (together with) her ten
sons and ten (lovely-haired) daughters by means of
their long-pointed arrows; and when he saw her
from heaven high-throned father Zeus pitied her,
(worn away) by her incurable griefs, and turned her
into a jagged stone and brought her respite from a
(misfortune) hard to bear ...

[1] With reference to suicide by means of a noose or a leap.
[2] Oenone, a nymph whom Paris deserted for Helen, took her life
after refusing to cure his mortal wounds. But the text, much dam-
aged, may have spoken of the suicide of Althaea, wife of Oeneus
and mother of Meleager.   [3] When Niobe boasted to Leto of
the number of her children, Artemis and Apollo, Leto's children,
killed them.

Aul. Gell. *Noct. Att.* 20. 7 (ii 301 Hosius)

Homerus (*Il.* 24. 602) pueros puellasque eius (sc. Niobae) bis senos dicit fuisse, Euripides (fr. 455 N²) bis septenos, Sappho (fr. 205) bis novenos, Bacchylides et Pindarus (fr. 65 Snell) bis denos, quidam alii scriptores tres fuisse solos dixerunt.

cf. schol. in Bacch., P.Oxy. 2081 (e) fr. 2

fr. 20E P.Oxy. 2362 fr. 1 col. iii + 1361 fr. 21 (vv. 5–10 fin.)

<pre>
              ]θρ[
           χά]λκεον[
            ]μέλαν[
            ]ανδ' αἶσα   [
5   π]άνδωρος ἀθαν[
            ]ῆϊταν λέλογχε·
         κερ]αυνοβίας ὕπατος[
            ]αλλ' ἀπ' ' Ολύμπου
            ]ομάχαν
10   Σαρ]πηδόνα πυροφόρ[
            ].ενον· χρυσοπλόκ[
            ]αν φάτιν εἴπαρα.[
            ]ἀνθρώπ[ο]υς ὁμι[
            ]ε.σι μὲν ἀθαν[ατ
15   ]αι τελευτάν·
         ἀ]ενάωι Σιμόε[ν]τι πε[
            ]..[...]εϊ χαλκῶ[ι].
                            ]
                         ]ι χρόνος
20   ]νει φρέν' αἴσιο[
            ]. ι θυμὸν α.[
            ]αλλοῖαι..[
</pre>

284

BACCHYLIDES

Aulus Gellius, *Attic Nights*[1]

Homer says Niobe had six sons and six daughters, Euripides says seven of each, Sappho nine, Bacchylides and Pindar ten, certain other writers only three of each.

[1] Similar material in the scholiast on Bacchylides.

fr. 20E Oxyrhynchus papyrus (*c.* 200 A.D.)

... bronze ... black ... all-giving Destiny ... immortal ... has won ...; but the highest god, mighty with his thunderbolt, sent (Sleep and Death?)[1] from (snowy?) Olympus (to the fearless) fighter Sarpedon, (leader of) wheat-bearing (Lycia); and the golden-haired (Far-worker?)[2] spoke words ... men ... immortal ... the end; (but he fell) at the ever-flowing Simois,[3] (laid low by) the (pitiless) bronze ... time ... just mind ... spirit ... different ...

[1] Snell's tentative supplement: cf. *Il.* 16. 671 ff.   [2] Apollo.
[3] River in the Troad.

2, 5 suppl. ed. pr. (Lobel)   6 λ]ηϊτάν Lobel   ν]ηϊταν Lloyd-Jones   7, 10 ed. pr.   7ss. "Υπνον δὲ κερ]. ὕπ. [Θάνατόν τε | νιφό-εντος ἴ]αλλ' ἀπ' 'Ολ. | εἰς τὸν ἀταρβ]ομάχαν | ... Σαρ]πηδόνα πυρο-φόρ[ου | Λυκίας ἁγού]μενον· χρυσοπλόκ[αμος | δ' 'Εκάεργος   ]αν φάτιν εἶπ' tent. Snell   9 schol.]ον   14]εροι vel]εσσι   14, 16, 17 ed. pr.   16s. ἀλλ' ὅ γ' ἐπ' ἀ]εν. Σιμ. πέ[σεν | δαμεὶς περ]ὶ ν[ηλ]έϊ χαλκῶ[ι e.g. Snell   20 ιγι in ισι corr.?

285

(b) 5]αἶδα ·   (c) 5]εὔβουλο[

fr. 20F

6 ἱμερτ[

fr. 20G

1 χλιδῆ[3 λεύκα[5 ἔρωτι δ[

fr. 21 Athen. 11. 500ab (iii 103 Kaibel)

μνημονεύει δὲ τῶν Βοιωτικῶν σκύφων Βακχυλίδης ἐν τούτοις,
ποιούμενος τὸν λόγον πρὸς τοὺς Διοσκούρους, καλῶν αὐτοὺς ἐπὶ
ξένια ·

οὐ βοῶν πάρεστι σώματ᾽ οὔτε χρυσὸς
οὔτε πορφύρεοι τάπητες,
ἀλλὰ θυμὸς εὐμενής
Μοῦσά τε γλυκεῖα καὶ Βοιωτίοισιν
ἐν σκύφοισιν οἶνος ἡδύς.

fr. 22 = fr. 4. 21–25

fr. 23 Clem. Alex. *Strom.* 5. 110. 1 (ii 400 Stählin)

ἀκούσωμεν οὖν πάλιν Βακχυλίδου τοῦ μελοποιοῦ περὶ τοῦ θείου
λέγοντος ·

οἱ μὲν ἀδμῆτες ἀεικελιᾶν
†νούσων εἰσὶ† καὶ ἄνατοι,
οὐδὲν ἀνθρώποις ἴκελοι.

cf. Euseb. *Praep. ev.* 13. 679

1 Neue: ἀεὶ καὶ λίαν Clem.   ἀεικελίων Euseb.   2 εἰσὶ νόσων
Bergk   Schäfer: ἀναίτιοι Clem., Euseb.

(b) 5 (from) Hades   (c) 5 wise

fr. 20F

lovely[1]

[1] From the last line of a poem.

fr. 20G

luxury[1] . . . white . . . love . . .

[1] Or 'insolence'; first word of a poem.

fr. 21 Athenaeus, *Scholars at Dinner*

Bacchylides mentions the Boeotian σκύφοι (large cups) in the following lines, where he is addressing the Dioscuri and inviting them to a feast[1]:

There are no whole oxen here, no gold, no crimson rugs; but there is a friendly heart, the pleasant Muse, and sweet wine in Boeotian cups.

[1] E.g. at Athens, where plain fare was set before them in the town-hall (Athen. 4. 137e, citing Chionides fr. 7 K.-A.); but B.'s feast may have been private rather than public.

fr. 22 = fr. 4. 21–25

fr. 23 Clement of Alexandria, *Miscellanies*

Let us listen once more to the lyric poet Bacchylides talking about divinity:

they are unsubdued by cruel diseases and unharmed, not at all like men.

fr. 24 Stob. 1. 5. 3 (i 74s. Wachsmuth) (περὶ εἱμαρμένης καὶ τῆς τῶν γινομένων εὐταξίας)

Βακχυλίδου·

θνατοῖσι δ' οὐκ αὐθαίρετοι
οὔτ' ὄλβος οὔτ' ἄκναμπτος Ἄρης
οὔτε πάμφθερσις στάσις,
ἀλλ' ἐπιχρίμπτει νέφος ἄλλοτ' ἐπ' ἄλλαν
5 γαῖαν ἁ πάνδωρος Αἶσα.

1 Neue: θνητοῖς codd.   2 Snell: ἄκαμπτος codd.   5 Boeckh: γᾶν codd.

fr. 25 Clem. Alex. *Strom.* 6. 14. 3 (ii 433 Stählin)

Βακχυλίδου τε εἰρηκότος·

παύροισι δὲ θνατῶν τὸν ἄπαντα χρόνον δαίμων ἔδωκεν
πράσσοντας ἐν καιρῷ πολιοκρόταφον
γῆρας ἱκνεῖσθαι πρὶν ἐγκύρσαι δύᾳ.

cf. Hsch. Π 3287 πρὶν ἐγκύρσαι <δύᾳ>· πρὶν πλησιάσαι τῆς κακοπαθείας

1 Stephanus: παρ' οἷσι cod.   Neue: θνητῶν cod.   Neue: τῷ δαίμονι δῶκε cod.   2 Sylburg: πράσσοντα cod.

fr. 26 Clem. Alex. *Paed.* 3. 100. 2 (i 290 Stählin)

οὐ γὰρ ὑπόκλοπον φορεῖ βροτοῖσι φωνάεντα λόγον
†ἔστε λόγος† σοφία,

ὥς φησι Βακχυλίδης.

ἔσται ante corr. cod., ἔστι δὲ λόγος in marg.   θεσπιῳδὸς Schwartz

fr. 24 Stobaeus, *Extracts* (on fate and the orderliness of events)

Bacchylides:

But mortals are not free to choose prosperity nor stubborn war nor all-destroying civil strife: Destiny, giver of all things, moves a cloud now over this land, now over that.

fr. 25 Clement of Alexandria, *Miscellanies*

Bacchylides said

But God has granted to only a few mortals that they have happy fortunes all their days and reach grey-templed age without encountering misery.

fr. 26 Clement of Alexandria, *The Schoolmaster*

For there is no deception in the voiced utterance brought to mortals by wisdom,[1]

as Bacchylides says.

[1] Possibly 'by the poet's skill'; with Schwartz's emendation, 'by prophetic skill'. Jebb, following Hill and Blass, placed the lines at 15(14). 30 f. on metrical grounds.

fr. 27 Plut. *Num*. 4. 11 (iii 2. 56 Ziegler)

εἰ δὲ λέγει τις ἄλλως, κατὰ Βακχυλίδην

πλατεῖα κέλευθος.

fr. 28 = 1. 13s.

fr. 29 *Et. Gen.* (p. 24 Calame) = *Et. Mag.* 295. 57

εἴδωλον· σκιῶδες ὁμοίωμα ἢ φαντασία σώματος· σκιά τις
ἀεροειδής, ὡς καὶ Βακχυλίδης·

μελαγκευθὲς εἴδωλον ἀνδρὸς Ἰθακησίου

cf. *Anecd. Gr.* i 208 Bachmann, *Lex. Sabb.* 14. 21, *Sud.* ΕΙ 45 (ii 521
Adler) (schol. B rec. in *Il.* 5. 449) +

Neue: μελαγκεθές *Ett., Anecd.*   μελαμβαφές *Sud.* (schol. *Il.*)

fr. 30 Athen. *epitom.* 1. 36 (i 44 Kaibel)

Μέμφιν . . . , περὶ ἧς Βακχυλίδης φησί·

τὰν ἀχείμαντόν τε Μέμφιν
καὶ δονακώδεα Νεῖλον

1 Neue: τὴν codd.

fr. 31 = fr. 1B

fr. 32 = 18. 2

fr. 33 Prisc. *De metr. Ter.* (iii 428 Keil, *Gramm. Lat.*)

similiter Bacchylides:

χρυσὸν βροτῶν γνώμαισι μανύει καθαρόν

hic quoque iambus in fine tribrachyn habet.

fr. 27 Plutarch, *Life of Numa*

But if anyone gives a different account, well, as Bacchylides has it,

wide is the path.

fr. 28 = 1. 13 f.

fr. 29 *Etymologicum Genuinum* +

εἴδωλον: a shadowy likeness or image of a body, a misty shadow, as in Bacchylides:

the dark-shrouded[1] ghost of the man[2] of Ithaca

[1] Or 'dark-dyed' (*Suda*).   [2] Odysseus.

fr. 30 Athenaeus, *Scholars at Dinner*

Memphis . . . , about which Bacchylides says,

stormfree Memphis and the reedy Nile[1]

[1] Blass suggested that the lines (with καὶ <τὸν> δον.) belong to 13.

fr. 31 = fr. 1B

fr. 32 = 18. 2

fr. 33 Priscian, *On the Metres of Terence*

Similarly[1] Bacchylides:

indicates pure gold to the minds of mortals.[2]

This iambic line also ends with a tribrach.[3]

[1] P. has quoted Pindar fr. 35c.   [2] Cf. fr. 14.   [3] The metre seems rather to be dactylo-epitrite.

fr. 34 Hsch. Δ 2017 (i 466 Latte)

δίχολοι· διάφοροι. Ἀχαιὸς Καταπείρᾳ (fr. 23a Snell) 'δίχολοι γνῶμαι'· παρὰ τὸ δίχα· ἢ δίτροποι, κατὰ μετάληψιν· χόλος γὰρ ἡ ὀργὴ καὶ <ὀργὴ ὁ> τρόπος. Βακχυλίδης·

> ὀργαὶ μὲν ἀνθρώπων διακεκριμέναι
> μυρίαι.

cf. Zenob. 3. 25 (i 64 Leutsch-Schneidewin), Erotian. fr. 11 (p. 102 Nachmanson) = schol. Hippocr. π. χυμῶν (v 484 Littré)

fr. 35 *Et. Mag.* 676. 25

πλημμυρίς·... εἰ μέντοι ὄνομά ἐστιν, εὔλογον βαρύνεσθαι αὐτὸ διὰ τὴν παρὰ Βακχυλίδην αἰτιατικήν, οἶον

> πλήμυριν πόντου φυγών

Wilamowitz: πλημμ. codd.

fr. 36 = 13. 208s.

frr. 37–37B = frr. 54–56

fr. 38 Amm. Marc. 25. 4. 3 (i 360s. Seyfarth)

item ut hoc propositum validius confirmaret, recolebat saepe dictum lyrici Bacchylidis, quem legebat iucunde, id asserentis quod ut egregius pictor vultum speciosum effingit, ita pudicitia celsius consurgentem vitam exornat.

BACCHYLIDES

fr. 34 Hesychius, *Lexicon*

δίχολοι: ('double-galled') means 'different', as in Achaeus, *The Attack,* 'different minds'; from δίχα ('twofold', 'differently'), or by transference of meaning = δίτροποι, 'of different temperaments'; for χόλος, 'gall' = ὀργή, 'anger', and ὀργή = τρόπος 'temperament', as in Bacchylides[1]:

Of the temperaments of men there are ten thousand distinct kinds.

[1] Attributed to Alcman by Erotianus.

fr. 35 *Etymologicum Magnum*

πλημμυρίς: . . . if however it is (not an adverb but) a noun, 'flood-tide', it is reasonable to accent it on the first syllable in view of the accusative case (πλήμμυριν) in Bacchylides:

having escaped the flood-tide of the sea

fr. 36 = 13. 208 f.

frr. 37–37B = frr. 54–56

fr. 38 Ammianus Marcellinus, *History*

Moreover, to give stronger support to this principle (of chastity) Julian would often repeat the saying of the lyric poet Bacchylides, whom he enjoyed reading, to the effect that

as an outstanding painter makes a face beautiful, so self-restraint[1] adorns a life that is climbing to the heights.

[1] Perhaps σωφροσύνη in B. (Jebb).

fr. 39 Ap. Dysc. *Adv.* 596 (i 183 Schneider)

ὃν τρόπον καὶ ἐπ' ὀνομάτων μεταπλασμοὶ γίνονται καθάπερ τὸ ἐρυσάρματες, τὸ λῖτα, τὸ παρὰ Σαπφοῖ αὖα, τὸ

$$πυργοκέρατα$$

παρὰ Βακχυλίδῃ . . .

cf. Pind. fr. 325 ὑψικέρατα πέτραν

fr. 40 Athen. 4. 174f (i 392 Kaibel)

τούτοις δὲ καὶ οἱ Κᾶρες χρῶνται ἐν τοῖς θρήνοις, εἰ μὴ ἄρα καὶ ἡ Καρία Φοινίκη ἐκαλεῖτο, ὡς παρὰ Κορίννῃ καὶ Βακχυλίδῃ ἔστιν εὑρεῖν.

fr. 41 Schol. Ar. *Av.* 1536 (p. 273s. White)

Εὐφρόνιος (fr. 27 Strecker)· ὅτι Διὸς θυγάτηρ ἡ Βασίλεια, καὶ δοκεῖ τὰ κατὰ τὴν ἀθανασίαν αὕτη οἰκονομεῖν, ἣν ἔχει καὶ παρὰ Βακχυλίδῃ ἡ Ἀθηνᾶ, τῷ Τυδεῖ δώσουσα τὴν ἀθανασίαν.

fr. 42 Schol. Pind. *Ol.* 1. 40a (i 30 Drachmann)

ὁ δὲ Βακχυλίδης τὸν Πέλοπα τὴν Ῥέαν λέγει ὑγιάσαι †καθεῖσαν διὰ λέβητος† (ἐγκαθεῖσαν πάλιν τῷ λέβητι ci. Bergk).

BACCHYLIDES

fr. 39 Apollonius Dyscolus, *Adverbs*

As metaplasms[1] occur in nouns, e.g. ἐρυσάρματες, 'drawing chariots', λῖτα, 'linen cloth', Sappho's αὔα, 'dawn' (175) and Bacchylides' πυργοκέρατα,

tower-horned[2] ...

[1] Forms derived from a non-existent nom. sing. acc. sing.: cf. Pindar's 'high-horned rock'.   [2] Perhaps

fr. 40 Athenaeus, *Scholars at Dinner* (on the γίγγρας, a small Phoenician pipe)

The Carians use these in their laments, unless of course the name Phoenice was being applied to Caria,[1] as one may find it in Corinna (686) and Bacchylides.

[1] I.e. unless the pipe was in fact Carian.

fr. 41 Scholiast on Aristophanes, *Birds* ('unless Zeus gives you Princess for your wife')

According to Euphronius,[1] this is because Princess is the daughter of Zeus; and she seems to look after business connected with immortality, the responsibility of Athena in Bacchylides, where she intends to give immortality to Tydeus.[2]

[1] Identity unknown; perhaps the 3rd c. B.C. poet.   [2] See 'Apollodorus' 3. 6. 8: she changed her mind when Tydeus disgusted her by eating the brains of his victim Melanippus.

fr. 42 Scholiast on Pindar, *Ol.* 1. 26 ('when Clotho took Pelops from the pure cauldron')

Bacchylides says that it was Rhea who restored Pelops[1] by lowering him (again?) into the cauldron.

[1] His father Tantalus had served his flesh to the gods to test their omniscience.

GREEK LYRIC

fr. 43 Himer. *Or.* 27. 30 (p. 126s. Colonna)

καὶ Σιμωνίδῃ (621) καὶ Βακχυλίδῃ ἡ 'Ιουλὶς (Wernsdorf: ἡ πόλις cod. Rom. πόλεις cod. Nap.) ἐσπούδασται.

fr. 44 Schol. Hom. *Od.* 21. 295 (p. 702 Dindorf)

Βακχυλίδης δὲ διάφορον οἴεται τὸν Εὐρυτίωνα. φησὶ γὰρ ἐπιξενωθέντα Δεξαμενῷ ἐν Ἤλιδι ὑβριστικῶς ἐπιχειρῆσαι τῇ τοῦ ξενοδοχοῦντος θυγατρί, καὶ διὰ τοῦτο ὑπὸ Ἡρακλέους ἀναιρεθῆναι καιρίως τοῖς οἴκοις ἐπιστάντος.

cf. Eust. *Od.* 1909. 61

fr. 45 Schol. Ap. Rhod. 2. 498–527a (p. 169 Wendel)

τινὲς δ' 'Αρισταίους γενεαλογοῦσιν, ὡς καὶ Βακχυλίδης· τὸν μὲν Καρύστου, ἄλλον δὲ Χείρωνος, ἄλλον δὲ Γῆς καὶ Οὐρανοῦ, καὶ τὸν Κυρήνης.

τὸν μὲν Καρύστου ὡς καὶ B. Hiller von Gaertringen

fr. 46 = fr. 20D (Aul. Gell.)

fr. 47 Schol. Hes. *Theog.* 914 (p. 113 Di Gregorio)

ἡρπάσθαι δὲ αὐτήν (sc. τὴν Περσεφόνην) φασιν οἱ μὲν ἐκ Σικελίας, Βακχυλίδης δὲ ἐκ Κρήτης.

BACCHYLIDES

fr. 43 Himerius, *Orations*

Simonides and Bacchylides speak of Iulis[1] with respect.

[1] Their native city: see test. 2.

fr. 44 Scholiast on *Odyssey* (on the centaur Eurytion, drunk at the marriage-feast of Peirithous)

Bacchylides regards his Eurytion as distinct from this one: according to him, Eurytion after being entertained by Dexamenus in Elis insolently assaulted his host's daughter and for this reason was killed by Heracles, who by good luck had stopped at the house.[1]

[1] Cf. fr. 66.

fr. 45 Scholiast on Apollonius of Rhodes (Aristaeus, son of Apollo and Cyrene, brought up by Chiron)

Some authorities give the parentage of four gods called Aristaeus, as Bacchylides[1] does: one the son of Carystus,[2] another the son of Chiron,[3] another the son of Earth and Heaven, and the son of Cyrene.[4]

[1] Perhaps the words 'as B.' should be placed after 'son of Carystus'. Aristaeus was worshipped on B.'s island, Ceos, which is not far south of Carystus in Euboea.   [2] Chiron's son.   [3] As being a healing god.   [4] In fact different authorities will have given different parentage to the rural god Aristaeus.

fr. 46 = fr. 20D (Aulus Gellius)

fr. 47 Scholiast on Hesiod, *Theogony*

Some say that it was from Sicily that Persephone was carried off, but Bacchylides says it was from Crete.[1]

[1] In 3. 2 she is associated with Sicily.

GREEK LYRIC

fr. 48 [Plut.] *Vit. Hom.* 5 (v 247 Allen, O.C.T. Homer)

κατὰ δὲ Βακχυλίδην καὶ Ἀριστοτέλην τὸν φιλόσοφον (fr. 76 Rose) Ἰήτης.

fr. 49 Str. 13. 1. 70 (iii 63 Kramer)

ὁ δὲ Κάϊκος οὐκ ἀπὸ τῆς Ἴδης ῥεῖ, καθάπερ εἴρηκε Βακχυλίδης
. . .

fr. 50 Schol. Ap. Rhod. 1. 1165a (p. 104 Wendel)

Ῥυνδακὸς ποταμός (Schaefer: τόπος codd.) ἐστι Φρυγίας, οὗ μνημονεύει Βακχυλίδης.

de accentu cf. schol. 1165b Ῥυνδακὸς δὲ ὡς Αἰακός; at Hdn. *Il. Pros.* ad 13. 759 (ii 88 Lentz) Λάμψακος, Ῥύνδακος· Ῥύνδακον ἀμφὶ βαθύσχοινον.

fr. 51 Schol. Ap. Rhod. 4. 973 (p. 300 Wendel)

ὀρείχαλκος·

εἶδος χαλκοῦ. . . . μνημονεύει καὶ Στησίχορος (260) καὶ Βακχυλίδης.

cf. Didym. Chalc. fr. 34a Schmidt, Ar. Byz. fr. 413 Slater

fr. 52 Tzetz. *Theog.* 80–86 (Matranga, *Anecd. Gr.* p. 580)

ἐκ δὲ τοῦ καταρρέοντος αἵματος τῶν μορίων
ἐν μὲν τῇ γῇ γεγόνασι τρεῖς Ἐρινύες πρῶτον,
ἡ Τεισιφόνη, Μέγαιρα, καὶ Ἀληκτὼ σὺν ταύταις,
καὶ σὺν αὐταῖς οἱ τέσσαρες ὀνομαστοὶ Τελχῖνες,
Ἀκταῖος, Μεγαλήσιος, Ὁρμενός τε καὶ Λύκος,
οὓς Βακχυλίδης μέν φησι Νεμέσεως Ταρτάρου,
ἄλλοι τινὲς δὲ λέγουσι τῆς Γῆς τε καὶ τοῦ Πόντου.

BACCHYLIDES

fr. 48 'Plutarch', *Life of Homer*

According to Bacchylides and the philosopher Aristotle[1] Homer was from Ios.

[1] In Book 3 of *On Poetry* A. said Homer's mother was born in Ios, Homer at Smyrna.

fr. 49 Strabo, *Geography*

But the Caicus does not flow from Mt. Ida, as Bacchylides has it.

fr. 50 Scholiast on Apollonius of Rhodes

The Rhyndacus is a river of Phrygia, mentioned by Bacchylides.[1]

[1] Herodian, talking of the accent, quotes the words 'by the deep-reeded Rhyndacus'; Schneidewin attributed them to B., Hecker to Callimachus (cf. fr. 459 Pfeiffer).

fr. 51 Scholiast on Apollonius of Rhodes

orichalc,[1]

a kind of copper. It is mentioned by Stesichorus (260)[2] and Bacchylides.

[1] 'Mountain-copper'.   [2] It is in Ibyc. 282(a). 42 f.

fr. 52 Tzetzes, *Theogony*

From the blood that flowed from the genitals (of Uranus) three Erinyes were born first in the earth, Teisiphone, Megaera and Alecto with them; and along with them the four famous Telchines, Actaeus, Megalesius, Ormenus and Lycus, whom Bacchylides calls the children of Nemesis and Tartarus,[1] but some others the children of Earth and Pontus (Sea).

[1] Or 'of Nemesis, daughter of Tartarus'. See p. 119 n. 1. The four names need not have been in B.

GREEK LYRIC

fr. 53: v. 15 n. 2 (schol. *Il.*)

DUBIA

fr. 53a Plut. *Quaest. conviv.* 3. 1. 2 (iv 82 Hubert)

ὦ τᾶν, ἢ καταθέσθαι δίκαιος εἶ μεθ' ἡμῶν τουτονὶ

τὸν καλ<ύκεσσι> φλέγοντα
ταῖς ῥοδίνοις στέφανον,

ἢ λέγειν ... ὅσας ἔχουσιν οἱ ἄνθινοι στέφανοι πρὸς τὸ πίνειν βοηθείας.

1 suppl. Wilamowitz   2 Wilamowitz: τοῖς codd.

fr. 54 Stob. 4. 34. 26 (v 833 Hense) (περὶ τοῦ βίου, ὅτι βραχὺς καὶ εὐτελὴς καὶ φροντίδων ἀνάμεστος)

ἐν ταὐτῷ (sc. Βακχυλίδῃ) · θνατοῖσι ... φέγγος (= 5. 160–2),

ὄλβιος δ' οὐδεὶς βροτῶν πάντα χρόνον.

fr. 55 = 959 *P.M.G.*   Clem. Alex. *Strom.* 5. 16. 8 (ii 336 Stählin)

οὐ γὰρ ἐν μέσοισι κεῖται
δῶρα δυσμάχητα Μοισᾶν
τὠπιτυχόντι φέρειν.

BACCHYLIDES

fr. 53: see n. 2 on p. 209 (schol. *Il.*)

Frr. 53a–66 are of uncertain authorship

fr. 53a Plutarch, *Table-talk*

Sir, you ought either to lay aside, as we do, this

garland aflame with rose buds,[1]

or tell us . . . all the benefits brought to the drinker by garlands of flowers.

[1] Ascribed to Simonides or B. by Wilamowitz, *Hermes* 60 (1925) 305; but D. S. Robertson, *C.R.* 65 (1951) 17, notes that the words may have been part of a pentameter (κ. φλέγων τ. ῥ. στέφανος).

fr. 54 Stobaeus, *Anthology* (that life is short, worthless and full of cares)

In the same source (viz. Bacchylides)[1]: 'Best for mortals . . . the sun's light' (= 5. 160–162),

and no mortal is prosperous all his days.[2]

[1] Or 'Bacchylides, *Epinicians*'. [2] Wrongly attached in Stobaeus to 5. 160–162; the same thought in fr. 20B. 23 ff., fr. 25.

fr. 55 = 959 *P.M.G.* Clement of Alexandria, *Miscellanies*

For the keenly-contested gifts of the Muses do not lie open to all for any comer to carry off.[1]

[1] Attributed to B. by Blass; Edmonds noted that the scraps of line-endings at fr. 20C. 42 f. fit vv. 1–2. Same turn of phrase at 15. 53 f. Clement has just quoted Hes. *Op.* 287 and Eur. *First Hippolytus* fr. 432 without naming the authors.

fr. 56 Clem. Alex. *Paed.* 1. 94. 1 (i 146 Stählin)

ἀρετὰ γὰρ ἐπαινεομένα δένδρον ὣς ἀέξεται.

ἀρετὰ δ' αἰνευμένα δένδρεον ὣς ἀ. Blass

fr. 57 Stob. 3. 11. 20 (iii 433 Hense)

'Ολυμπιάδος·

'Αλάθεια θεῶν ὁμόπολις
μόνα θεοῖς συνδιαιτωμένα.

1 θεῶν: βροτῶν ci. Bergk, sed v. M. L. West, *Z.P.E.* 37 (1980) 144
2 μόνη, -μένη codd.

fr. 58 Schol. Ael. Arist. *Or.* 1. 350 (iii 317 Dindorf)

ἄλλοι δὲ λέγουσιν ὡς ἐκ Σικελίας ἐφάνη (sc. τὸ ἅρμα) τὴν
ἀρχήν· Βακχυλίδης γὰρ καὶ Πίνδαρος (v. fr. 106) Ἱέρωνα καὶ
Γέλωνα, τοὺς Σικελίας ἄρχοντας, ὑμνήσαντες καὶ πλεῖστα θαυμά-
σαντες ἐν ἱππηλασίᾳ, πρὸς χάριν αὐτῶν εἶπον ὡς Σικελιῶται
πρῶτοι ἅρμα ἐξεῦρον.

fr. 56 Clement of Alexandria, *The Schoolmaster*

For excellence when commended flourishes like a tree.[1]

[1] Attributed to Bacch. 1 by Blass, *Hermes* 36 (1901) 285, although his version scarcely fits the metre; same comparison in Pindar *Nem.* 8. 39 f.

fr. 57 Stobaeus, *Anthology* (on truth)

Truth is from the same city as the gods; she alone lives with the gods.[1]

[1] Attributed to B. by Bergk. The citation follows fr. 14, which is ascribed to B.'s Dance-songs. The word 'Olympias' which introduces it may refer to an Olympian ode of B. (or of Pindar: *Ol.* 10. 65 was cited a few lines earlier). Text probably corrupt.

fr. 58 Scholiast on Aelius Aristides, *Panathenaicus* ('since the chariot too came originally from Athens and not from Sicily')

Others say the chariot appeared first in Sicily: Bacchylides and Pindar, when they sang the praises of Hiero and Gelo, the rulers of Sicily, and found a great deal to admire in their horse-driving, said by way of gratifying them that Sicilians invented the chariot.[1]

[1] P. in fact merely commends the Theban chariot and the Sicilian mule-cart (fr. 106). Another version of the scholion said more guardedly that B. and P. gave the impression that Sicilians invented horsemanship.

fr. 59 Comes Natalis, *Myth*. 9. 8 (p. 987 ed. Francof. 1581)

dicitur Polyphemus non modo amasse Galateam sed etiam Galatum ex illa suscepisse, ut testatus est Bacchylides.

fr. 60 *P.S.I.* x 1181

2 fin.]ἴδον δέμας

7 ὑ]περ ἀμετέρ[ας]
    τ]ατος ἐράτυ[. . . .]ματα
    δ[υσμενέω[ν . . .]χοίμεθα
10 ἀκρίτοις ἀλι[άστοις]
    ὑπὸ πένθε[σιν ἤ]μεναι·
    κρυόεντι γὰρ [ἐμ π]ολέμω<ι>
    δίμενακα . [. . .]αι παν
    κιχέταν λι[. . . .] . [. .] . υ
15 . τερι πατρι . [. . . .]οι
    αι σφιν θο[. . .]δ[. . .]ν
    εὐανθέο[ς .] αρε[. ἐλ]ευθερίας
    Ἀχέρον[τι .] ρου θεων ἀδαεῖ
    εὐηρατ[. . .]ναι [.]ομων
20 τ' Ἀίδαο . [. . .]ν

6 φυλάσ]σων? Snell   7 ed. pr. (Vogliano)   7s. νεό-|τατος Lobel
8 ἐράτυ[εν vel [ον, [σε(ν), [σαν ed. pr.   ἄρ]ματα vel ὄμ]ματα Lobel
9 ἀνε]χοίμεθα ed. pr.   ἀκα]χοίμεθα Pfeiffer   10 Diehl   11 ed. pr.
12 ἐμ Maas   13 δύμεναι Maas   fin. κ]αι πᾶν ed. pr.   15 περὶ
πατρία[ισι Milne   16 αἴ σφιν . . . δ[ῶκε]ν ed. pr.   17 -θέος Maas,
Snell   fin. ed. pr.   18 init. ed. pr.   θεῶν Snell   19 εὐηράτων
δῦναι (Pfeiffer) δόμων (ed. pr.)   20 λ[αχεῖ]ν Snell

fr. 59 Natale Conti, *Mythology*

Polyphemus is said not only to have loved Galatea but to have fathered a son Galatus[1] on her, as Bacchylides testified.

[1] Timaeus fr. 37 (566 F69 *F.Gr.H.*) (= *Et. Mag.* 220.5) mentions a son Galates, Appian, *Illyr.* 2 a son Galas, who gave his name to the Galatians. Pfeiffer *Call.* i 305 suggests that Conti, a notoriously unreliable writer, took his information from *Et. Mag.* and wilfully substituted Bacchylides for Timaeus.

fr. 60 Italian papyrus (2nd or 3rd c. A.D.)

'... form ... for the sake of our (youth?) (he? they?) checked the (chariots?) of the enemy, we[1] should endure to sit under a load of uncountable unabating sorrows; for in chilling war ... (the two) came ... father('s) ... (to) them ... (of) flourishing freedom to Acheron that has no knowledge of (the gods?) ... lovely ... of Hades ...'

[1] The speakers are female.

μάλ' ἔγε[. . .] τοι[α]ύτα φάτις·
ἐπεὶ δοκ[ὸν σ]κια[ρῶ]ν
ξπ[[ε]]ὶ πολυ[δεν]δρέ[ω]ν ἀκτῶν
κῦμα πό[ρευσ'] ἀπ' Ἰλίου,
25 θεῶν τι[ς ἀ]μ-
φανδὸ[ν
αὖθι μένε[ιν . . . . .]ερ . μίδι
τὸν δ' οὐλόμε[νον . .]έιμεν
προφυγεῖν θά[νατ]ον.
30 ἐ]πασσύτεραι δ' ἰα[χαί]
οὐρανὸν ἶξον [
ἀ̣έλπτω<ι> περὶ χάρ[μα]τι [   ]
οὐδ' ἀνδρῶν
θώκοισι μετε[.] . [.]ʹτω[ν στόμα
35 ἄναυδον ἦν,
νέαι δ' ἐπεύχο[ν]τ[ο] . [.] . λλαι
ἰὴ ἰή.

21 ἔγε[ιφε Page ἔγε[ντο Diehl   22 fin. Diehl   23 ἐπὶ Snell   πολ.
Maas   ἀκτῶν agn. Milne   24–26 Maas   26 εἶπε τὸν μὲν
Page   27 ἐν γᾶι Π]εραμιδι Diehl   28 ἔν]ειμεν ed. pr.   29 ed.
pr.   30 fin. Maas   31 [γυναικῶν vel sim. ed. pr.   34 στόμα
Snell   36 νέαι nom. pl. vel dat. s.

fr. 61 *P.S.I.* x 1181 (cont.)

ΛΕΥΚΙΠΠΙΔΕΣ

ἰοδερκέϊ τελλόμεναι
Κύπριδι νεοκέλαδον
ε]ὐειδέα χορόν·

Such the utterance that (aroused? occurred?);
when the wave carried the ship from Troy on to the
shadowy forested headlands, a god (said) openly
that (one?) should remain there . . . , while the other
should escape accursed death.[1] Many cries (of
women?) reached heaven in unexpected joy, nor was
(the mouth) of men unheard . . . on the benches; and
young women prayed . . . iē, iē![2]

[1] With reference to the Dioscuri or to the Cabiri?   [2] Poem
ends with the cry of the paean. Vogliano, the first editor of frr. 60
and 61 (1932), ascribed them to B., J. A. Davison, *C.R.* 48 (1934)
205 ff., to Simonides.

fr. 61 Same papyrus

LEUCIPPIDES[1]

For violet-eyed Cypris[2] we[3] establish a beautiful
choral dance of new song, and . . .[4]

[1] Daughters of Leucippus, wives of Castor and Polydeuces.
[2] Aphrodite.   [3] The speakers are female.   [4] See fr. 60
last note.

fr. 62 P.Oxy. 680

(a) 1]τοισι βροτῶν   2]ερχομένοισιν ὑποσ[3s.
τα]λακάρδιος ἔπλε[το   4]ντα χαλκου   5]ων
ἐπιόντ' ἐρεμναι[6]ελλαις   7]τ' ἀλκάν.
8 ἕ]καστος ἀνήρ   9 π]ατρίδος αἵ σφισιν ο[10]ν
μεγαλοκλέα δο[13]ντες αἰνῶς   14]τα πᾶσαν
ε �․ ͒ λλοβ[15]αρ τὸν ἔχον[τ'] ε[16 ἀ]νδρὶ γὰρ
οὐδ[

(b) 1]δεδορ[κ   4]ρ ὅρματ[7 μενεπ]τολέμων
8]εν πυκινὰς στίχα[ς   9]καὶ ἐμ<ε>ίξατον λ[
10 ὅ]πλοις

5s. ἐρεμναῖ[ς . . . ἀ]έλλαις vel θυ]έλλαις edd. prr. (Grenfell, Hunt)
14 ε[ὶς ἄ]λλο? Snell

fr. 63 P.Oxy. 673

1 Πιερ]ίδων θερα[π   2 ὀβρι]μοπάτρας [3]μενα
γλυκ[4] ͘ ἱππόβοτο[5]νόμοις · Ὀλυμ[π
6]ντος ὑπὸ π[7]ρ ἀϊόνων ε[8 π]οντιάδεσσι[
9 π]λοκάμοις θεαῖς[10]εν ἀνιοκουρ[11]φνε τοξ[

1s. Blass   cetera edd. prr. (Grenfell, Hunt)   11 κατέπε]φνε
τόξ[ωι e.g. Snell

fr. 64 P. Berol. 16140 col. 2

5 ο[
Ἀλ[κ]μήν[ας υἱὸς
ἄγει τ' ἐκ κ[

6 vel Ἀλκ[μ]ήν[ιος ἥρως Snell   7 Κ[αλυδῶνος Snell

fr. 62 Oxyrhynchus papyrus (1st or early 2nd c. A.D.)

... of mortals ... to (them) coming ... (he) was stout-hearted ... bronze ... (him) approaching ... dark (storms?) ... valour ... each man ... (of) his native land ... who to them ... of great glory ... dreadfully ... all ... the man who has ...; for to a man not ... (has seen?) ... (rushed?) ... (steadfast in) battle ... tight ranks ... and the two joined (battle) ... (with) their arms ...[1]

[1] Attributed to B. by the first editors, Grenfell and Hunt, on grounds of vocabulary.

fr. 63 Oxyrhynchus papyrus (3rd c. A.D.)

... servant of the Pierians[1] ... (of) the mighty father's daughter[2] ... sweet ... horse-pasturing ... (customs?); Olympus ... (of) shores ... (lovely-) haired sea goddesses ... (reins?) ... (killed with the bow) ...

[1] The Muses.   [2] Mnemosyne (daughter of Heaven and Earth and mother of the Muses)?

fr. 64 Berlin papyrus (1st or 2nd c. A.D.)[1]

... Alcmena's (son)[2] ... and brings from (Caly-

[1] First published in 1935 by Bowra as Pindar (O.C.T.) fr. 341 (incerti auctoris); attributed to B. by Snell, *Hermes* 75 (1940) 177 ff.   [2] Heracles.

```
       τ̣ονας ἔνθεν[
     πορθμευοντ[
10   νήϊδα ῥοδόπ[αχυν . . . με-
       τα χερσὶ πεδά[ρσιον
     διὰ ποταμὸν ἔ[
     ἵπποις ἔχων [παῖδ’ ἐν ἀγκάλαις·
     ἀλλ’ ὅτε δὴ πέλ[ασσεν ὄχθαις,
15   ἀφροδισιᾶν μ[ανιᾶν πλησθείς

     Κένταυρος ἄϊ[ξ’ ἐπὶ νύμφαν·
     κελάδησε δὲ δ[
     φίλον πόσιν ἱκ[ετευ
     σπεύδ[ει]ν ἐπ̣η̣[
20   γυναικὸ̣ς̣ φον[
     πυριδαὲς ὄμμα[
     φόνον τε καὶ δ[
     ἄφατος· οὐ προ[
     ἐν δαῒ βρομωχ[
25   ἐν δὲ χειρὶ δεξ[ιᾶι
     ῥόπαλον μέγα [
     φη[ρ]ὸς ἀγρίου [ κεφαλὰν ἐπ’
     οὔατος μέσσαν [
     συνάραξέ τε π[
30   ὀμμάτων τε σ[
     ὀφρύων τε· πε[
     πόδεσσιν αθα[
     νυπ[ . . ]ξιν· επε[
     . . . . ]ανδροσ[
35   . . . . . . ] .ο[
```

don?) ... (from?) there ... as he[1] carried the rosy-
armed woman, inexperienced in (guile?), (raised
high) in his arms ... across the river ... his horses
... holding[2]. .... But when (he approached the bank)
the Centaur, (filled with) Aphrodite's (madness),
rushed (at the young woman); and she cried out and
begged her dear husband to hurry ... his wife's ...
his blazing eye ... death and ..., the prodigious
(hero?); ... not ... in battle ... (din?) ..., and
(brandishing) his great club[3] in his right hand he
(struck) the middle of the savage beast's (head over)
the ear and smashed ... (from) his eyes and brows;
... with his feet ... of the man(-) ...[4]

[1] The centaur Nessus, to whom Heracles entrusted his wife
Deianeira when crossing the river Lycormas (Euenus); see 16. 23 ff.
with n. 2 on p. 215.   [2] Perhaps '(Heracles) went across the
river in his horse-drawn chariot, holding their child in his arm'
(Snell): cf. Philostratus, *Imag.* 16.   [3] Since H. does not use
bow and arrow in this version, there will have been no mention of
the love-charm given by Nessus to Deianeira.   [4] The letter Ξ
opposite v. 23 marks v. 1400 of the book.

8s. ἔνθ' ἐπ[έτραπε Νέσσωι | πορθμεύοντ[ι δόλων Snell, Maehler
10 Diehl   11–13 Snell   14 Diehl   15–18 Snell   19 Roberts
21 [δινάσας Maehler   22 δ[εtν- Maehler   25 ed. pr. (Bowra);
vel δεξιτερᾶι   26 [τινάσσων Snell   27 Roberts   28 [ἔπλαξε
Snell   29 π[αμβίαι κράνιον e.g. Snell

fr. 65 (a)(b) P.Oxy. 2365   (c) *P.S.I.* ined. inv. 2011

(a)

> δόξα]ν τέ μοι ἀθάν[ατον
> καὶ κ]ῦδος ὀπάσσατ[ε
>   . .] . . γε λειμῶ[
>   .]ιξιαν χρυσάνιο[ν
> 5 .] . τωτ᾿ ἀπενθητα . [
>   . . . .]ντ᾿ Ἄρτεμιν τ[
>   ]ε σύν τ᾿ ὄλβωι κ[
> σύν] τ᾿ ἐπιζήλωι τ[ύχαι
>   . . . .] . υ Δᾶλον ποτ . [
> 10 . . . . .] ὶ ὑπ᾿ ἀνθρωπο[

> ἁγναὶ ἀν]αξίχοροι
> Μοῦσαι Δ]ιὸς ἀργικε[ραύνου
> παρθέν]οι χρυσάμ[πυκες,
> δεῦθ᾿ Ἐλι]κῶνα λιπ[οῦσαι

(b) 1 ἀ]γακλέΐ[4]σελασεν . [6]ἐπίμοιρ[ο
9]ἄγαλμα   10]ων κὰλων .   11] . σε βίου
12 τέ]θαλεν βιά[13 ἀκερ]σεκόμα

(c) 1]ν φραδαῖς

(a) 1 init. Barrett fin. Snell   2 καὶ? Snell   cet. ed. pr. (Lobel)
4, 8 ed. pr.   11 ἁγναὶ Barrett   ἀν]αξ. ed. pr.   12 Μοῦσαι
Barrett   cet. ed. pr.   13 παρθέν]οι Barrett   fin. ed. pr.   14 δεῦθ᾿
Barrett   Ἐλι]κῶνα ed. pr.   fin. Snell   (b) 1, 12 ed. pr.   13
Snell

fr. 65 Oxyrhynchus papyrus (3rd c. A.D.)[1]

... grant me undying (fame and) glory ... (meadow?) ... of the golden reins[2] ... carefree ... Artemis ... with prosperity and with enviable fortune ... Delos ... (at the hands of men?)

(Holy),[3] dance-ruling (Muses) with golden headbands, (daughters) of thunder-flashing Zeus, (come hither), leaving Helicon ... far-famed ... (radiance?) ... partaking ... adornment ... beautiful ... life ... flourishes ... (with uncut) locks[4] ... counsels ...

---

[1] Hesitantly ascribed to B. by the first editor, Lobel.　　[2] Apollo?
[3] Beginning of a new poem.　　[4] Addressed to Apollo?

fr. 66 P.Oxy. 2395 fr. 1 = *P.M.G.* 924 (fr. adesp.)

θ]υμῶι [
]αῦ βίαι χ[

]δυσφορέω[
] . [   ] . δ' ὁ . [
5 ο]ύδ' ἐσῆλ[υθε]ν . [
ἔ]ειπε δὲ τοῦτο . [
ἄ]χομα[ι] θυμὸν ζ . . [
α]ύτόματον τ[
ἐραννὰν ἐπὶ δ[αῖτα
10 ὁρικοίτας Κένταυρ[ος
αἰτεῖ δέ με παῖδα τα[
ἐθέλων ἄγεσθαι
πρὸς Μαλέαν · ἐμοὶ δ'[

ἀέκοντι δ[ὲ] πικροτε[ρ
15 ασεπιτ λά[. .]αι μέγ' ἀά[
ἀλλά σ' ἐγ[ὼ . . .] . όντ' . [
ὡς ὄφελ[.] . ἀμυμ[

1 ed. pr. (Lobel)   5 init. Page: α]ῦ δ' ἐσῆλ[θε vel ἐσῆλ[υθε]ν
Snell   ]υδ . ς 'Ηλ[εἰω]ν tent. Barrett (cf. fr. 44)   ο]ύδέ σ' vel
κ]ῦδος Maehler   6 init., 7–10 ed. pr.   6ss. τοῦτο π[ατὴρ βαρέα
στενάχων · | ἄ]χομαι θυμὸν ζαμ[ενεῖ περὶ λύπαι · | α]ύτόματον τ[οι Θεσ-
σαλίαθεν] ἐραννὰν | ἐπὶ δ[αῖτα μολὼν] ὁρικοίτας | Κένταυρ[ος ἀτάσθαλα
βάζει tent. Page   11 παῖδ pap.   τα[νίσφυρον Barrett   11ss.
τα[ν . εὐναίαν ἐ. ἄ. | π. Μ.· ἐμοὶ δ' [ἀποθύμια μήδεται (vel γίνεται) · |
ἀέκοντι δὲ πικρότε[ρον καταπειλεῖ | Page   15 μέγ' ἀά[σθης Page

fr. 66 Oxyrhynchus papyrus (early 3rd c. A.D.)[1] = *P.M.G.* 924

... at heart ... again with violence ... vexed ... nor did (he?)[2] approach ...; and he[3] said this: 'I am grieved at heart ...: uninvited (he came) to the lovely feast, the Centaur[4] whose bed is in the mountains ... and he asks me for my (slender-ankled?) daughter, wishing to take her as his bride to Malea; but to me (this is repellent), and since I am unwilling (he threatens me) more harshly (saying?) ... "(You) acted very foolishly; but I ... you ... Would that ... blameless ..."'

1 Ascribed to B. by Page, Lloyd-Jones, *C.R.* 73 (1959) 22; see fr. 44.
2 Heracles?   3 Dexamenus.   4 Eurytion.

EPIGRAMMATA

I *F.G.E.*   *Anth. Pal.* 6. 53, Plan. (Βακχυλίδου)

Εὔδημος τὸν νηὸν ἐπ᾿ ἀγροῦ τόνδ᾿ ἀνέθηκεν
τῷ πάντων ἀνέμων πιοτάτῳ Ζεφύρῳ·
εὐξαμένῳ γάρ οἱ ἦλθε βοαθόος, ὄφρα τάχιστα
λικμήσῃ πεπόνων καρπὸν ἀπ᾿ ἀσταχύων.

cf. *Sud.* Π 1632 (1 τόνδ᾿ – 2), Π 1013 (3 ὄφρα – 4)

2 πιστοτάτῳ Unger, Schneidewin   3 βοηθόος Plan.

II *F.G.E.*   *Anth. Pal.* 6. 313 (Βακχυλίδου)

κούρα Πάλλαντος πολυώνυμε, πότνια Νίκα,
πρόφρων †Κρανναίων† ἱμερόεντα χορόν
αἰὲν ἐποπτεύοις, πολέας δ᾿ ἐν ἀθύρμασι Μουσᾶν
Κηίῳ ἀμφιτίθει Βακχυλίδῃ στεφάνους.

2 Καρθαιῶν Bergk   Κραναΐδων Meineke

BACCHYLIDES

EPIGRAMS[1]

I *F.G.E.*   *Palatine Anthology*

Eudemus dedicated this temple on his land to Zephyrus, richest (?) of all winds; for in answer to his prayer he came to help him, so that he might winnow most speedily the grain from the ripe ears.

[1] Both epigrams are likely to be of Hellenistic date. See test. 13.

II *F.G.E.*   *Palatine Anthology*

Far-famed daughter of Pallas,[1] lady Victory, may you always look with favour on the lovely chorus of (the Carthaeans?[2] the sons of Cranaus?[3]) and in the pastimes of the Muses[4] crown Bacchylides of Ceos with many garlands.

[1] An obscure figure, son of Crius and Eurybia; see West on Hesiod, *Theog.* 376, 383 ff.   [2] Carthaea was a town in Ceos.   [3] I.e. the Athenians.   [4] I.e. musical contests.

LAMPROCLES

TESTIMONIA VITAE ATQUE ARTIS

1 Schol. Plat. *Alcib.* 118c (p. 95 Greene)

Πυθοκλείδης μουσικὸς ἦν, τῆς σεμνῆς μουσικῆς διδάσκαλος, καὶ Πυθαγόρειος, οὗ μαθητὴς Ἀγαθοκλῆς, οὗ Λαμπροκλῆς, οὗ Δάμων.

2 [Plut.] *Mus.* 16. 1136de (p. 118 Lasserre, vi 3. 13s Ziegler)

ἐν δὲ τοῖς ἱστορικοῖς οἱ ἁρμονικοὶ (Einarson–De Lacy: τοῖς ἁρμονικοῖς codd.) Πυθοκλείδην φασὶ τὸν αὐλητὴν εὑρετὴν αὐτῆς (sc. τῆς Μιξολυδίου ἁρμονίας) γεγονέναι, αὖθις (Westphal: λύσις codd., Λύσις Bernardakis) δὲ Λαμπροκλέα τὸν Ἀθηναῖον, συνιδόντα ὅτι οὐκ ἐνταῦθα ἔχει τὴν διάζευξιν ὅπου σχεδὸν ἅπαντες ᾤοντο, ἀλλ' ἐπὶ τὸ ὀξύ, τοιοῦτον αὐτῆς ἀπεργάσασθαι τὸ σχῆμα οἷον τὸ ἀπὸ παραμέσης ἐπὶ ὑπάτην ὑπατῶν.

LAMPROCLES

1 Scholiast on Plato, *Alcibiades* I ('Pericles consorted with wise men, e.g. Pythocleides and Anaxagoras')

Pythocleides was a musician, a teacher of the dignified style of music and a Pythagorean; his pupil was Agathocles, whose pupil was Lamprocles,[2] whose pupil was Damon.

---

[1] See also P.Oxy. 1611 (at 735 below), Athen. 11. 491c (= 736).
[2] L. will have worked in the early 5th c. In Athen. 1. 20e, where the young Sophocles is said to have been taught dancing and music by Lamprus, Lamprus may be an error for Lamprocles; see Lamprus test. 2.

2 'Plutarch', *On Music*

In their historical accounts the writers on harmonics say that Pythocleides the aulete was the inventor of the Mixolydian *harmonia,* and that later Lamprocles the Athenian, realising that its disjunction is not where almost everyone had thought but at the top of its range, shaped it so as to run from *paramesē* (b) to *hypatē hypatōn* (B).[1]

---

[1] I.e., he saw that it had two conjunct tetrachords, BCDE/EFGa, with a disjunct tone, ab, 'at the top'. The text of 'Plutarch' is uncertain at more than one point.

LAMPROCLES

735 = Stesichorus 274   P.Oxy. 1611 frr. 5 + 43

ταις Φ[ρύ]ν[ιχος] … ἀφηγο[ύ]μεν[ος] … ‘Πα[λ]λά[δα]
περ[σέπολιν κλήιζ]ω π[ολεμαδόκο]ν ἁγνὰν π[αῖδα Διὸς] μεγάλου
δ[αμάσιπ]πον’ οὕτω παρα[ποιεῖ ?]· διαπορούσι γὰρ ο[ὐκ ὀ]λίγοι
π[ε]ρὶ τ[ού]των κα[θ]άπερ Χαμαιλέων (fr. 29c Wehrli) πότερόν
ποτε Στη[σι]χόρου ἐστὶν ἢ Λαμπροκλ[έο]υς, κ[αίπ]ερ τοῦ
Φρυν[ίχου Λαμ]προκλεῖ μα[θη<τηι ?> Μίδωνος ?] προσνέμον[τος·
καὶ Ἀ]ριστοφάνης [δὲ ? παραπ]οιεῖ λέγων· ‘[Παλλάδα] π[ε]ρσέ-
[π]ο(λιν)’.

Schol. RV Ar. *Nub.* 967 (I 3. 1. 186 Holwerda)

Παλλάδα περσέπολιν δεινάν· ἀρχὴ ἄσματος Στησιχόρου (van
Leeuwen: Φρυνίχου cod. R), ὡς Ἐρατοσθένης φησίν. Φρύνιχος
δὲ αὐτοῦ τούτου τοῦ ἄσματος μνημονεύει ὡς Λαμπροκλέους ὄντος·

**Παλλάδα περσέπτολιν κλήζω πολεμαδόκον ἁγνάν
παῖδα Διὸς μεγάλου <δαμάσιππον>**

cf. schol. E (p. 186 Holwerda), ubi Π. π. δ. θεὸν ἐγρεκύδοιμον

320

LAMPROCLES

FRAGMENTS

735 = Stesichorus 274   Oxyrhynchus papyrus (early 3rd
c. A.D.) containing literary criticism

... Phrynichus ... telling ... 'Pallas, sacker of cities, I
summon, the warlike, the pure, child of great Zeus, horse-
tamer': he[1] takes the words over in this form. For many
scholars, Chamaeleon[2] among them, are vexed over these
lines: were they by Stesichorus or by Lamprocles? Yet
Phrynichus attributes them to Lamprocles, pupil[3] of
Midon. Aristophanes also takes them over, saying 'Pallas,
sacker of cities, the grim'.

[1] Phrynichus, presumably the 5th c. comic poet.   [2] Peripatetic
grammarian, c. 350–after 281 B.C.   [3] 'Son of Midon' or 'son
or pupil of Midon' in the scholia on Ar. *Clouds* 967 (p. 185 f.
Holwerda).

Scholiast (RV) on Aristophanes, *Clouds* 967

'Pallas, sacker of cities, the grim'[1]: the beginning of a
song of Stesichorus,[2] as Eratosthenes[3] says. Phrynichus
mentions this same song as being by Lamprocles:

Pallas, sacker of cities, I summon, the warlike,
the pure, child of great Zeus.

[1] Used by Aristophanes as a sample of traditional song taught in
the old-style education.   [2] So van Leeuwen: the mss. have
'Phrynichus'.   [3] Geographer and literary critic of Alexandria,
3rd c. B.C.

Schol. Aristid. *Or.* 46. 162 (= 3. 155 Behr) (iii 538 Dindorf)

Παλλάδα περσέπολιν· . . . τὸν δὲ ποιητὴν αὐτοῦ Ῥοῦφος καὶ Διονύσιος ἱστοροῦσιν ἐν τῇ Μουσικῇ Φρύνιχόν τινα, ἄλλοι δέ φασι Λαμπροκλέα ἢ Στησίχορον. τὸ δὲ δεινὰν γελοίως ἀντίκειται <παρὰ τῷ κωμικῷ add. cod. Oxon.>· τὸ γὰρ ᾆσμα οὕτως ἔχει· Παλλάδα περσέπολιν κλεισοπολεμοδόκον ἁγνὴν παῖδα Διὸς μεγάλου δαμνηπῶλον ἄιστον (ἄριστον cod. Oxon.) παρθένον.

cf. Tzetz. *Chil.* 1. 686 (p. 31 Leone), schol. ad loc. (p. 553 Leone), Dion. Chrys. *Or.* 13. 19 (i 184 von Arnim), *Sud.* T 490 (iv 539 Adler)

736 Athen. 11. 491c (iii 83 Kaibel)

Λαμπροκλῆς δ' ὁ διθυραμβοποιὸς καὶ ῥητῶς αὐτὰς (sc. τὰς Πλειάδας) εἶπεν ὁμωνυμεῖν ταῖς περιστεραῖς ἐν τούτοις·

αἵ τε ποταναῖς
ὁμώνυμοι πελειάσιν αἰθέρι κεῖσθε.

cf. Eust. *Od.* 1713. 5 καὶ Λαμπροκλῆς· αἱ ποταναῖς ὁμώνυμοι πελειάσιν ἐν αἰθέρι κεῖνται.

1 τε om. E   2 κεῖνται E: νεῖσθε ci. Meineke

LAMPROCLES

Scholiast on Aelius Aristides ('Pallas, sacker of cities')

... the composer of this song, according to Rufus[1] and Dionysius[2] in their *Music,* was a certain Phrynichus, but according to others it was Lamprocles or Stesichorus.[3] The word 'grim' is a comic substitution in Aristophanes, for the song runs 'Pallas, sacker of cities, I summon ...'

[1] Scholar of Greek literature, date unknown (*R.E.* Rufus 17).
[2] D. of Halicarnassus, Greek literary critic, *fl. c.* 20 B.C.   [3] The testimonia are badly confused: the truth may be that there were poems by Stesichorus and by Lamprocles (a century later), both of which began 'Pallas, sacker of cities'; that Stesichorus continued with 'the grim goddess, rouser of war', the text from which Aristophanes quoted three words; and that Aristophanes' contemporary Phrynichus quoted 'Pallas, sacker of cities, I summon ... of great Zeus', naming Lamprocles as author. See K. J. Dover on *Clouds* 967, D. L. Page at *P.M.G.* 735.

736 Athenaeus, *Scholars at Dinner*

Lamprocles, the dithyrambic poet, said expressly that the Pleiades have the same name as the pigeons in these lines:

you who are set in the sky, bearing the same name as the winged doves.

CEDEIDES

TESTIMONIA VITAE ATQUE ARTIS

1 Ar. *Nub.* 984s.

ἀρχαῖά γε καὶ Διπολιώδη καὶ τεττίγων ἀνάμεστα
καὶ Κηδείδου καὶ Βουφονίων.

2 Nauck: Κηκείδου, Κηκίδου, Κικίδου, Κυκείδου, Κείδου, Κηκιδίου,
Κηδίου codd.

Schol. RV ad loc. (985a.β : p. 190 Holwerda) = *Sud.* K 1500
(Κηκίδιος) (iii 108 Adler)

Κηδείδης (Κηκείδης, Κηκίδης codd.)· διθυράμβων
ποιητὴς πάνυ ἀρχαῖος. μέμνηται δὲ αὐτοῦ Κρατῖνος ἐν
Πανόπταις (fr. 168 K.-A.).

cf. Phot. s.v. Κηδίδης (i 338 Naber), Hsch. K 2476 (Κηθείδης), *Et.
Mag.* 166. 4 (Κηδείδης, nomen patronymicum)

2 *I.G.* i² 770

Κλεισθένης ἐχορέγε Αὐτοκράτος Ἐρεχθῆιδι Αἰγῆι-
δι, Κεδείδης ἐδίδασκε.

CEDEIDES[1]

1 Aristophanes, *Clouds* (423 B.C.) (Wrong Argument describes old-style education)

Old-fashioned stuff, like the festival of Dipolia, chock-full of cicadas and Cedeides and the Bouphonia.

Scholiast on the passage (= *Suda* s.v. Cecidius)

Cedeides: a very early[2] dithyrambic poet. Cratinus mentions him in his *See-alls.*

[1] There is doubt about the spelling of his name: see Dover on *Clouds* 985.   [2] Or 'very old-fashioned'.

2 Athenian inscription (not before *c.* 415 B.C.)

Cleisthenes, son of Autocrates, was choregus for the Erechtheid and Aegeid tribes.[1] Cedeides trained the chorus.

[1] His dithyrambic victory was won at the Thargelia festival: see Pickard-Cambridge, *D.T.C.*[2] 30, 37.

SOPHOCLES

Sud. Σ 815 (iv 402 Adler)

Σοφοκλῆς· . . . καὶ ἔγραψεν ἐλεγείαν τε καὶ παιᾶνας . . .

Philostr. *Vit. Apoll.* 3. 17 (i 96 Kayser)

οἱ δὲ ᾖδον ᾠδὴν ὁποῖος ὁ παιὰν ὁ τοῦ Σοφοκλέους ὃν Ἀθήνησι τῷ Ἀσκληπιῷ ᾄδουσιν.

[Lucian.] *Encom. Demosthen.* 27 (iii 274 Macleod)

οὐδὲ γὰρ τἀσκληπιῷ μεῖόν τι γίγνεται τῆς τιμῆς εἰ μὴ τῶν προσιόντων αὐτῶν ποιησάντων ὁ παιὰν Ἰσοδήμου (Macleod: ὅπλα ἀναλισοδήμου codd.) τοῦ Τροιζηνίου καὶ (ἢ Harmon) Σοφοκλέους ᾄδεται.

737 (a)   ΠΑΙΑΝ · ΑΣΚΛΗΠΙΟΣ

Philostr. *Imag.* 13. 4 (ii 415 Kayser)

Ἀσκληπιὸς δὲ οἶμαι οὗτος ἐγγὺς παιάνά που παρεγγυῶν γράφειν καὶ

326

SOPHOCLES

Suda, Sophocles

. . . he wrote elegiacs and paeans . . .

Philostratus, *Life of Apollonius*

And they began singing a song like the paean of Sophocles which is sung to Asclepius[1] at Athens.

[1] For Sophocles' relations with Asclepius see Plut. *Mor.* 1103b, *Numa* 4, *Et. Mag.* 256.5.

'Lucian', *Encomium of Demosthenes*

Nor does any less honour accrue to Asclepius if the worshippers themselves compose nothing and the paean of Isodemus of Troezen or that of Sophocles is sung.

737 (a)   PAEAN FOR ASCLEPIUS

Philostratus the Younger, *Pictures* (on a painting of Sophocles)

This is Asclepius nearby, I think, no doubt exhorting you to write a paean and not disdaining to be called

327

κλυτομήτης

οὐκ ἀπαξιῶν παρὰ σοῦ (sc. τοῦ Σοφοκλέους) ἀκοῦσαι . . .

κλυτόμητις ci. Bergk (cf. *P.M.G.* 934)

(b) *I.G.* ii² 4510 + James H. Oliver, *Hesperia* 5 (1936) 109ss.

ΣΟΦΟΚΛΕΟΥΣ [ΠΑΙ]ΑΝ

(i)

(ὦ) **Φλεγύα**] κούρα περιώνυμε, μᾶτερ ἀλεξιπό[ν]ο[ιο
    θεοῦ

ὃν ἔφυσ]ας ἀκειρεκόμα<ι>, σέ[θ]εν ἄρξομαι [ὕμ]νον
    ἐγερσιβόαν

(.) . . . . .]νεσι[ν] εὐεπί[η . . . .] . [. . .] . [.]αν[. . .
    οβοα

               ]συρίγμασι μιγνύ[μεν]ον

5   ]σι Κεκροπιδῶν [ἐπ]ιτάρροθο

             ] . μόλοις τὸν [χρυσο]κόμα[

             ]ν αὐτον[

10   'Ολύ]μπιον

desunt vv. vi

17   ]τερα

(ii) 4 λυρ[

1 init. Buecheler, fin. Oliver   2 init. Page, cett. Oliver   3 Ditten-
berger   fort. αὐλ]οβόα Page   4 Oliver   5 Wilhelm   6, 10 Oliver

SOPHOCLES

skill-famed

by you.[1]

[1] James H. Oliver, *Hesperia* 5 (1936) 121 f. argues convincingly that Phil.'s ascription of the epithet to Sophocles is mistaken, and that it belongs rather to the famous 'Erythraean' paean (*P.M.G.* 934), which begins 'Sing of skill-famed Paean'.

(b) Inscription from the Asclepieum at Athens[1] (200–250 A.D.)

PAEAN OF SOPHOCLES

Wide-famed daughter of Phlegyas, mother of the god who wards off pain, (whom you bore to) the Unshorn,[2] yours is the shout-raising hymn which I shall begin ... (euphony?) ... -shouting ... mingled with pipings ... helper of the Cecropidae[3] ... may you come ... the Golden-haired[4] ... him(self) ... Olympian ...

[1] Photographs in Oliver, *loc. cit.* pp. 110, 112. The paean was performed in Athens *c.* 174/5 A.D. It is addressed to Coronis, mother of Asclepius.   [2] Apollo.   [3] Cecrops was a mythical king of Athens.   [4] Apollo. Another piece of the stone (ii), which preserves a few letters of line-beginnings, has 'lyre', perhaps 'lyre-singer' of Apollo.

ELEGI

fr. eleg. 1 Heph. *Ench.* 1. 5 (p. 3s. Consbruch)

ἐν δὲ τοῖς ἔπεσι σπανιώτερον, οὕτως ὥστε τὸ τοῦ Ἀρχελάου
ὄνομα Σοφοκλῆς ἐν ταῖς ἐλεγείαις οὐκ ᾤετο ἐγχωρεῖν οὔτε εἰς ἔπος
οὔτε εἰς ἐλεγεῖον. φησὶ γοῦν·

Ἀρχέλεως· ἦν γὰρ σύμμετρον ὧδε λέγειν.

cf. Eust. in *Il.* p. 264. 20 (i 402 van der Valk)

fr. eleg. 2 Harp. (i 60s. Dindorf)

'ἀρχὴ ἄνδρα δείκνυσι'· Δημοσθένης προοιμίοις δημηγορικοῖς
(48. 2). Σοφοκλῆς μὲν οὖν ἐν ταῖς ἐλεγείαις Σόλωνός φησιν αὐτὸ
εἶναι ἀπόφθεγμα, Θεόφραστος δὲ ἐν τῷ <περὶ> παροιμιῶν καὶ
Ἀριστοτέλης (*Eth. Nic.* 5. 1. 1130a) Βίαντος.

Σοφοκλῆς <Ἀντιγόνη . . .> Leutsch, *Corp. Paroem. Gr.* i 212

fr. eleg. 3 Erotian. *Lex Hippocr.* X 2 (p. 93 Nachmanson)

χάριτες· αἱ χαραί, ὡς καὶ Σοφοκλῆς ἐν ἐλεγείᾳ μέμνηται.

SOPHOCLES

ELEGIACS

fr. eleg. 1 Hephaestion, *Handbook on Metres*

Internal corruption is less common in dactylic hexameters; indeed Sophocles in his elegiacs thought that the name Archelaus fitted neither hexameter nor pentameter[1]; at any rate he says

Archeleōs—for this form fitted the metre.

[1] I.e. he would not allow the α to count as short before the -ος.

fr. eleg. 2 Harpocration, *Lexicon of the Ten Attic Orators*

'Office shows the man': quoted by Demosthenes in his *Exordia to Public Speeches*. Sophocles in his elegiacs[1] makes it a saying of Solon, but Theophrastus *On Proverbs* and Aristotle make it a saying of Bias.

[1] With Leutsch's emendation, 'Sophocles in his *Antigone* refers to it; X in his elegiacs . . .'; see *Antig.* 175 ff.

fr. eleg. 3 Erotianus, *Glossary to Hippocrates*

χάριτες ('graces') can be used to mean

joys;

so Sophocles in a poem in elegiacs.

GREEK LYRIC

fr. eleg. 4 = i *F.G.E.* Athen. 13. 604d–f (iii 333s. Kaibel)

Ἱερώνυμος δὲ ὁ Ῥόδιος ἐν τοῖς ἱστορικοῖς ὑπομνήμασίν (fr. 35
Wehrli) φησιν ὅτι Σοφοκλῆς εὐπρεπῆ παῖδα ἔξω τείχους ἀπήγαγε
χρησόμενος αὐτῷ. ὁ μὲν οὖν παῖς τὸ ἴδιον ἱμάτιον ἐπὶ τῇ πόα
ὑπέστρωσεν, τὴν δὲ τοῦ Σοφοκλέους χλανίδα περιεβάλοντο. μετ᾽
οὖν τὴν ὁμιλίαν ὁ παῖς ἁρπάσας τὸ τοῦ Σοφοκλέους χλανίδιον
ᾤχετο, καταλιπὼν τῷ Σοφοκλεῖ τὸ παιδικὸν ἱμάτιον. οἷα δὲ εἰκὸς
διαλαληθέντος τοῦ συμβεβηκότος, Εὐριπίδης πυθόμενος καὶ ἐπιτω-
θάζων τὸ γεγονὸς καὶ αὐτός ποτε ἔφη τούτῳ κεχρῆσθαι τῷ παιδί,
ἀλλὰ μηδὲν προεθῆναι (West: προσθεῖναι cod.), τὸν δὲ Σοφοκλέα
διὰ τὴν ἀκολασίαν καταφρονηθῆναι. καὶ ὁ Σοφοκλῆς ἀκούσας
ἐποίησεν εἰς αὐτὸν τὸ τοιοῦτον ἐπίγραμμα, χρησάμενος τῷ περὶ τοῦ
ἡλίου καὶ Βορέου λόγῳ, καί τι πρὸς μοιχείαν αὐτοῦ παραινιττό-
μενος·

> ἥλιος ἦν, οὐ παῖς, Εὐριπίδη, ὅς με χλιαίνων
>   γυμνὸν ἐποίησεν· σοὶ δὲ φιλοῦντι †ἑταίραν†
> Βορρᾶς ὡμίλησε. σὺ δ᾽ οὐ σοφός, ὃς τὸν Ἔρωτα,
>   ἀλλοτρίαν σπείρων, λωποδύτην ἀπάγεις.

2 τάλαν West

fr. eleg. 5 = ii *F.G.E.*   Plut. *an seni sit gerenda resp.* 3.
785b (V. i. 26 Hubert)

τουτὶ δὲ ὁμολογουμένως Σοφοκλέους ἐστὶ τὸ ἐπιγραμμάτιον·

> ᾠδὴν Ἡροδότῳ τεῦξεν Σοφοκλῆς ἐτέων ὢν
>   πέντ᾽ ἐπὶ πεντήκοντα

2 vel πεντήκονθ᾽ in pentamentro

332

SOPHOCLES

fr. eleg. 4 = i *F.G.E.*   Athenaeus, *Scholars at Dinner*

Hieronymus of Rhodes[1] says in his *Historical Notes* that Sophocles took a good-looking boy outside the city wall to have intercourse with him: the boy spread his own cloak on the grass, and they wrapped themselves in Sophocles' cape. When they had finished, the boy grabbed Sophocles' cape and went off with it, leaving him his boy's cloak. As was to be expected, people gossiped about the incident, and when Euripides heard of it he joked about it, saying that he had once had intercourse with this boy but that nothing had been taken off, whereas Sophocles had been treated with contempt because of his licentious behaviour. When Sophocles heard this, he addressed the following epigram to him, using the fable of Helius and Boreas[2] and making riddling reference to his adultery:

It was the sun, Euripides, and no boy that made me hot and stripped me, but when *you* made love, it was Boreas who kept you company; and you are unwise to bring Love to court as a clothes-stealer while you sow another man's field.

[1] Philosopher and literary historian, 3rd c. B.C.   [2] The sun and the north wind competed to see who could more quickly make a man remove his cloak.

fr. eleg. 5 = ii *F.G.E.*   Plutarch, *Should an old man govern?*

And this little epigram is universally accepted as the work of Sophocles:

Sophocles fashioned a song for Herodotus[1] when he was five and fifty years of age.

[1] The historian?

DIAGORAS

TESTIMONIA VITAE ATQUE ARTIS

1 *Sud.* Δ 523 (ii 53 Adler)

Διαγόρας, Τηλεκλείδου ἢ Τηλεκλύτου, Μήλιος,
φιλόσοφος καὶ ἀσμάτων ποιητής· ὃν εὐφυᾶ θεασάμενος
Δημόκριτος ὁ Ἀβδηρίτης ὠνήσατο αὐτὸν δοῦλον ὄντα
μυρίων δραχμῶν καὶ μαθητὴν ἐποιήσατο. ὁ δὲ καὶ τῇ
λυρικῇ ἐπέθετο, τοῖς χρόνοις ὢν μετὰ Πίνδαρον καὶ
Βακχυλίδην, Μελανιππίδου δὲ πρεσβύτερος· ἤκμαζε
τοίνυν οη΄ Ὀλυμπιάδι. καὶ ἐπεκλήθη Ἄθεος διότι
τοῦτο ἐδόξαζεν, ἀφ᾽ οὗ τις ὁμότεχνος αἰτιαθεὶς ὑπ᾽
αὐτοῦ ὡς δὴ παιᾶνα ἀφελόμενος, ὃν αὐτὸς ἐπεποιήκει,
ἐξωμόσατο μὴ κεκλοφέναι τοῦτον, μικρὸν δὲ ὕστερον
ἐπιδειξάμενος αὐτὸν εὐημέρησεν. ἐντεῦθεν οὖν ὁ Δια-
γόρας λυπηθεὶς ἔγραψε τοὺς καλουμένους Ἀποπυργί-
ζοντας λόγους, ἀναχώρησιν αὐτοῦ καὶ ἔκπτωσιν ἔχον-
τας τῆς περὶ τὸ θεῖον δόξης. κατοικήσας δὲ Κόρινθον ὁ
Διαγόρας αὐτόθι τὸν βίον κατέστρεψεν.

cf. [Hesych. Mil.] *De viris illustr.* 17

DIAGORAS

BIOGRAPHY[1]

1 *Suda* (1st notice)

Diagoras, son of Telecleides or Teleclytus, from Melos, philosopher and composer of songs; he was a slave, and Democritus[2] of Abdera, noticing that he was talented, bought him for 10,000 drachmae and made him his pupil. He devoted himself to lyric poetry also, coming after Pindar and Bacchylides[3] but before Melanippides. He flourished in the 78th Olympiad (468/464 B.C.).[4] He was called 'the atheist', since this was his belief from the day when a fellow-poet, accused by him of stealing a paean which he had composed, denied the theft, but soon after produced the paean successfully as his own work. Diagoras, pained, wrote the so-called *Tower-wrecking Discourses*,[5] which told of his apostasy and defection from his belief in God. He settled in Corinth and ended his days there.[6]

---

[1] For the many testt. which have no relevance to D.'s dates or poetry see Winiarczyk's edition. [2] The tale is told to link 'the atheist' with the physicist (c. 460–c. 356 B.C.). [3] Cf. test. 2(b). Schol. Ar. *Frogs* (see test. 6) makes him a contemporary of Simonides and Pindar. [4] Cf. test. 2(b) with n. 2. [5] Translation of title uncertain; seemingly a prose work, perhaps known also as *Phrygian Discourses* (Tatian, *Against the Greeks* 27); authenticity doubtful. [6] The last sentence may show confusion with Diagoras of Eretria.

2 Euseb. *Chron.*

(a) Ol. 74.3 (p. 109 Helm, ii 103 Schöne)

Diagoras agnoscitur et sectatores eius physici philosophi.

(b) Ol. 78.1 (p. 110 Helm, ii 103 Schöne)

Bacchylides et Diagoras atheus plurimo sermone celebrantur.

3 Diod. Sic. 13. 6. 7 (iii 13 Vogel)

τούτων δὲ πραττομένων Διαγόρας ὁ κληθεὶς ἄθεος, διαβολῆς τυχὼν ἐπ' ἀσεβείᾳ καὶ φοβηθεὶς τὸν δῆμον, ἔφυγεν ἐκ τῆς Ἀττικῆς. οἱ δ' Ἀθηναῖοι τῷ ἀνελόντι Διαγόραν ἀργυρίου τάλαντον ἐπεκήρυξαν.

CHRONOLOGY[1]

2 Eusebius, *Chronicle*

(a) Olympiad 74.3 (482/481 B.C.): Diagoras is well-known together with his followers, the physicist philosophers.

(b) Olympiad 78.1 (468/467 B.C.): Bacchylides and Diagoras the atheist are much spoken of.[2]

[1] See also test. 1.   [2] Both dates may originally have been transmitted as the year of his birth. The first may synchronise him with Protagoras, the second may mark him as a successor of Simonides, who died in 468.

3 Diodorus Siculus, *World History* (on the year 415/414 B.C.)[1]

While this was going on, Diagoras, known as 'the atheist', was accused of impiety and in fear of the people fled from Attica. The Athenians proclaimed the reward of a talent of silver for his killer.

[1] The 11th c. Arab writer Mubaššir, drawing on the *Philosophic History* of Porphyry of Tyre, similarly puts the decree in the archonship of Charias (415/414 B.C.) (Eng. tr. in *F.Gr.H*. IIIb, Suppl. i 198).

4 Ar. *Nub.* 826–831

ΣΤΡ.   ὁρᾷς οὖν ὡς ἀγαθὸν τὸ μανθάνειν;
       οὐκ ἔστιν, ὦ Φειδιππίδη, Ζεύς.

ΦΕΙΔ.   ἀλλὰ τίς;

ΣΤΡ.   Δῖνος βασιλεύει τὸν Δι' ἐξεληλακώς.

ΦΕΙΔ.   αἰβοῖ, τί ληρεῖς;

ΣΤΡ.   ἴσθι τοῦθ' οὕτως ἔχον.

ΦΕΙΔ.   τίς φησι ταῦτα;

ΣΤΡ.   Σωκράτης ὁ Μήλιος
       καὶ Χαιρεφῶν, ὃς οἶδε τὰ ψυλλῶν ἴχνη.

Schol. ad loc. (p. 167 Holwerda)

830a Σωκράτης ὁ Μήλιος· παρ' ἱστορίαν. Ἀθηναῖος γὰρ ὁ Σωκράτης· ἀλλ' ἐπειδὴ Διαγόρας Μήλιος ὢν διεβάλλετο ὡς θεομάχος, καὶ τὸν Σωκράτην δὲ ὡς ἄθεον διαβάλλει, διὰ τοῦτο αὐτὸν Μήλιον ἔφη.

830c.a Διαγόρας (Hermann: Ἀρισταγόρας cod.) ἐγένετο Μήλιος διθυραμβοποιός, ὃς τὰ ἐν Ἐλευσῖνι μυστήρια ἐξορχησάμενος καὶ ἐξειπὼν ἀσεβέστατος ἐκρίθη. ἀπ' ἐκείνου οὖν τοὺς Μηλίους ἐπὶ ἀσεβείᾳ κωμῳδοῦσιν.

DIAGORAS

ARISTOPHANES AND THE SCHOLIA

4 Aristophanes, *Clouds* (423 B.C., revised version *c.* 418–416)

Strepsiades: So you see what a blessing learning is? There is no Zeus, Pheidippides.

Pheidippides: Then who *is* there?

Str.: Vortex is king, having expelled Zeus.

Ph.: Ugh! What *is* this nonsense?

Str.: I assure you it's the truth.

Ph.: Who says all that?

Str. Socrates the Melian and Chaerephon, who knows about fleas' footprints.

Scholiast on the passage

(1) 'Socrates the Melian': not so in fact, for Socrates was Athenian; but Diagoras, who was a Melian, was accused of hostility towards the gods, and Aristophanes is accusing Socrates of atheism: that is why he called him a Melian.

(2) Diagoras[1] was a dithyrambic poet from Melos, who divulged the Eleusinian Mysteries in dance and word and was judged to be a most impious man. That is why they make fun of the Melians for impiety.

1 The mss. have 'Aristagoras', presumably in error.

5 Ar. *Av.* 1072–1078

τῆδε μέντοι θἠμέρᾳ μάλιστ' ἐπαναγορεύεται·
'ἢν ἀποκτείνῃ τις ὑμῶν Διαγόραν τὸν Μήλιον,
λαμβάνειν τάλαντον, ἤν τε τῶν τυράννων τίς τινα
τῶν τεθνηκότων ἀποκτείνῃ, τάλαντον λαμβάνειν.'
βουλόμεσθ' οὖν νῦν ἀνειπεῖν ταὐτὰ χἠμεῖς ἐνθάδε·
'ἢν ἀποκτείνῃ τις ὑμῶν Φιλοκράτη τὸν Στρούθιον,
λήψεται τάλαντον· ἢν δὲ ζῶντ' ἀπαγάγῃ, τέτταρα
. . .'

Schol. ad loc. (p. 199s. White)

(b) ἄλλως· ταῦτα ἐκ τοῦ ψηφίσματος εἴληφεν. οὕτως
γὰρ ἐκήρυξαν, τῷ μὲν ἀποκτείναντι αὐτὸν τάλαντον
λαμβάνειν, τῷ δὲ ἄγοντι δύο. ἐκηρύχθη δὲ τοῦτο διὰ
τὸ ἀσεβὲς αὐτοῦ, ἐπεὶ τὰ μυστήρια πᾶσι διηγεῖτο
κοινοποιῶν αὐτὰ καὶ μικρὰ ποιῶν καὶ τοὺς βουλομέ-
νους μυεῖσθαι ἀποτρέπων, καθάπερ Κράτερος (*F.Gr.H.*
342 F16) ἱστορεῖ. ἐκκεκήρυκται δὲ μάλιστα ὑπὸ τὴν
ἅλωσιν τῆς Μήλου, οὐδὲν γὰρ κωλύει πρότερον.
Μελάνθιος δὲ ἐν τῷ Περὶ μυστηρίων (*F.Gr.H.* 326 F3)
προφέρεται τῆς χαλκῆς στήλης ἀντίγραφον, ἐν ᾗ
ἐξεκήρυξαν καὶ αὐτὸν καὶ τοὺς <μὴ> ἐκδιδόντας Πελ-
λανεῖς, ἐν ᾗ γέγραπται καὶ ταῦτα· 'ἐὰν δέ τις
ἀποκτείνῃ Διαγόραν τὸν Μήλιον, λαμβάνειν ἀργυρίου
τάλαντον· ἐὰν δέ τις ζῶντα ἀγάγῃ, λαμβάνειν δύο.'

DIAGORAS

5 Aristophanes, *Birds* (414 B.C.)

Chorus-leader of the birds: Now on this day in particular proclamation is made that if any of you kills Diagoras the Melian, he will receive a talent; and if anyone kills one of the dead tyrants, he will receive a talent. So we too wish to make the same proclamation here: if any of you kills Philocrates[1] the Sparrovian, he will receive a talent, and if he brings him here alive, four talents.

[1] A bird-catcher.

Scholiast (b) on the passage

Aristophanes has taken this from the decree; for their proclamation was as follows: the man who kills him will receive a talent, the man who brings him two. This proclamation was made on account of his impiety, since he described the Mysteries to everyone, divulging and belittling them and dissuading people who wished to be initiated, as Craterus[1] tells. The proclamation was made roughly about the time of the capture of Melos (i.e. winter 416/415): 'roughly', since there is nothing to exclude an earlier date. Melanthius[2] in his work *On Mysteries* provides a text of the bronze column on which they outlawed both him and the citizens of Pellene[3] who refused to expatriate him: on it was inscribed, 'Whoever kills Diagoras the Melian will receive a talent of silver; whoever brings him alive, two talents.'

[1] 3rd c. B.C. author of *Collection of (Athenian) Decrees.*   [2] C. 350–270 B.C.   [3] City of E. Achaea, where D. took refuge; cf. *Birds* 1421.

6 Ar. *Ran.* 316–320

XOP.   Ἴακχ᾽, ὦ Ἴακχε.
         Ἴακχ᾽, ὦ Ἴακχε.

ΞΑΝ.   τοῦτ᾽ ἐστ᾽ ἐκεῖν᾽, ὦ δέσποθ᾽ · οἱ μεμυημένοι
         ἐνταῦθά που παίζουσιν, οὓς ἔφραζε νῷν.
         ᾄδουσι γοῦν τὸν Ἴακχον ὅνπερ Διαγόρας.

δι᾽ ἀγορᾶς cod. V

Schol. ad loc. (p. 284 Dübner)

    Διαγόρας μελῶν ποιητὴς ἄθεος, ὃς καὶ καινὰ
δαιμόνια εἰσηγεῖτο, ὥσπερ Σωκράτης . . .

6 Aristophanes, *Frogs* (405 B.C.)

Chorus: Iacchus, o Iacchus! Iacchus, o Iacchus!

Xanthias: That's it, master! That must be the initiates he told us about, enjoying themselves here. At any rate they are singing the Iacchus-song that Diagoras sang.[1]

[1] Some edd. read 'di' agorās': 'the Iacchus-song sung as they pass through the agora'.

Scholiast on the passage

Diagoras was a composer of songs, an atheist who like Socrates tried to introduce new divinities . . .[1]

[1] The scholiast goes on to say that the critic Aristarchus took the 'singing' of D. to mean 'mockery', and says (with no regard for chronology) that Aristophanes is inciting the Athenians, who thereupon passed their decree against Diagoras and the people of Pellene; Craterus' *Collection of the Decrees* is again cited.

DIAGORAS

FRAGMENTA

738 Philodem. *De Piet.* (p. 85s. Gomperz: v. A. Henrichs, *Cronache ercolanesi* 4 (1974) 21s.)

... ἀνθρωπ[ο]ε[ι]δεῖς γὰρ ἐκεῖνό γε <οὐ> νομίζουσιν ἀλλὰ ἀέρας καὶ πνεύματα καὶ αἰθέρας, ὥστ᾽ ἔγωγε [κ]ἂν τεθαρ[ρ]ηκότως εἴπαιμι τούτους Διαγόρου [μ]ᾶλλον πλημμελεῖν· ὁ μὲν γὰρ ἔπαιξεν, εἴπερ ἄρα καὶ τοῦθ᾽ ὑ[γι]ές ἐστ[ι]ν ἀλλ᾽ οὐκ ἐπενήνεκται, καθάπ[ερ ἐ]ν τοῖς Μα[ν]τινέων Ἐθε[σ]ιν Ἀριστόξενός φησιν (fr. 127a Wehrli), ἐν δὲ τῆι ποιήσει τῆι μόνηι δοκούσηι κατ᾽ ἀλήθειαν ὑπ᾽ αὐτοῦ γεγράφθαι τ[ο]ῖς ὅλοις οὐ[δ]ὲν ἀσεβὲς παρενέφ[ην]εν ἀλλ᾽ ἐστὶν εὔφημος ὡς [π]οιητὴς εἰς τὸ δ[α]μόνιον, καθάπερ ἄλλα τε μαρτυρεῖ καὶ τὸ γεγρα[μ]μένον εἰς Ἀριάνθην τὸν Ἀργεῖον·

(1) θεὸς θεὸς πρὸ παντὸς ἔργου βροτείο[υ]
νωμᾶι φρέν᾽ ὑπερτάταν,
<αὐτοδαὴς δ᾽ ἀρετὰ βραχὺν οἶμον ἕρπει>,

καὶ τὸ εἰς Νικόδωρον τὸν Μαντινέα·

(2) κατὰ δαίμονα καὶ τύχαν
τὰ πάντα βροτοῖσιν ἐκτελεῖται.

τὰ παραπλήσια δ᾽ αὐτῶι περι[έ]χει [καὶ τ]ὸ Μαντινέω[ν] ἐγκώμιον.

cf. Didym. Alexandr. *De Trinit.* III 1 (*P.G.* 39. 784s.) ὥς που καὶ Διαγόρας ὁ Μήλιος ἔφησεν· θεὸς πρὸ παντὸς ἔργου βροτείου νομαφρενα (sic) ὑπερτάταν· αὐτοδαὴς δεαρεταβραχυν (sic) οἶμον ἕρπειν.

(1) 3 ἕρπει Mingarelli
(2) 2 Schneidewin: ἐκτελεῖσθαι Philodem.

DIAGORAS

FRAGMENTS

738 Philodemus, *On Piety*

For they (sc. the Stoics) do not regard the gods as having human form but as airs and breaths and skies; and so I can confidently assert that their offence is greater than that of Diagoras: for Diagoras spoke in jest—if indeed this[1] is correct, not merely imputed to him as Aristoxenus has it in his *Customs of the Mantineans*; in his poetry, on the other hand, which alone seems genuinely to have been composed by him, he gave not the slightest hint of impiety, but speaks of divinity with a poet's reverence. His lines to Arianthes of Argos are particularly good evidence:

(1) It is God, God, who wields his supreme mind before any mortal deed is done; man's excellence of itself makes little headway[2];

and by his words to Nicodorus[3] of Mantinea:

(2) It is in accordance with God and fortune that all the deeds of mortals are performed.

There is similar material in his *Encomium of the Mantineans*.

[1] The business of D.'s atheism.   [2] The last sentence is quoted only by the Christian apologist Didymus.   [3] Famous boxer and later (*c.* 425?) lawgiver at Mantinea; see Aelian, *V. H.* 2. 23, who says that D. collaborated with Nicodorus in drawing up the laws, having become his lover.

GREEK LYRIC

Sext. Emp. *Adv. mathem.* 9. 53 (p. 225 Mutschmann)

Διαγόρας δὲ ὁ Μήλιος διθυραμβοποιὸς ὥς φασι τὸ πρῶτον γενόμενος ὡς εἴ τις καὶ ἄλλος δεισιδαίμων, ὅς γε καὶ τῆς ποιήσεως ἑαυτοῦ κατήρξατο τὸν τρόπον τοῦτον· κατὰ δαίμονα καὶ τύχην πάντα τελεῖται· ἀδικηθεὶς δὲ ὑπό τινος ἐπιορκήσαντος καὶ μηδὲν ἕνεκα τούτου παθόντος μεθηρμόσατο εἰς τὸ λέγειν μὴ εἶναι θεόν.

739 (dub.) Schol. Vat. in Ael. Arist. *Rhet.* (Or. 2 Behr) 258 = ii 80 Dindorf, ed. B. Keil, *Hermes* 55 (1920) 63ss.

Διαγόρας οὗτος φιλόσοφος ἦν. κληθεὶς δέ ποτε εἰς ἑστίασιν ὑφ' ἑτέρου φιλοσόφου, ἕψοντος ἐκείνου φακῆν καὶ κατά τινα χρείαν ἔξω ⟦ἐκείνου⟧ χωρήσαντος, τῆς φακῆς μὴ τελέως ἑψηθῆναι δυναμένης διὰ τὸ μὴ ὑπέκκαυμα ἔχειν τὸ ὑποκείμενον πῦρ, αὐτός τε περιστραφεὶς ὧδε κἀκεῖσε καὶ τὸ τοῦ Ἡρακλέους ἄγαλμα προχείρως εὑρὼν καὶ συντρίψας ἐνίησι τῷ πυρὶ ἐπειπὼν ἐπ' αὐτό· δώδεκα τοῖσιν (Keil: δωδεκάτοισιν cod.) ἄθλοις τρισκαιδέκατον τόνδ' ἐτέλεσεν Ἡρακλῆς δῖος.

numeros ita restituit Keil: πρὸς δώδεκα τοῖσιν ἄθλοις | τρισκαιδέκατον τόνδ' ἐτέλεσσεν Ἡρακλῆς δῖος.

cf. Clem. Alex. *Protr.* 2. 24. 2–4 (p. 8 Stählin), Athenag. *Supplic. pro Christ.* 4, Epiphan. *Ancor.* 103 (i 124 Holl), *Theosoph. Tubing.* 70 (p. 184 Erbse), *Gnomolog. Vat.* 276, schol. Ar. *Nub.* 830g, Tzetz. *Chil.* 369ss., Ibn Durayd, Kitāb al-muǧtanā (p. 74 Krenkow: v. F. Rosenthal, *Orientalia* n.s. 27 (1958) 51s.)

DIAGORAS

Sextus Empiricus, *Against the Physicists*

Diagoras of Melos, the dithyrambic poet, was at first, they say, as god-fearing as anyone; for he began his poem in this way: 'It is in accordance with God and fortune that all deeds are performed'; but when he had been wronged by someone who perjured himself and did not come to grief because of it, he changed his tune and said that God does not exist.

739 (dub.) Scholiast on Aelius Aristides

This Diagoras was a philosopher. He was once invited to a banquet by another philosopher; the host was boiling lentils and had gone outside for some purpose, and the lentils could not be properly boiled since the fire under them had no fuel; so Diagoras looked this way and that and finding the statue of Heracles nearby broke it up and threw it on the fire, saying, 'On top of his twelve labours the godlike Heracles has performed this one, his thirteenth.'[1]

[1] The editor of the scholium, B. Keil, thought that this was verse; few would agree.

ION OF CHIOS

TESTIMONIA VITAE ATQUE ARTIS

1 *Sud.* I 487 (ii 653 Adler)

Ἴων, Χῖος, τραγικὸς καὶ λυρικὸς καὶ φιλόσοφος, υἱὸς Ὀρθομένους, ἐπίκλησιν δὲ Ξούθου. ἤρξατο δὲ τὰς τραγῳδίας διδάσκειν ἐπὶ τῆς πβ' ὀλυμπιάδος. δράματα δὲ αὐτοῦ ιβ', οἱ δὲ λ', ἄλλοι δὲ μ' φασιν. οὗτος ἔγραψε περὶ μετεώρων, καὶ συνθέτους λόγους. ὃν παίζων Ἀριστοφάνης ὁ κωμικὸς Ἀοῖόν φησι (*Pax* 837). οὗτος τραγῳδίαν νικήσας Ἀθήνησιν ἑκάστῳ τῶν Ἀθηναίων ἔδωκε Χίου (Casaubon: Χῖον codd.) κεράμιον.

cf. A 731 (i 69 Adler)

348

ION OF CHIOS

LIFE AND WORKS

1 *Suda*

Ion of Chios,[1] tragedian, lyric poet and philosopher, son of Orthomenes but nicknamed son of Xuthus.[2] He began to produce tragedies in the 82nd Olympiad (452/448 B.C.); some say he composed 12, others 30, others 40.[3] He wrote on astronomical phenomena[4] and invented compound adjectives for them.[5] The comic poet Aristophanes makes fun of him by calling him Dawn.[6] When he won the tragic prize at Athens, he presented every Athenian with a jar of Chian wine.[7]

---

[1] Strabo 14. 1. 35 lists him among distinguished Chiots. The Tydeus, son of Ion, who was executed by the Spartans in 412/411 for his pro-Athenian views (Thuc. 8. 38. 3) may have been his son.   [2] The mythical Ion was son of Xuthus.   [3] He figured in the Alexandrian canon of tragedians; he won 3rd prize at Athens in 428, when Euripides was first with *Hippolytus*. The tragic fragments are in Snell, *T.G.F.* i 96 ff. 'Longinus' 33. 5 says that although his plays were impeccable and beautifully written in the smooth style, no one in his right mind would accept the whole corpus in exchange for the *Oedipus* of Sophocles.   [4] In the *Triagmos* (*Triad*) or *Triagmoi*: *F.Gr.H.* 392 T24–26, Diels-Kranz, *Vorsokratiker* 36 (i 377 ff.).   [5] See Ar. *Peace* 831.   [6] See test. 2, *P.M.G.* 745.   [7] So Athenaeus 1. 3 f.

2 Ar. *Pax* 832ss.

ΟΙ.   οὐκ ἦν ἄρ᾽ οὐδ᾽ ἃ λέγουσι, κατὰ τὸν ἀέρα
        ὡς ἀστέρες γιγνόμεθ᾽, ὅταν τις ἀποθάνῃ;
ΤΡ.   μάλιστα.
ΟΙ.   καὶ τίς ἐστιν ἀστὴρ νῦν ἐκεῖ;
ΤΡ.   Ἴων ὁ Χῖος, ὅσπερ ἐποίησεν πάλαι
        ἐνθάδε τὸν ἀοῖόν ποθ᾽· ὡς δ᾽ ἦλθ᾽, εὐθέως
        ἀοῖον αὐτὸν πάντες ἐκάλουν ἀστέρα.

Schol. ad loc. (p. 129 Holwerda)

Ἴων ὁ Χῖος· διθυράμβων ποιητὴς καὶ τραγῳδίας
καὶ μελῶν. ἐποίησε δὲ ᾠδὴν ἧς ἡ ἀρχή 'ἀοῖον — πρό-
δρομον' (*P.M.G.* 745). φαίνεται δὲ τετελευτηκὼς ἐκ
τούτων. παίζων οὖν ὁ Ἀριστοφάνης ἀοῖον αὐτόν
φησιν ἀστέρα κληθῆναι. περιβόητος δὲ ἐγένετο.
ἔγραψε δὲ καὶ κωμῳδίας καὶ ἐπιγράμματα καὶ
παιᾶνας καὶ ὕμνους καὶ σκολιὰ καὶ ἐγκώμια καὶ
ἐλεγεῖα, καὶ καταλογάδην τὸν πρεσβευτικὸν λεγό-
μενον, ὃν νόθον ἀξιοῦσιν εἶναί τινες καὶ οὐχὶ αὐτοῦ.
φέρεται δὲ αὐτοῦ καὶ κτίσις καὶ κοσμολογικὸς καὶ ὑπο-
μνήματα καὶ ἄλλα τινά. καὶ πάνυ δόκιμος ἦν. φασὶ δὲ
αὐτὸν ὁμοῦ διθύραμβον καὶ τραγῳδίαν ἀγωνισάμενον
ἐν τῇ Ἀττικῇ νικῆσαι, καὶ εὐνοίας χάριν προῖκα Χῖον
οἶνον πέμψαι Ἀθηναίοις. καὶ Σωκράτους δὲ τοῦ φιλο-

2 Aristophanes, *Peace* (421 B.C.)

Slave: So after all it isn't true what they say, that
   when we die we turn into stars in the sky?
Trygaeus: Oh yes, it is.
Sl.: Well, who's a star up there now?
Tr.: Ion of Chios, who once down here wrote 'the
   Dawn-star'; and when he arrived, they all
   immediately started calling him 'Dawn-star'.

Scholiast on the passage

   Ion of Chios: composer of dithyrambs, tragedy
and lyric poems. He wrote a song which begins
(*P.M.G.* 745 below). Aristophanes' lines show that
Ion was dead, so it is a joke when he says he
was called 'Dawn-star'. Ion became very famous;
he wrote comedies,[1] epigrams,[2] paeans, hymns,
drinking-songs, encomia, elegiac poems,[3] and in
prose the work called *Account of the Embassy,* which
some believe to be spurious. He was also the author
of the *Foundation of Chios, Cosmology,*[4] *Memoirs*[5]
and some other works. He was highly esteemed.
They say that he competed in Attica with a dithy-
ramb and a tragedy at the same time and when he
was victorious showed his goodwill by sending the
Athenians a gift of Chian wine. He features in a

---

[1] Perhaps his satyr-plays are meant.   [2] See Page, *F.G.E.*
p. 157 ff.   [3] West, *I.E.G.* p. 77 ff.   [4] The *Triagmos*: test.
1 n. 4.   [5] Or *'Notes'*, probably the same as the *Visits* (Ἐπιδη-
μίαι: *F.Gr.H.* 392 F4–7).

σόφου ἐστὶν εἰς αὐτὸν λόγος λεγόμενος Ἴων. μέμνη-
ται αὐτοῦ καὶ Καλλίμαχος ἐν τοῖς Χωλιάμβοις, ὅτι
πολλὰ ἔγραψεν (fr. 203 Pfeiffer).

cf. *Sud.* Δ 1029 (ii 91 Adler)

3 Plut. *Cim.* 9. 1 (I. i. 343 Ziegler)

συνδειπνῆσαι δὲ τῷ Κίμωνί φησιν ὁ Ἴων παντά-
πασι μειράκιον ἥκων εἰς Ἀθήνας ἐκ Χίου παρὰ Λαο-
μέδοντι . . .

4 Athen. 13. 603e (iii 331 Kaibel)

Ἴων γοῦν ὁ ποιητὴς ἐν ταῖς ἐπιγραφομέναις Ἐπι-
δημίαις γράφει οὕτως· ʻΣοφοκλεῖ τῷ ποιητῇ ἐν Χίῳ
συνήντησα, ὅτε ἔπλει εἰς Λέσβον στρατηγός . . .ʼ

dialogue of the philosopher Socrates called the *Ion*.[1]
Callimachus mentions him in his *Choliambics,* saying that he wrote a great amount.[2]

[1] This confuses him with the rhapsode Ion of Ephesus.
[2] Call. says he resembles Ion in his literary versatility (πολυείδεια) (fr. 203 Pfeiffer with Diegesis 9. 32 ff.). In his Catalogue of the Alexandrian Library Call. noted disagreement over the authorship of the *Triagmos* (fr. 449 Pf.).

3 Plutarch, *Cimon*

Ion says he dined with Cimon at Laomedon's house when he had come from Chios to Athens, still only a youth.[1]

[1] *C.* 465 B.C.: see F. Jacoby, *C.Q.* 41 (1947) 2 f.

4 Athenaeus, *Scholars at Dinner*

At any rate Ion the poet in his work called *Visits* writes as follows: I met the poet Sophocles in Chios, when he was sailing as general to Lesbos.[1]

[1] In 441/440 B.C.; see Simon. 585. Ion also visited the Isthmian Games with Aeschylus (Plut. *Mor.* 79e) (before 458, the year of A.'s departure from Athens to Sicily), and may have met Archelaus and the young Socrates *c.* 450 (Diog. Laert. 2. 23).

ION OF CHIOS

FRAGMENTA

740 Argum. Soph. *Antig.* (Σαλουστίου ὑπόθεσις) (Jebb, *Antig.* p. 5)

στασιάζεται δὲ τὰ περὶ τὴν ἡρωίδα ἱστορούμενα καὶ τὴν ἀδελφὴν αὐτῆς Ἰσμήνην· ὁ μὲν γὰρ Ἴων ἐν τοῖς Διθυράμβοις καταπρησθῆναί φησιν ἀμφοτέρας ἐν τῷ ἱερῷ τῆς Ἥρας ὑπὸ Λαοδάμαντος (Brunck: Λαομέδοντος codd.) τοῦ Ἐτεοκλέους.

741 Schol. Ap. Rhod. 1. 1165c (p. 106 Wendel)

καὶ Ἴων φησὶν ἐν διθυράμβῳ ἐκ μὲν τοῦ πελάγους αὐτὸν (sc. τὸν Αἰγαίωνα) παρακληθέντα ὑπὸ Θέτιδος ἀναχθῆναι φυλάξοντα τὸν Δία· Θαλάσσης δὲ παῖδα.

ION OF CHIOS

FRAGMENTS

740–746A are from Ion's lyric poetry: 740, 741 and 745 are from dithyrambs, 742 from his hymn to Opportunity, 743 from an encomium.

740 Sallustius' introduction to Sophocles, *Antigone*

There is discrepancy in the stories told of the heroine and her sister Ismene. Ion in his Dithyrambs says they were both burned to death in Hera's temple by Laodamas,[1] son of Eteocles.

[1] In this version L., not Creon, must have become king of Thebes on the death of Eteocles and Polyneices and will have punished his aunts for giving burial to Polyneices.

741 Scholiast on Apollonius of Rhodes ('the great cairn of Aegaeon')

Ion says in a dithyramb that Aegaeon[1] was summoned from the ocean by Thetis and taken up to protect Zeus,[2] and that he was the son of Thalassa (Sea).[3]

[1] Another name for the hundred-handed giant Briareus: see Kirk on *Il.* 1. 403–4, West on Hesiod, *Theog.* 149. [2] When Poseidon, Hera and Athena led a revolt against Zeus. [3] In Hesiod he is son of Uranus and Gaia (Heaven and Earth).

742 Paus. 5. 14. 9 (ii 36 Rocha-Pereira)

Ἴωνι δὲ οἶδα τῷ Χίῳ καὶ ὕμνον πεποιημένον Καιροῦ· γενεα-
λογεῖ δὲ ἐν τῷ ὕμνῳ νεώτατον παίδων Διὸς Καιρὸν εἶναι.

743 Zenob. Ath. 2. 35 (iv 270ss. Bühler)

Αἰγιέες οὔτε τρίτοι οὔτε τέταρτοι· Μνασέας ὁ Πατρεὺς ἐξηγού-
μενος τοῦ ἔπους τούτου τὸν νοῦν λέγει (fr. 50, *F.H.G.* iii 157) ὅτι
οἱ Αἰγιεῖς οἱ ἐν Ἀχαΐᾳ νικήσαντες Αἰτωλοὺς τὴν Πυθίαν ἐπηρώτων
τίνες εἶεν κρείττους τῶν Ἑλλήνων, ἡ δὲ Πυθία εἶπεν· 'ὑμεῖς δ'
Αἰγιέες οὔτε τρίτοι οὔτε τέταρτοι.' ὅτι γὰρ τούτοις ἐχρήσθη καὶ οὐ
Μεγαρεῦσι καὶ Ἴων μέμνηται ἐν τῷ εἰς Σκυθιάδην ἐγκωμίῳ.

cf. Zenob. *Cent.* 1. 48 (i 19 Leutsch-Schneidewin), Phot. *Lex.* (ii
238s. Naber)

744 Athen. 2. 35de (i 82 Kaibel)

Ἴων δ' ὁ Χῖός φησιν·

> ἄδαμον
> παῖδα ταυρωπόν, νέον οὐ νέον,
> ἥδιστον πρόπολον βαρυ-
> γδούπων Ἐρώτων,
> οἶνον ἀερσίνοον
> 5   ἀνθρώπων πρύτανιν.

2 ταυρῶπα cod. E ut vid.   4 Casaubon: -πνοον codd.

742 Pausanias, *Description of Greece* (on the altar to Opportunity at Olympia)

I know that a hymn to Opportunity was composed by Ion of Chios; in his hymn he makes Opportunity the youngest of the children of Zeus.[1]

[1] See H. J. Rose in *O.C.D.*[2] s.v. Kairos.

743 Zenobius *Proverbs*

'Aegians neither third nor fourth': Mnaseas of Patrae,[1] explaining the meaning of the expression, says that the men of Aegium in Achaea defeated the Aetolians and then asked the priestess at Delphi who were the best of the Greeks; and she said, 'But you Aegians are neither third nor fourth.' That the oracle was given to them and not to the Megarians[2] is shown by Ion's mention of it in his encomium for Scythiades.

[1] Or rather of Patara in Lycia, geographer and writer on oracles, *c.* 200 B.C. [2] As in Theocr. 14. 48 f. with schol., Callim. *Epigr.* 11. 5 f. (Page-Gow, *H.E.* 1095 f.).

744 Athenaeus, *Scholars at Dinner* (on wine)

Ion of Chios says,

... the untamed child, bull-faced, young and not young, sweetest attendant of loud-roaring Loves, wine that makes thoughts soar, ruler of mankind.

745 Schol. Ar. *Pax* 832ss. (v. test. 2)

Ἴων ὁ Χῖος· . . . ἐποίησε δὲ ᾠδὴν ἧς ἡ ἀρχή·

ἀοῖον ἀεροφοίταν
ἀστέρα μείναμεν, ἀελίου
λευκοπτέρυγα πρόδρομον.

schol. b ἔν τινι τῶν διθυράμβων

1 ἀώιον ci. Bergk   ἠερο- cod. R, *Sud*. Δ 1029   2 Bentley: μείνωμεν
V Ald., μῆνα μὲν R *Sud*.   3 Bentley: λευκῇ πτέρυγι codd.

746 Philo, *qu. omn. prob.* 132–4 (vi 38 Cohn-Reiter)

Μιλτιάδης ὁ τῶν Ἀθηναίων στρατηγός, ἡνίκα βασιλεὺς ὁ Περ-
σῶν ἅπασαν τὴν ἀκμὴν τῆς Ἀσίας ἀναστήσας μυριάσι πολλαῖς δι-
έβαινεν ἐπὶ τὴν Εὐρώπην ὡς ἀναρπάσων αὐτοβοεὶ τὴν Ἑλλάδα,
συναγαγὼν ἐν τῷ παναθηναϊκῷ τοὺς συμμάχους ὀρνίθων ἀγῶνας
ἐπέδειξε, λόγου παντὸς δυνατωτέραν ὑπολαμβάνων ἔσεσθαι τὴν
διὰ τῆς τοιαύτης ὄψεως παρακέλευσιν. καὶ γνώμης οὐχ ἥμαρτε·
θεασάμενοι γὰρ τὸ τλητικὸν καὶ φιλότιμον ἄχρι τελευτῆς ἐν
ἀλόγοις ἀήττητον, ἁρπάσαντες τὰ ὅπλα πρὸς τὸν πόλεμον ὥρμη-
σαν. . . . τοῦ δὲ περὶ τοὺς ὄρνιθας ἐναγωνίου μέμνηται καὶ ὁ τραγι-
κὸς Ἴων διὰ τούτων·

οὐδ' ὅ γε σῶμα τυπεὶς διφυεῖς τε κόρας ἐπι-
λάθεται ἀλκᾶς,
ἀλλ' ὀλιγοδρανέων φθογγάζεται·
θάνατον δ' ὅ γε δουλοσύνας προβέβουλε.

1 τυπτεὶς codd. FHP   ἀλκῆς MQT   3 δ' ὅτε A, δέ γε M   -σύνης
AQT

745 Scholiast on Aristophanes, *Peace* (see test. 2)

Ion wrote a song which begins,

We waited for the Dawn-star, air-roaming, white-winged fore-runner of the sun.[1]

[1] From a dithyramb (schol. b).

746 Philo, *Every good man is free*

When the king of the Persians had mobilised the finest fighting men of Asia and was crossing over to Europe with hundreds of thousands, expecting to storm Greece without striking a blow, Miltiades, the Athenian general, gathered the allies in the panathenaic stadium and put on a display of cock-fighting in the belief that the exhortation provided by such a spectacle would be more effective than any speech-making. He was right; for when they saw the endurance of mere birds and their gallantry, indomitable to the point of death, they seized their arms and rushed to war.... The cock-fight is mentioned by the tragedian Ion in these lines[1]:

not even when struck on the body and on his two eyes does he forget his valour, but despite his failing strength he utters his call; his choice is death rather than slavery.[2]

[1] Perhaps from a tragedy: F53 in Snell, *T.G.F.* i 110.   [2] The defeated cock was thought of as 'slave' to the winner: 'Phrynichus' F17 Snell, Ar. *Birds* 70 with schol., Theocr. 22. 71 f. with Gow's note.

746A = 316 *S.L.G.*   P.Oxy. 2737 fr. 1 col. i 19–27 (v. Ar. fr. 590 K.-A.)

κύκνος ὑπὸ πτερύγων τοιόνδε [τι] · τὸ μὲν Ἀριστάρ-
χειον δο[κο]ῦν ὅτι Τερπάνδρου ἐστὶν [ἡ] ἀρχή, Εὐφρόνιος δὲ ὅτι ἐκ
[τ]ῶν Ἴ[ω]νος μελῶν, ὁ δὲ τὴν [π]αραπλοκὴν ὅτι ἐκ τῶν
Ἀλ[κ]μᾶνος · ἔστι δ᾽ ἐκ τῶν εἰς Ὅμη[ρ]ον <ἀναφερομένων>
ὕμνων.

ELEGI

fr. eleg. 26 Athen. 10. 447d (ii 473 Kaibel)

τῷ δὲ ἡμετέρῳ χορῷ (Dindorf: χρόνῳ cod.) οἶνος φίλος

ὃν <πόρε> θυρσοφόρος μέγα πρεσβεύων Διόνυσος,

φησὶν Ἴων ὁ Χῖος ἐν τοῖς ἐλεγείοις ·

αὕτη γὰρ πρόφασις παντοδαπῶν λογίων,
ᾗ τε Πανελλήνων ἀγοραὶ θαλίαι τε ἀνάκτων,
ἐξ οὗ βοτρυόεσσ᾽ οἰνὰς ὑποχθόνιον
5 πτόρθον ἀνασχομένη θαλερῷ ἐπορέξατο πήχει
αἰθέρος, ὀφθαλμῶν δ᾽ ἐξέθορον πυκινοὶ
παῖδες, φωνήεντες ὅταν πέσῃ ἄλλος ἐπ᾽ ἄλλῳ·
πρὶν δὲ σιωπῶσιν · παυσάμενοι δὲ βοῆς
νέκταρ ἀμέλγονται, πόνον ὄλβιον ἀνθρώποισιν,
10 ξυνὸν τοῦ χαίρειν φάρμακον αὐτοφυές.

verba ἡμετέρῳ δὲ χορῷ fortasse poetae   1 suppl. Hiller   Musu-
rus: μέτα cod. A   3 Edmonds: αἴ τε codd.   4 epit.: ὑποχθονίων
cod. A   5 Lobeck: ἐπτήξατο cod. A, ἐπήξατο epit.   ἐπτύξατο
Casaubon   9 Meineke: μόνον codd.

---

[1] Text of opening lines uncertain.   [2] Or 'buds'.   [3] The grapes.

ION OF CHIOS

746A = 316 *S.L.G.* Oxyrhynchus papyrus (late 2nd c. A.D.): commentary on Aristophanes

The swan to the accompaniment of his wings (sings a song) such as this:

the view of Aristarchus is that the beginning (sc. of the Aristophanic stanza) is by Terpander (fr. 1), Euphronius[1] thinks it is from Ion's songs, the author of the *Paraploke*[2] thinks it comes from Alcman's songs (fr. 12B); but it comes from the hymns ascribed to Homer (*Homeric hymn* 21.1).

[1] Alexandrian scholar, 3rd c. B.C.   [2] *Quotation*? Author unknown.

ELEGIACS

fr. eleg. 26 Athenaeus, *Scholars at Dinner*

But to our chorus wine is dear, the wine which the thyrsus-bearer, greatly honoured Dionysus, (provided?),

says Ion of Chios in his elegiacs:

for it has been the theme of chroniclers from all lands[1] where there have been gatherings of all Greeks and feasts of princes, ever since the vine with her clusters lifted her stem from under the earth and stretched out for the sky with her luxuriant arm; and from her eyes[2] there jumped a crowd of children,[3] noisy when they fall on top of each other, but silent till then. When they stop their shouting, they are milked of their nectar, a blessed toil for mankind, a self-grown remedy, common to all men,

361

τοῦ θαλίαι φίλα τέκνα φιλοφροσύναι τε χοροί τε·
τῶν <δ'> ἀγαθῶν βασιλεὺς οἶνος ἔδειξε φύσιν.
τῷ σύ, πάτερ Διόνυσε, φιλοστεφάνοισιν ἀρέσκων
ἀνδράσιν, εὐθύμων συμποσίων πρύτανι,
15 χαῖρε· δίδου δ' αἰῶνα, καλῶν ἐπιήρανε ἔργων,
πίνειν καὶ παίζειν καὶ τὰ δίκαια φρονεῖν.

12 suppl. Hartung; post τῶν ἀγαθῶν lacunam stat. West
13 Bergk: τοῦ cod. A, deest epit.

fr. eleg. 27 Athen. 11. 463a–c (iii 8 Kaibel)

καὶ Ἴων δὲ ὁ Χῖός φησιν·

χαιρέτω ἡμέτερος βασιλεὺς σωτήρ τε πατήρ τε·
ἡμῖν δὲ κρητῆρ' οἰνοχόοι θέραπες
κιρνάντων προχύταισιν ἐν ἀργυρέοις· ὁ δὲ χρυσοῦν
δῖνον ἔχων χειροῖν νιζέτω εἰς ἔδαφος.
5 σπένδοντες δ' ἁγνῶς Ἡρακλεῖ τ' Ἀλκμήνῃ τε,
Προκλεῖ Περσείδαις τ' ἐκ Διὸς ἀρχόμενοι
πίνωμεν, παίζωμεν· ἴτω διὰ νυκτὸς ἀοιδή,
ὀρχείσθω τις· ἑκὼν δ' ἄρχε φιλοφροσύνης.
ὄντινα δ' εὐειδὴς μίμνει θήλεια πάρευνος,
10 κεῖνος τῶν ἄλλων κυδρότερον πίεται.

cf. 496c προχύτης εἶδος ἐκπώματος. . . . Ἴων δὲ ὁ Χῖος ἐν ἐλεγείοις, vv.
2–3 (ἀργυρέοις).

3 προχοαῖσιν ἐν ἀργυρεαις 463b cod. A   West: χρυσὸς codd.
4 Haupt: οἶνον . . . χειρῶν codd.

362

for the bringing of joy. Its dear children are feasts and jollities and dancing choirs. King wine shows up the nature of good men. And so, father Dionysus, you who give pleasure to garlanded banqueters and preside over cheerful feasts, my greetings to you! Helper in noble works, grant me a lifetime of drinking, sporting and thinking just thoughts.

fr. eleg. 27 Athenaeus, *Scholars at Dinner*

Ion of Chios says:

Greetings to our king, our saviour and father[1]; and for us let the wine-pouring attendants mix the bowl from silver pitchers; and let him who holds in his hands the golden jug wash our hands on to the floor.[2] Let us make holy libation to Heracles and Alcmena, to Procles and Perseus' descendants,[3] beginning with Zeus, and let us drink and play; let the singing last all night, let there be dancing; begin the jollity with a will; and if any one has a shapely woman waiting to share his bed, he will drink more confidently than the rest.

[1] Dionysus or wine (cf. 'king wine' in 26. 16) rather than the Spartan king.   [2] Text of this sentence very insecure.   [3] Ion lists the ancestors of the Spartan king Archidamus: Perseus was great-grandfather of Heracles (son of Alcmena), whose descendants, the Heracleidae, carried out the Dorian invasion of the Peloponnese; Procles established the Eurypontid line of kings. Jacoby, *C.Q.* 41 (1947) 9 dated the poem to 463/2, when Cimon led Athenian troops to help Archidamus against the Messenians; West, *B.I.C.S.* 32 (1985) 74 to *c.* 450, when Cimon was in Sparta to negotiate the 5-year truce.

fr. eleg. 28 Athen. (epit.) 2. 68b (i 160 Kaibel)

ὅτι εἴρηται ἀρσενικῶς . . . ὁ ὀρίγανος. . . . ˝Ιων·

αὐτὰρ ὅ γ' ἐμμαπέως τὸν ὀρίγανον ἐν χερὶ κεύθει.

cf. *Et. Gen.* (Miller, *Mélanges* 227), *Et. Mag.* 630.46

Musurus: χειρὶ codd.

fr. eleg. 29 Plut. *Thes.* 20. 2 (i 1. 17 Ziegler)

ἔνιοι δὲ καὶ τεκεῖν ἐκ Θησέως Ἀριάδνην Οἰνοπίωνα καὶ Στάφυ-
λον· ὧν καὶ ὁ Χῖος ˝Ιων ἐστὶν περὶ τῆς ἑαυτοῦ πατρίδος λέγων·

τήν ποτε Θησείδης ἔκτισεν Οἰνοπίων.

fr. eleg. 30 Diog. Laert. 1. 120 (i 55 Long)

˝Ιων δ' ὁ Χῖός φησιν περὶ αὐτοῦ·

ὣς ὁ μὲν ἠνορέῃ τε κεκασμένος ἠδὲ καὶ αἰδοῖ
καὶ φθίμενος ψυχῇ τερπνὸν ἔχει βίοτον,
εἴπερ Πυθαγόρης ἐτύμως σοφός, ὃς περὶ πάντων
ἀνθρώπων γνώμας ᾔδεε κἀξέμαθεν.

3 σοφός, ὃς Sandbach   ὁ σοφὸς codd.   4 Diels: εἶδε καὶ ἐξ- codd.

fr. eleg. 30A Philodem. *De Piet.* (p. 13 Gomperz: v. A.
Henrichs, *Cronache ercolanesi* 5 (1975) 12)

καὶ Μουσα[ῖο]ν μὲν Ὀρφεὺς υ[ἱὸν] αὐτῆς (sc. Σελήνης)
γενέσ[θ]αι φησίν . . .

σεληνο[πε]τῆ

δ' ˝Ιων αὐτὸν [λέγ]ει

-[πε]τῆ suppl. West, *Z.P.E.* 50 (1983) 46

ION OF CHIOS

fr. eleg. 28 Athenaeus, *Scholars at Dinner*

ὀρίγανον ('origanum') can be masculine[1]; so . . . Ion:

but he quickly hides the origanum in his hand.

[1] Also feminine, ἡ ὀρίγανος.

fr. eleg. 29 Plutarch, *Theseus*

Some say Ariadne actually bore Oenopion and Staphylus to Theseus. Among them is the Chiot Ion, who says of his native city

which once Theseus' son Oenopion founded.

fr. eleg. 30 Diogenes Laertius, *Life of Pherecydes of Syros*[1]

Ion of Chios says of him:

Thus, excellent in manhood and modesty, he has a pleasant life for his soul, even although he is dead—if indeed Pythagoras was really wise, who above all others knew and learned true opinions.[2]

[1] Philosopher and prose-writer *c.* 550 B.C.   [2] Text and tr. uncertain.

fr. eleg. 30A Philodemus, *On Piety*

And Musaeus[1] is said by Orpheus to have been her son (i.e. son of Selene, Moon); Ion calls him

moon-fallen.

[1] Mythical singer.

GREEK LYRIC

fr. eleg. 31 Athen. 10. 436f (ii 449s. Kaibel)

Βάτων δὲ ὁ Σινωπεὺς ἐν τοῖς περὶ Ἴωνος τοῦ ποιητοῦ
(F.Gr.H. 268 F6) φιλοπότην φησὶν γενέσθαι καὶ ἐρωτικώτατον
τὸν Ἴωνα. καὶ αὐτὸς δὲ ἐν τοῖς ἐλεγείοις ἐρᾶν μὲν ὁμολογεῖ Χρυ-
σίλλης τῆς Κορινθίας, Τελέου δὲ θυγατρός· ἧς καὶ Περικλέα τὸν
Ὀλύμπιον ἐρᾶν φησι Τηλεκλείδης ἐν Ἡσιόδοις (fr. 18 K.-A.).

fr. eleg. 32 'Cleonides' Isag. harm. 12 (p. 202 Jan, Euclid.
viii 216 Menge)

ἐπὶ μὲν οὖν τοῦ φθόγγου χρῶνται τῷ ὀνόματι (sc. τόνῳ) οἱ
λέγοντες ἑπτάτονον τὴν φόρμιγγα, καθάπερ Τέρπανδρος καὶ Ἴων.
ὁ μὲν γάρ φησιν (fr. 6), ὁ δέ·

> ἑνδεκάχορδε λύρα, δεκαβάμονα τάξιν ἔχουσα
> καὶ συμφωνούσας ἁρμονίας τριόδους·
> πρὶν μέν σ᾽ ἑπτάτονον ψάλλον διὰ τέσσαρα πάντες
> Ἕλληνες, σπανίαν μοῦσαν ἀειράμενοι.

1 Hermann: τὴν δεκαβ. codd.   Meibom: ἔχοις ἀεὶ fere codd.
ἔχοισα Diels   2 West: τὰς συμφ. codd.   3 δὶς Bergk

fr. eleg. 32A Phot. Lex. (i 218 Theodoridis)

ἀπειρόκαλος· Ἴων εἴρηκεν καὶ Πλάτων (Legg. 6. 775b) καὶ
Δημοσθένης (22. 75, 24. 183).

fr. eleg. 31 Athenaeus, *Scholars at Dinner*

Baton of Sinope[1] in his work *On Ion the Poet* says he was a keen drinker[2] and very prone to love affairs. Indeed Ion himself admits in his elegiacs that he loves the Corinthian Chrysilla, daughter of Teleas; Teleclides in his *Hesiods* says Pericles the Olympian also loved her.

[1] 3rd c. B.C.   [2] So Aelian, *V. H.* 2. 41.

fr. eleg. 32 'Cleonides', *Introduction to Harmony*

The word τόνος ('tuning, tone') is used to mean 'note' by those who call the lyre ἑπτά-τονος ('seven-toned'), as Terpander and Ion do: Terpander says (fr. 6), Ion says,

Eleven-stringed lyre, with your arrangement of ten steps and your concordant junctions of tuning, previously you were seven-toned and all Greeks plucked you four by four, raising a meager music.[1]

[1] To put it in crude terms, the seven-stringed lyre abcdefg had only two conjunct tetrachords, a-d, d-g; the eleven-stringed lyre added a disjunct tetrachord, e.g. D-G, giving DEFG/abcdefg. The 'junctions' at G and d are 'concordant' in that they produce octaves, D-d, G-g. See F. R. Levin, *T.A.P.A.* 92 (1961) 295 ff., West, *Studies* 174.

fr. eleg. 32A Photius, *Lexicon*

Ion used the word ἀπειρόκαλος,[1]

lacking in good taste,

as did Plato and Demosthenes.

[1] Included among Ion's elegiac frr. by Gentili-Prato, but it almost certainly belongs to the prose writings, e.g. the *Visits*.

EPIGRAMMATA

i *F.G.E.*   *Anth. Pal.* 7. 43 (Plan.)

῎Ιωνος ·

χαῖρε, μελαμπετάλοις, Εὐριπίδη, ἐν γυάλοισι
  Πιερίας τὸν ἀεὶ νυκτὸς ἔχων θάλαμον,
ἴσθι δ' ὑπὸ χθονὸς ὢν ὅτι σοι κλέος ἄφθιτον ἔσται,
  ἴσον Ὁμηρείαις ἀενάοις χάρισιν.

cf. *Sud.* E 1152 (ii 271 Adler) (1–2 Πιερίας)

1 Lobeck: -πέπλοις codd.

ii *F.G.E.*   *Anth. Pal.* 7. 44 (Plan., Syll. Σ)

῎Ιωνος (Syll. Σ)

εἰ καὶ δακρυόεις, Εὐριπίδη, εἷλέ σε πότμος,
  καί σε λυκορραῖσται δεῖπνον ἔθεντο κύνες,
τὸν σκηνῆς μελίγηρυν ἀηδόνα, κόσμον Ἀθηνῶν,
  τὸν σοφίῃ Μουσέων μιξάμενον χάριτα,
5 ἀλλ' ἔμολες Πελλαῖον ὑπ' ἠρίον, ὡς ἂν ὁ λάτρις
  Πιερίδων ναίῃς ἀγχόθι Πιερίης.

3 Desrousseaux: σκηνῇ codd.   4 Μουσέων *A.P.*   τραγικὴν Plan.,
Σ 6 Πιερίης Σ   Πιερίδων *A.P.*, Plan.

368

ION OF CHIOS

EPIGRAMS[1]

i *F.G.E.*   *Palatine Anthology*

Ion

Greetings, Euripides, you who possess night's eternal chamber among the dark-leaved hollows of Pieria[2]; although you are under the earth, be assured that you will have undying glory, the equal of Homer's everlasting graces.

[1] Euripides did not die till *c.* 406 B.C.; both epigrams are probably Hellenistic.   [2] In Macedonia, where Eur. died; birthplace and home of Muses.

ii *F.G.E.*   *Palatine Anthology*

Ion

Even if a tearful fate took you, Euripides, and wolf-rending dogs made you their supper, you, the honey-voiced nightingale of the stage, the adornment of Athens, who mingled with wisdom the Muses' grace, at least you reached a tomb in Pella,[1] so that you, the servant of the Pierians, should dwell near Pieria.

[1] Capital of Macedonia; see n. 2 above.

PRAXILLA

1 Euseb. *Chron.* Ol. 82.2 (p. 112 Helm, ii 105 Schöne)

Crates comicus et Telesilla ac Bacchylides lyrici clari habentur. Praxilla quoque et Cleobulina sunt celebres.

cf. Sync. p. 297 Mosshammer

2 Athen. 15. 694a (iii 535 Kaibel)

καὶ Πράξιλλα δ᾽ ἡ Σικυωνία ἐθαυμάζετο ἐπὶ τῇ τῶν σκολίων ποιήσει.

3 *Anth. Pal.* 9. 26. 1ss. = Antipater of Thessalonica xix 1ss. Gow-Page

τάσδε θεογλώσσους Ἑλικὼν ἔθρεψε γυναῖκας
ὕμνοις καὶ Μακεδὼν Πιερίας σκόπελος,
3 Πρήξιλλαν, Μοιρώ . . .
8 πάσας ἀενάων ἐργατίδας σελίδων.
ἐννέα μὲν Μούσας μέγας Οὐρανὸς ἐννέα δ᾽ αὐτά
10 Γαῖα τέκεν, θνατοῖς ἄφθιτον εὐφροσύναν.

370

PRAXILLA

LIFE AND WORK

1 Eusebius, *Chronicle*

Olympiad 82.2 (451/450 B.C.)[1]: the comic poet
Crates and Telesilla and the lyric poet Bacchylides
are regarded as famous. Praxilla also and Cleobu-
lina are renowned.

[1] The Armenian version gives 449/8.

2 Athenaeus, *Scholars at Dinner*

Praxilla of Sicyon also was admired for her com-
position of drinking-songs.[1]

[1] 'Scolia': see frr. 749, 750. Was she a hetaera?

3 *Palatine Anthology*: Antipater of Thessalonica

These divine-tongued women were nourished on
songs by Helicon and the Macedonian rock of Pieria:
Praxilla, Moero ..., craftswomen all of immortal
pages. Nine Muses were created by great Heaven,
nine by Earth herself to be an undying joy for mor-
tals.[1]

[1] Eustathius, *Il.* 326.43 lists 5 poetesses, Praxilla among them.

4 Tat. *Or. ad Gr.* 33 (p. 61 Whittaker)

Πράξιλλαν μὲν γὰρ Λύσιππος ἐχαλκούργησεν
μηδὲν εἰποῦσαν διὰ τῶν ποιημάτων χρήσιμον.

PRAXILLA

4 Tatian, *Against the Greeks*

Lysippus[1] made a bronze statue of Praxilla, although she said nothing worth-while in her poetry.

[1] Famous sculptor from Sicyon, *fl.* 328 B.C. Tatian says mockingly that statues were made of 13 other poetesses also; on his veracity see A. Kalkmann, *Rh. Mus.* 42 (1887) 489 ff.

PRAXILLA

FRAGMENTA

747 Zenob. 4. 21 (i 89 Leutsch-Schneidewin) (cod. Coisl.)

ἠλιθιώτερος τοῦ Πραξίλλης Ἀδώνιδος· ἐπὶ τῶν ἀνοήτων.
Πράξιλλα Σικυωνία μελοποιὸς ἐγένετο, ὥς φησι Πολέμων (F.H.G.
iii 147)· αὕτη ἡ Πράξιλλα τὸν Ἄδωνιν ἐν τοῖς ὕμνοις εἰσάγει ἐρω-
τώμενον ὑπὸ τῶν κάτω τί κάλλιστον καταλιπὼν ἐλήλυθεν, ἐκεῖνον
δὲ λέγοντα οὕτως·

κάλλιστον μὲν ἐγὼ λείπω φάος ἠελίοιο,
δεύτερον ἄστρα φαεινὰ σεληναίης τε πρόσωπον
ἠδὲ καὶ ὡραίους σικύους καὶ μῆλα καὶ ὄγχνας·

εὐήθης γάρ τις ἴσως ὁ τῷ ἡλίῳ καὶ τῇ σελήνῃ τοὺς σικύους καὶ τὰ
λοιπὰ συναριθμῶν.

cf. Diogenian. 5. 12 (i 251 L.-S.) (ἥλιος, ἔφη, καὶ σῦκα), Apostol. 8. 53
(ii 445 L.-S.) (ἥλιον σελήνην σῦκα καὶ μῆλα), Sud. H 220 (ii 562 Adler),
Liban. *Ep.* 707. 4 (x 717 Foerster)

3 Schneidewin: ὄχνους cod.

PRAXILLA

FRAGMENTS

747   HYMN TO ADONIS

Zenobius, *Proverbs*

'Sillier than Praxilla's Adonis': used of stupid people. Praxilla of Sicyon was a lyric poetess, according to Polemon.[1] In her hymn this Praxilla represents Adonis as being asked by those in the underworld what was the most beautiful thing he left behind when he came, and giving as his answer:

The most beautiful thing I leave behind is the sun's light; second, the shining stars and the moon's face; also ripe cucumbers[2] and apples and pears.

For anyone who lists cucumbers and the rest alongside sun and moon can only be regarded as feeble-minded.

[1] Geographer, *c.* 200 B.C.   [2] 'Figs' in some versions. The name of her city Sicyon means 'cucumber-bed'.

748 Heph. *Ench.* 2. 3 (p. 9 Consbruch) (περὶ συνεκφωνή-σεως)

... ἢ δύο βραχεῖαι εἰς μίαν βραχεῖαν (sc. παραλαμβάνονται)
...· ἔστι μέντοι καὶ ἐν ἔπει, ὡς παρὰ Κορίννῃ ἐν τῷ πέμπτῳ
(Corinna 657) καὶ παρὰ Πραξίλλῃ ἐν διθυράμβοις ἐν ᾠδῇ ἐπιγρα-
φομένῃ Ἀχιλλεύς (codd. DI, Ἀχιλεύς cod. A)·

ἀλλὰ τεὸν οὔποτε θυμὸν ἐνὶ στήθεσσιν ἔπειθον.

cf. schol. B (p. 287C.), schol. Dion. Thrac. (p. 210 Hilgard), Drac.
Stratonic. (p. 146 Hermann), *Anecd. Gr.* ii 180 Bachmann, Eust. *Il.*
12.25, 805.21, 1372.9

ἔπειθον, ἔπειθεν codd.

749 Ar. *Vesp.* 1236ss.

τί δ᾽ ὅταν Θέωρος πρὸς ποδῶν κατακείμενος
ᾄδῃ Κλέωνος λαβόμενος τῆς δεξιᾶς·

Ἀδμήτου λόγον ὦ ἑταῖρε μαθὼν τοὺς ἀγαθοὺς φίλει,

τούτῳ τί λέξεις σκόλιον;

Schol. ad loc. (p. 194ss. Koster)

Ἀδμήτου λόγον· καὶ τοῦτο ἀρχὴ σκολίου. ἐξῆς δέ ἐστι·

τῶν δειλῶν δ᾽ ἀπέχου γνοὺς ὅτι δειλῶν ὀλίγα χάρις.

... τοῦτο οἱ μὲν Ἀλκαίου, οἱ δὲ Σαπφοῦς· οὐκ ἔστι δέ, ἀλλ᾽ ἐν τοῖς
Πραξίλλης φέρεται παροινίοις.

cf. *P.M.G.* 897 (= Athen. 15. 695c), Ar. fr. 444 K.-A., Cratin. fr. 254
K.-A., Eust. *Il.* 326.38ss. (i 509 van der Valk), Paus. *Lex. Att.* A 25
Erbse, Phot. *Lex.* p. 32 Reitzenstein, *Sud.* A 493, Π 737 (i 52, iv 64
Adler)

748   DITHYRAMB: ACHILLES

Hephaestion, *Handbook on Metres* (on synizesis)

. . . or two short syllables are run together to give one short . . . : this occurs even in a hexameter, as in Corinna in Book 5 (fr. 657) and in Praxilla[1] in her Dithyrambs in a song entitled 'Achilles':

but they never persuaded[2] the heart in your breast.

[1] τεὸν is to be scanned as one short syllable.   [2] In some mss. 'he never persuaded'.

749 and 750 are drinking-songs

749 Aristophanes, *Wasps*

And when Theorus, reclining at Cleon's feet, grasps his right hand and sings,

Learn the story of Admetus, my friend, and love the good,[1]

what drinking-song will you sing in answer to him?

Scholiast on the passage: this too is the beginning of a drinking-song (cf. *P.M.G.* 897); it goes on,

and keep away from the worthless, knowing that the worthless have little gratitude.

. . . Some attribute it to Alcaeus, some to Sappho ('Sappho or Alcaeus' 25C: i 455); but it is not by either of them: it is included in Praxilla's drinking-songs.

[1] Referred to elsewhere by the comic poets, Cratinus in *Chirons*, Aristophanes in *Storks*.

750 Ar. *Thesm.* 528ss.

τὴν παροιμίαν δ' ἐπαινῶ | τὴν παλαιάν· ὑπὸ λίθῳ γὰρ | παντί που χρὴ | μὴ δάκῃ ῥήτωρ ἀθρεῖν.

Schol. ad loc. (p. 268 Dübner)

ἐκ τῶν εἰς Πράξιλλαν ἀναφερομένων·

ὑπὸ παντὶ λίθῳ σκορπίον ὦ ἑταῖρε φυλάσσεο.

cf. *P.M.G.* 903 (Athen. 15. 695d), Zenob. 6. 20, Diogenian. 8. 59 (i 166, 317 L.-S.), *Sud.* Υ 554 (iv 674 Adler), Hsch. Υ 717 (iv 215 Schmidt), *Anecd. Gr.* (de Villoison ii 177)

751 Athen. 13. 603a (iii 329 Kaibel)

Πράξιλλα δ' ἡ Σικυωνία ὑπὸ Διός φησιν ἁρπασθῆναι τὸν Χρύσιππον.

752 Hsch. Β 128 (i 309 Latte)

Πράξιλλα δὲ ἡ Σικυωνία 'Αφροδίτης παῖδα τὸν θεὸν (sc. Διό-νυσον) ἱστορεῖ.

753 Paus. 3. 13. 5 (i 232 Rocha-Pereira)

Πραξίλλῃ μὲν δὴ πεποιημένα ἐστὶν ὡς Εὐρώπης εἴη καὶ <Διὸς ὁ suppl. Rinckh> Κάρνειος καὶ αὐτὸν ἀνεθρέψατο 'Απόλλων καὶ Λητώ.

Schol. Theocr. 5. 83 (p. 170s. Wendel)

τὰ δὲ Κάρνεα· Πράξιλλα μὲν ἀπὸ Κάρνου φησὶν ὠνομάσθαι τοῦ Διὸς καὶ Εὐρώπης υἱοῦ, ὃς ἦν ἐρώμενος τοῦ 'Απόλλωνος.

cf. Hsch. Κ 842 (ii 415 Latte), schol. Callim. *h. Apoll.* 71 (ii 48s. Pfeiffer)

PRAXILLA

750 Aristophanes, *Thesmophoriazusae*

And I approve of the old proverb: under every stone we should look in case we are bitten by—a politician.

Scholiast on the passage: from the words attributed to Praxilla:

Under every stone, my friend, look out for a scorpion.[1]

[1] See drinking-song *P.M.G.* 903.

751 Athenaeus, *Scholars at Dinner*

But Praxilla of Sicyon says that it was Zeus[1] who carried off Chrysippus.

[1] Not Laius, who in other versions was cursed by Pelops for abducting his son Chrysippus.

752 Hesychius, *Lexicon*

Praxilla of Sicyon makes the god (Dionysus) the son of Aphrodite.[1]

[1] Not of Semele.

753 Pausanias, *Description of Greece*

Praxilla's version is that Carneius was the son of Europa and Zeus, and that Apollo and Leto brought him up.

Scholiast on Theocritus

The Carnea[1]: Praxilla says the festival took its name from Carnus, Apollo's beloved boy, son of Zeus and Europa.

[1] Dorian festival of Apollo; see Alcm. 52.

754 Heph. *Ench.* 7. 8 (p. 24 Consbruch)

ἔστι δέ τινα καὶ λογαοιδικὰ καλούμενα δακτυλικά, ἅπερ ἐν μὲν ταῖς ἄλλαις χώραις δακτύλους ἔχει, τελευταίαν δὲ τροχαϊκὴν συζυγίαν. ἔστι δὲ αὐτῶν ἐπισημότατα τό τε πρὸς δύο δακτύλοις ἔχον τροχαϊκὴν συζυγίαν, καλούμενον δὲ Ἀλκαϊκὸν δεκασύλλαβον (Alc. 328) καὶ τὸ πρὸς τρισὶ καλούμενον Πραξίλλειον·

ὦ διὰ τᾶς θυρίδος καλὸν ἐμβλέποισα
παρθένε τὰν κεφαλὰν τὰ δ᾽ ἔνερθε νύμφα

cf. schol. A (p. 130 C.) (v. 1), schol. B (p. 275 C.) (vv. 1–2), Trich. (p. 379s. C.), vasculum ap. P. Jacobsthal, *Göttinger Vasen* 59ss. cum tab. 22 = *Athen. Mitteil.* 65 (1940) tab. 3 (οδιατεσθυριδοσ)

1 Renehan: τῶν θυρίδων codd.   τῆς θυρίδος vasc.

PRAXILLA

754 Hephaestion, *Handbook on Metres*

There are also the 'logaoedic dactylic' lines, which have dactyls in the other positions but end with a trochaic syzygy. The most remarkable are the one beginning with two dactyls, the 'Alcaic decasyllable' (Alc. 328), and the one beginning with three, the 'Praxilleion' ($-\cup\cup-\cup\cup-\cup\cup-\cup-\cup$)[1]:

You who look so beautifully in through the window,[2] with a virgin's head but a married woman's body beneath . . .

[1] Trichas says Praxilla used the metre often; for other units labelled Praxilleion see Sapph. 154, *R.E.* s.v.   [2] The first four words ('O . . . through the window') are on a vase dated *c.* 450.

EURIPIDES

755 Plut. *Vit. Alcib.* 11 (i 2. 236 Ziegler)

αἱ δ' ἱπποτροφίαι περιβόητοι μὲν ἐγένοντο καὶ τῷ πλήθει τῶν ἁρμάτων· ἑπτὰ γὰρ ἄλλος οὐδεὶς καθῆκεν Ὀλυμπίασιν ἰδιώτης οὐδὲ βασιλεύς, μόνος δ' ἐκεῖνος. καὶ τὸ νικῆσαι δὲ καὶ δεύτερον γενέσθαι καὶ τέταρτον, ὡς Θουκυδίδης φησίν (6. 16), ὡς δ' Εὐριπίδης τρίτον, ὑπερβάλλει λαμπρότητι καὶ δόξῃ πᾶσαν τὴν ἐν τούτοις φιλοτιμίαν. λέγει δ' Εὐριπίδης ἐν τῷ ᾄσματι ταῦτα·

> σὲ δ' ἄγαμαι,
> ὦ Κλεινίου παῖ· καλὸν ἁ νίκα,
> κάλλιστον δ', ὃ μηδεὶς ἄλλος Ἑλλάνων,
> ἅρματι πρῶτα δραμεῖν καὶ δεύτερα καὶ τρίτα\<τα\>,
> 5 βῆναί τ' ἀπονητὶ Διὸς στεφθέντ' ἐλαίᾳ
> κάρυκι βοὰν παραδοῦναι.

cf. Athen. 1. 3de (i 6 Kaibel)

1 Lindskog: ἄγαμε cod. N, ἀείσομαι UA   3 δ' N, om. UA   μήτις Page   4 Bergk: τρίτα codd.   5 -ναί τ' UA, -ναι δ' N   Hermann: δὶς codd.   6 βοᾶν Bergk

EURIPIDES

755 Plutarch, *Life of Alcibiades*

His horse-breeding was famous and especially so for the number of his chariots: no one else, neither private citizen nor king, ever entered seven at the Olympic games; and to come first, second and fourth, as Thucydides says (6. 16)—third, according to Euripides[1]—outshines in the brilliance of its renown all that ambition strives for in these contests. This is what Euripides says in his song:

But of you, son of Cleinias, I stand in awe: victory is a fine thing, but finest of all to do what no other Greek has done, to run first and second and third with the chariot and arrive without labour, wreathed with the olive of Zeus, to provide the theme for the herald's cry.[2]

[1] Isocrates 16. 34 follows Euripides, Athenaeus 1. 3e Thucydides. The date was almost certainly 416.   [2] See C. M. Bowra, *Historia* 9 (1960) 68 ff.

GREEK LYRIC

756 Plut. *Vit. Demosth.* 1. 1 (i 2. 280 Ziegler)

ὁ μὲν γράψας τὸ ἐπὶ τῇ νίκῃ τῆς Ὀλυμπίασιν ἱπποδρομίας εἰς
Ἀλκιβιάδην ἐγκώμιον, εἴτ᾽ Εὐριπίδης, ὡς ὁ πολὺς κρατεῖ λόγος,
εἴθ᾽ ἕτερός τις ἦν, ὦ Σόσσιε Σενεκίων, φησὶ χρῆναι τῷ εὐδαίμονι
πρῶτον ὑπάρξαι

τὰν πόλιν εὐδόκιμον.

τὰν NU, τὴν A   incert. utrum verba εὐδ. πρῶτ. ὑπάρξαι poetae sint

EPIGRAMMATA

i *F.G.E.*   Plut. *Vit. Nic.* 17. 4 (i 2. 108 Ziegler)

ὁ μὲν γὰρ Εὐριπίδης μετὰ τὴν ἧτταν αὐτῶν καὶ τὸν ὄλεθρον
γράφων ἐπικήδειον ἐποίησεν·

οἵδε Συρακοσίους ὀκτὼ νίκας ἐκράτησαν
ἄνδρες, ὅτ᾽ ἦν τὰ θεῶν ἐξ ἴσου ἀμφοτέροις.

ii *F.G.E.*   Athen. 2. 61ab (i 143 Kaibel)

Ἐπαρχίδης (*F.Gr.H.* 437 F2) Εὐριπίδην φησὶ τὸν ποιητὴν
ἐπιδημῆσαι τῇ Ἰκάρῳ καὶ γυναικός τινος μετὰ τέκνων κατὰ τοὺς
ἀγρούς, δύο μὲν ἀρρένων τελείων, μιᾶς δὲ παρθένου, φαγούσης
θανασίμους μύκητας καὶ ἀποπνιγείσης μετὰ τῶν τέκνων ποιῆσαι
τουτὶ τὸ ἐπίγραμμα·

ὦ τὸν ἀγήρατον πόλον αἰθέρος, Ἥλιε, τέμνων,
ἆρ᾽ εἶδες τοιόνδ᾽ ὄμματι πρόσθε πάθος,
μητέρα παρθενικήν τε κόρην δισσούς τε συναίμους
ἐν ταὐτῷ φέγγει μοιραδίῳ φθιμένους;

4 μοιριδίῳ Musurus

384

EURIPIDES

756 Plutarch, *Life of Demosthenes*

The writer of the encomium for Alcibiades on his victory in the chariot-racing at Olympia, whether it was Euripides, as is generally held, or some other, says, Sosius Senecio, that the happy man must in the first place belong to

a city of high repute.[1]

[1] Cf. Simon. 640.

EPIGRAMS

i *F.G.E.* Plutarch, *Life of Nicias*

For Euripides, writing a lament[1] after their defeat and destruction,[2] said:

These men won eight victories over the Syracusans, while the gods showed equal favour to both sides.

[1] The lines are rather an epitaph (or the beginning of one). [2] The Athenian disaster at Syracuse, 413 B.C. It is uncertain whether Eur. was in fact the author: see Page, *F.G.E.* 129, 155 f.

ii *F.G.E.* Athenaeus, *Scholars at Dinner*

Eparchides[1] says that the poet Euripides made a visit to the island of Icarus and that when a woman and her children, two grown males and one girl, ate poisonous mushrooms in the countryside and all died, he composed this epigram:

Sun, cleaving the ageless vault of heaven, did you ever cast your eye on such a disaster, a mother and a maiden daughter with her two brothers meeting their fate on the same day?[2]

[1] 3rd c. B.C.? [2] A Hellenistic composition.

COMPARATIVE NUMERATION

Except in the case of Bacchylides, the numeration of the present edition is that of the margin of *P.M.G.* The numbers given in the second column below are the internal numbers for Corinna etc. in *P.M.G.*

CORINNA

Loeb/*P.M.G.* (margin)	*P.M.G.* (Corinna)	Bergk	Diehl
654	1	(28)	4,5
655	2	(20,13)	2,19
656	3	7	—
657	4	9	1
658	5	1	6
659	6	6	7
660	7	19	8
661	8	5	9
662	9	2	11
663	10	4	12
664(a)	11(a)	21	15
664(b)	11(b)	10	16
665	12	32	—
666	13	11	14
667	14	—	—
668	15	29	—
669	16	8	18
670	17	30	—
671	18	31	—

COMPARATIVE NUMERATION

Loeb/*P.M.G.* (margin)	*P.M.G.* (Corinna)	Bergk	Diehl
672	19	33	—
673	20	3	—
674	21	23	3
675	22	14–18	20–24
676(a)	23(a)	—	—
676(b)	23(b)	26	10
677	24	24	13
678	25	22	25
679	26	25	26
680	27	35	—
681	28	36	—
682	29	37	—
683	30	38	—
684	31	12,39	17
685	32	40	—
686	33	27	—
687	34	41	—
688	35	34	—
689	36	42	—
690	37	—	5ab
691–695	38–42	—	—
695A	—	—	—

* * * * * * * * * * * * *

Bergk	Loeb/*P.M.G.* (margin)	Bergk	Loeb/*P.M.G.* (margin)
1	658	8	669
2	662	9	657
3	673	10	664(b)
4	663	11	666
5	661	12	684
6	659	13	655
7	656	14	675(a)

388

CORINNA

Bergk	Loeb/*P.M.G.* (margin)	Bergk	Loeb/*P.M.G.* (margin)
15	675(b)	29	668
16	675(c)	30	670
17	675(d)	31	671
18	675(e)	32	665
19	660	33	672
20	655	34	688
21	664(a)	35	680
22	678	36	681
23	674	37	682
24	677	38	683
25	679	39	684
26	676(b)	40	685
27	686	41	687
28	654 n.5	42	689

* * * * * * * * * * * * * *

Diehl	Loeb/*P.M.G.* (margin)	Diehl	Loeb/*P.M.G.* (margin)
1	657	13	677
2	(655)	14	666
3	674	15	664(a)
4	654	16	664(b)
5	654	17	684
5ab	690	18	669
6	658	19	(655)
7	659	20	675(a)
8	660	21	675(b)
9	661	22	675(c)
10	676(b)	23	675(d)
11	662	24	675(e)
12	663	25	678
		26	679

COMPARATIVE NUMERATION

TELESILLA

Loeb/*P.M.G.* (margin)	*P.M.G.* (Teles.)	Bergk	Diehl
717	1	1	1
718	2	2	—
719	3	3	—
720	4	4	—
721	5	5	—
722	6	6	—
723	7	7	—
724	8	8	—
725	9	9	—
726	10	—	—

* * * * * * * * * * * * * *

TIMOCREON

Loeb/*P.M.G.* (margin)	*P.M.G.* (Timocr.)	Bergk	Diehl
727	1	1	1
728	2	2	2
729	3	3	3
730	4	5	3a
731	5	8	5
732	6	6	4
733	7	7	7
734	8	4	—
9 West	—	9	6
10 West	—	10	8

BACCHYLIDES

The numeration used in the present volume is that
of the 10th edition of Snell-Maehler (Teubner).
Jebb's numbering of the major poems, used also in
LSJ, differs in that he joined poems 7 and 8, so that
8 Jebb = 9 Snell-Maehler and so to 19 Jebb = 20
Snell-Maehler. The following table deals with the
fragments (fr. 1, fr. 2 etc.).

Loeb/Snell-Maehler	Bergk	Jebb	Edmonds
1	4	1	42
1A	57	37,42	5,28
1B	40	23	2
2	11	2	1
3	12	36	4
4	33+13	18+3	46+66A+7
5	14	4	8
6	15	5	9
7	16	39	21
8	18	38	17
9	32	51	18
10	56	47	44
11	19	7	22.1–5
12	20	8	22.6–7
13	21	9	23
14	22	10	25
15	23	11	26
15A	23n.	—	26A
16	31	12	27
17	24	13	68
18	25	14	69A
19	26	15	69B
20	—	—	—

COMPARATIVE NUMERATION

Loeb/Snell-Maehler	Bergk	Jebb	Edmonds
20A	—	—	—
20B	27	16	70
20C	—	—	71
20D–20G	—	—	—
21	28	17	6
22	33	18	46
23	34	19	47
24	36	20	48
25	3	21	49
26	35	(=14.30f.)	(=10.30f.)
27	37	29	50
28	7	(p.437)	(=29.13f.)
29	38	25	51
30	39	22	52
31	40	23	2
32	(42)	(26)	(53)
33	43	27	54
34	44	24	55
35	45	30	56
36	46	(=12.208f.)	(=40.208f.)
(37)	2.3	28	57
(37A)	adesp.86	32	72
(37B)	—	—	58
38	50	41	59
39	51	31	44A
40	53	60	45
41	54	45	20
42	55	54	19
43	58	59	p.81n.
44	60	48	43
45	62	44	60
(46)	63	52	61
47	64	53	3
48	65	58	62
49	66	57	63
50	67	61	64

Loeb/Snell-Maehler	Bergk	Jebb	Edmonds
51	68	43	65
52	69	55	p.127
(53)	59	56	p.93n.
53a	—	—	—
54	2.3	28	57
55	adesp.86	32	72
56	—	—	58
57	—	p.415	—
58	5	p.409	42A
59	p.588	50	66
60–66	—	—	—

* * * * * * * * * * * * *

BACCHYLIDES' FRAGMENTS: REVERSE INDEX

Read: 3 Bergk = 25 Loeb/Snell-Maehler; 4 Jebb = 5 Loeb/Snell-Maehler. An asterisk denotes an epinician or dithyramb from the British Museum papyrus.

Loeb/Snell-Maehler	Bergk	Jebb	Edmonds
1	*5.50ff.	1	2
2	*5.160ff.+54	2	1B
3	25	4.61ff.	47
4	1	5	3
5	58	6	(1A)
6	*5.37ff.	*21	21
7	*1.13f.	11	4.61ff.
8	*1.76	12	5
9	*11.1ff.	13	6
10	test.11	14	*15

COMPARATIVE NUMERATION

Loeb/Snell-Maehler	Bergk	Jebb	Edmonds
11	2	15	*16
12	3	16	*17
13	4.61ff.	17	*18
14	5	18	*19
15	6	19.1f.	*20
15A	—	—	*20n.3
16	7	20B.6ff.	*21
17	*17n.1	21	8
18	8	4.21ff.	9
19	11	23	42
20	12	24	41
21	13	25	7
22	14	30	11 + 12
23	15	1B	13
24	17	34	before 14
25	18	29	14
26	19.1f.	*(18.2)	15
26A	—	—	15A
27	20B.6ff.	33	16
28	21	54	(1A)
29	*15.50ff.	27	*1
30	*1.159ff.	35	*2
31	16	39	*3
32	9	55	*4
33	4.21ff.	epigr.II	*5
34	23	epigr.I	*6
35	26	test.11	*7 + 8
36	24	3	*9
37	27	(1A)	*10
38	29	8	*11
39	30	7	*12
40	1B	before 14	*13
41	*21.1f.	38	*14
42	*(18.2)	(1A)	1
42A	—	—	58
43	33	51	44

BACCHYLIDES REVERSE

Loeb/Snell-Maehler	Bergk	Jebb	Edmonds
44	34	45	10
44A	—	—	39
45	35	41	40
46	*13.208f.	*23	4.21ff.
47	*5.26f.	10	23
48	epigr.II	44	24
49	epigr.I	*20n.3	25
50	38	59	27
51	39	9	29
52	*13.58	20D	30
53	40	47	*18.2
54	41	42	33
55	42	52	34
56	10	*15n.2	35
57	(1A)	49	54
57A	—	—	*5.160
58	43	48	56
59	*15n.2	43	38
60	44	40	45
61	*20n.3	50	20D
62	45		48
63	20D		49
64	47		50
65	48		51
66	49		59
66A	—		4.39ff.
67	50		before 17
68	51		17
69	52		—
69A			18
69B			19
70			20B
71			20C
72			55

ION

Lyric poetry

Loeb/*P.M.G.* (margin)	*P.M.G.* (Ion)	Bergk	Diehl
740	1	12	—
741	2	11	—
742	3	14	—
743	4	15	—
744	5	9	8
745	6	10	9
746	7	16	10

Elegiac poetry (West's numeration is that of von Blumenthal)

Loeb/West *I.E.G.*	Bergk	Diehl
26	1	1
27	2	2
28	5	3
29	6	4
30	4	5
31	7	—
32	3	6

PRAXILLA

Loeb/*P.M.G.* (margin)	*P.M.G.* (Praxilla)	Bergk	Diehl
747	1	2	2
748	2	1	1
749	3	3	—
750	4	4	—
751	5	6	—
752	6	8	—
753	7	7	—
754	8	5	3

INDEX OF AUTHORS AND SOURCES

INDEX OF AUTHORS AND SOURCES

400

INDEX OF AUTHORS AND SOURCES

INDEX OF AUTHORS AND SOURCES

INDEX OF AUTHORS AND SOURCES

405

GENERAL INDEX

GENERAL INDEX

GENERAL INDEX

Julian, Roman emperor, 332–363 A.D.: 293
Justice (Dike): 137, 199, 211, 219

Kairos: *see* Opportunity

Lacedaemonians, Spartans: 237, 269
Lachon, sprinter: 155, 157
Laconia, district of S.E. Peloponnese, dominated by Sparta: 231
Ladon, earlier name of river Ismenus: 55
Laertes, father of Odysseus: 209
Laius, father of Oedipus: 379
Lampon, father of pancratiast Pytheas: 191, 201
Laocoon, priest of Apollo in Troy: 263
Laodamas, son of Eteocles: 355
Laomedon, father of Priam: 197
Laomedon, Ion's host in Athens: 353
Larissa, principal city of Thessaly: 207
Lemnos, volcanic island in N.E. Aegean: 231, 261
Leotychidas, king of Sparta 491–469 B.C.: 4, 88, 89
Lesbos, largest island off Asia Minor: 77, 269, 353
Leto, mother of Apollo and Artemis: 31, 33, 81, 89, 129, 147, 177, 183, 283, 379
Letrini, place in Elis: 79
Leucippides (daughters of Leucippus), wives of Dioscuri: 307
Libya = Africa; nymph, ancestor of Cadmus: 37

Liparion of Ceos, athlete: 159
Liparus, father of Liparion: 159
Love: *see* Eros
Loxias, title of Apollo: 133, 197, 251
Lusi, place in N. Arcadia: 179
Lusus, river of Lusi: 183
Lycambes, attacked by Archilochus: 87
Lycia, country in S.W. Asia Minor: 197, 285
Lycormas, Aetolian river, later called Euenus: 215, 277, 311
Lydia, kingdom of W. Asia Minor: 129, 161, 267
Lynceus, king of Argos, father of Abas: 181
Lysagora, daughter of Damon?: 117, 119
Lysippus of Sicyon, sculptor, *fl.* 328 B.C.: 373

Macedonia, region of N.W. Aegean: 5, 6, 277, 369, 371
Macelo, mother or sister of Dexithea: 119
Maia, mother of Hermes: 31, 233
Mantinea, city of Arcadia: 7, 237, 345
Marpessa, daughter of Euenus and wife of Idas: 237, 275, 277
Mecisteus, one of Seven against Thebes: 61, 63
Medes: *see* Persians
Megara, coastal city between Corinth and Athens: 93, 357
Meidon, Meidylus, father of Bacchylides: 5, 101, 103
Melampus, mythical seer: 257

415

GENERAL INDEX

Pleuron, city of Aetolia: 147, 149, 237

Poeëessa, city of Ceos: 101

Polyneices, son of Oedipus and Jocasta: 63, 161, 163, 355

Polypemon, father of Procoptes?: 229

Polyphemus, the Cyclops: 305

Porthanides (grandson of Porthaon), Meleager: 143

Poseidon, god of sea, earthquakes and horses: 31, 33, 41, 115, 119, 123, 171, 203, 205, 213, 219, 221, 223, 229, 237, 275, 355

Priam, king of Troy: 185, 197, 211

Procaon, brother of Althaea, uncle of Meleager: 243

Procatia, mother of Corinna: 19

Procles, established Eurypontid line of Spartan kings: 363

Procoptes or Procrustes, Attic brigand killed by Theseus: 229

Proetus, king of Tiryns: 179, 181, 183

Protogoras of Abdera, sophist, c. 490–c. 420 B.C.: 337

Proteus, sea-god: 241

Ptoios, Boeotian mountain with sanctuary of Apollo (Ptoion): 33, 67

Ptous, eponymous hero of Mt. Ptoios: 63

Pyrrhichus, father of Cleoptolemus: 205

Pytha(i)eus, son of Apollo; also title of Apollo: 79, 255, 257

Pythagoras of Samos,

philosopher, *fl.* 532/1 B.C.: 365

Pytheas of Aegina, pancratiast: 189, 199, 201

Pythian Games at Delphi: 121, 137, 141, 177

Pytho, name for Delphi: 131, 141, 159, 187, 213, 249, 257

Pythocleides of Ceos, musician and philosopher, early 5th c. B.C.: 319

Report (Pheme) personified: 125, 171

Rhadamanthys, son of Zeus and Europa: 263

Rhea, wife of Cronus: 27, 295

Rhodes, island of S.E. Aegean: 4, 85, 89, 93, 95, 97

Rhyndacus, river of Phrygia: 299

Salamis, island W. of Piraeus, scene of Greek naval victory over Persians, 480 B.C.; regarded as daughter of Asopus: 31, 88, 89

Sardis, capital of Lydia: 129

Sarpedon, son of Zeus and Europa, commander of Lycians at Troy: 263, 285

Scamander, river of Troy: 197, 245

Sciron, brigand near Megara, killed by Theseus: 229

Scopelinus, aulete, teacher and in some versions father of Pindar: 2, 69

Scythiades, subject of encomium by Ion: 357

Seasons (Horai), goddesses of the seasons: 59, 199, 211

419